The World of
Hannah More

The
World
of
Hannah More

❀❀

PATRICIA DEMERS

THE UNIVERSITY PRESS OF KENTUCKY

frontispiece: Hannah More. A painting by John Opie
(Bristol Museum and Art Gallery).

Copyright © 1996 by The University Press of Kentucky

Scholarly publisher for the Commonwealth, serving Bellarmine College,
Berea College, Centre College of Kentucky, Eastern Kentucky University,
The Filson Club, Georgetown College, Kentucky Historical Society,
Kentucky State University, Morehead State University, Murray State
University, Northern Kentucky University, Transylvania University,
University of Kentucky, University of Louisville,
and Western Kentucky University

Editorial and Sales Offices: The University Press of Kentucky
663 South Limestone Street, Lexington, Kentucky 40508-4008

Library óf Congress Cataloging-in-Publication Data
Demers, Patricia, [date]
   The world of Hannah More / Patricia Demers.
      p.   cm.
   Includes bibliographical references and index.
   ISBN 0-8131-1978-2 (cloth : alk. paper)
   1. More, Hannah, 1745–1833. 2. Women and literature—England—
History—18th century. 3. Women and literature—England—
History—19th century. 4. Women authors, English—18th century—
Biography. 5. Women authors, English—19th century—Biography.
6. Women educators—Great Britain—Biography. I. Title.
PR3605.M6D46   1996
828'.609—dc20
[B]   96-11179

Contents

Illustrations

Preface

A colleague specializing in eighteenth- and nineteenth-century women's writing once cautioned me that I could not hope to give Hannah More "a place in the sun." If not scorched, especially by the ultraviolet index of some criticism, I thought, what about at least allowing her to lounge in slightly more benign shade? While this project is not really a rescue mission, it is an attempt to take Hannah More seriously. Although she has acquired a certain infamy on account of the grimness and solemnity of her moral high ground and has become the embodiment of conservative, reactionary antifeminism, most stereotypes about her have been based on a selective sample of her writing. By examining the complete span of her career, by situating her major texts in relation to the works of contemporaries and events in her own life, and by considering her effect on readers in her day and our own, I plan to pursue a form of literary biography anchored in the work itself. It seems an appropriate and a just response to a woman who took pride in living to some purpose. Aware that this cultural warrior and her female moral imperialism often defy comparison and provoke extremely heated reactions, I propose to shed some light on the reasons why. By neither idealizing nor dismissing More, I wish to examine her as a complex human phenomenon—warts and all.

Acknowledgments

I am grateful to the Social Sciences and Humanities Research Council of Canada for a grant to assist in my research trips and to the University of Alberta for the privilege of a McCalla Research Professorship to allow me to concentrate on this project. Librarians at every step of the way have been immensely helpful and accommodating: at our own interlibrary loan office and Bruce Peel Special Collections Library, the British Library, the Bodleian, the City of Bristol Record Office, the Folger Shakespeare Library, the Huntington, the New York Public Library, the Osborne Collection, and the Pierpont Morgan Library. In my search for documents and information, the people I met throughout Somersetshire were exceptionally generous. The Curator of Fine Art at the Bristol Museum and Art Gallery, Francis Greenacre, gave me access to drawers of More prints. While I was scanning the memorials at the Bristol Cathedral, a chance encounter with Eileen Jenkins of Swindon led to her sending me holiday snapshots of a visit to Barley Wood. Dulcey Dibley of Cheddar opened up Hannah More Cottage for me and showed me around well after regular hours. Daphne Outhwaite invited me to lunch to talk about "Hannah." Joan Bentley sent me a copy of the dramatized anthology she had prepared from More's diaries and letters, and the Reverend Chris Moorsom of St. Andrew's, Banwell, provided other leads. Rosalie Brooker took time to give me a tour of Barley Wood. Closer to home, Isobel Grundy suggested additional sources and my now-transatlantic colleague, Gary Kelly, orchestrated many instructive discussions about Hannah More. Along with the kind encouragement of staff at the University Press of Kentucky, the detailed suggestions of the anonymous readers were truly magnanimous. As always, students have taught me a great deal; I am especially endebted to Bonnie Herron and Tania Smith.

❀ 1 ❀

More Is Less

On a sparkling June day, I walked up the steep drive from the Wrington Road to visit Barley Wood, the home Hannah More built and occupied for more than twenty-five years. Having pored over the early engravings, prints of which the American Board of Missions marketed to help pay for its girls' school in Ceylon—also called Barley Wood—I tried to superimpose mental transparencies of additions and expansions to the original two-story, double roofed, thatched, rectangular house. I was prepared for the rolling grassland sloping up the wooded hillside and for the considerable architectural changes that subsequent owners had effected on More's romantic *cottage orné*,[1] with two bow windows from the southern front and eastern side and a trellised verandah supported by tree trunks and fringed with thick hedges of roses, jessamine, woodbine, and clematis. On these grounds Marianne Thornton and her siblings romped, as had young Tom Macaulay. The sisters' cats, Non-resistance and Passive Obedience, had moused freely. Carriages conveying such guests as William Wilberforce, Elizabeth Fry, the Duke of Gloucester, Anna Barbauld, Lady Gladstone and her six-year-old son, Sarah Siddons, and Rowland Hill, along with scores of loyal readers from as far as Persia and America, had trundled up this path. Afternoon teas for two hundred had been spread out on these lawns.

Surrounded by majestic gingko and yew trees, the house is at least double in size, fronted by a formal garden and pavilion where, in a niche, a bust of Hannah More is enshrined. Upright trellises support the verandah in place of the rustic trunks. Wistaria vines cover the added stone porches. The roof is tiled. Among the remnants are the bellcote that Hannah used to summon the family and servants to prayer and the crumbling urns: simple, vase-shaped stones on plain plinths. One, the present of More's Bluestocking friend Elizabeth Montagu, is dedicated to John Locke, a Wrington native, and the other, with a more legible inscription, commemorates her "long and faithful friendship" with the Bishop of London, Beilby Porteus. On this brilliant morning, at the start of my Mendip pilgrimage, I thought the view of the lush Wrington vale with the Bristol Channel in the far distance as

1

A drawing by the Reverend Henry Thompson from his *Life of Hannah More* (1838).

spectacular and breathtaking as it must have been almost two centuries ago when the clear-sighted, independent More sisters planned their fourth and final house. Hannah knew where to build!

But the scene is now vastly different. Barley Wood is the home of residents in the ADAPT (Alcohol and Drug Abuse Problems Treatment) program. The grounds are not manicured. The statuary in the gardens has been vandalized, yet curiously the bust and urns are intact. Rosalie Brooker, the nurse-counsellor who gave me a quick tour, admitted she found real peace in the house and gardens and believed, with only a slight wavering of conviction, that Hannah would approve of the estate's present use. Speculating on More's reaction formed a tidy parallel to my own continuing questions about how to accord justice to this once lionized writer and activist, who is—and, as some would argue, always was—so devastatingly out of step. How would Hannah, memorialized in the south porch of All Saints Church, Wrington, for devoting "her time and talents to the cause of pure religion, sound morality and wide culture" and in the Hannah More Window depicting "Faith, Hope and Charity (1 Corinthians 13.13)" on the north wall of the sanctuary, respond to the problem of addiction? The question is truly impossible; by cutting across class lines, addiction vitiates More's central belief in a natural hierarchical social order, which is now angering in its condescension and immobility. While her benevolence and activism made Hannah More "the most influential female philanthropist of her day," who elevated the "religious and domestic skills of women [as] ideally suited to . . . moral reformation,"[2] her philanthropy also "perpetuated old-style paternalism" with its "discipline suited to a quiescent work force."[3] In this light her house on the hill, peering "down from . . . parklands at the corn-fields in which . . . labourers hungered,"[4] is the perfect emblem of her moral economy. However, there is something facile and ready-made about the linkage between architecture and attitude. Because "socially hierarchical, spiritually egalitarian Tories who foster radical causes like anti-slavery and lower-class education fit uneasily into conventional political schemes,"[5] allowance must be made for what does not fit, what continues to unsettle. Though it is too simple to label her benevolence "self-congratulatory,"[6] trying to deal justly with Hannah More means admitting both the expansiveness and the limitations of her charity, methodology, and vision.

At every turn in my Mendip journey, the anomalies of such justice—interrogating the subject herself and the strategies of her denouncers—were driven home. The mould-cracked tombstone in All Saints churchyard marks "the mortal remains of five sisters" who lived together for fifty years. "It is not given to every woman to be a hero to her sisters,"[7] observes one of Hannah's most perceptive and thorough critics. We continue to find the story of five spinsters living harmoniously either incredible or uninteresting. The second youngest of the daughters of Jacob and Mary (Grace) More, Hannah was gifted and cossetted. The figures of her father, headmaster of a foundation school at Fishponds in the parish of Stapleton, Bristol, and Hannah's first teacher, and her farmer's-daughter mother are spectral in her letters, possibly because of the decision of the official editor of her correspondence to suppress "what has seemed to belong to the more private recesses of the bosom."[8] However vexing this decision may be, it is one with which More would have concurred.[9] Born at Thorpe Hall, Harleston, in Norfolk, Jacob More had planned to enter the church, but the outcome of a family lawsuit and its award of a sizeable inheritance to a cousin instead of himself led to his move to Gloucestershire and to his appointment to the charity school endowed by Norborne Berkeley of Stoke Park. The early twentieth-century biographer Annette Meakin credits More's mother, "the daughter of a respectable Gloucestershire farmer," with "a sound judgment and plenty of common sense, which afterwards showed itself in her wise management and careful upbringing of a family of five daughters."[10] Although no letters to or about her mother have come to light, we do know that Hannah considered her father "exemplary" and registered real pleasure when the eighty-one-year-old Jacob translated Bishop Lowth's Latin verses in honor of his daughter, *"Hannae Morae, Virgini Piae Eruditae, Eleganti, Ingenio, Facundia et Sapientia Pariter Illustri."*[11] In 1777 she visited his birthplace, and at the time of his death, in 1783, when More was with Eva Marie Garrick at Hampton, she mourned indoors for three weeks.

Some readers have teased incriminating innuendo out of Hannah's relationships with her parents and sisters. Elizabeth Kowaleski-Wallace's reading of More as a case study "in complicity" presents a daddy's girl under patriarchy, who saw "the real mother" as seemingly "inconsequential" and who "disencumbered herself of her real father only to involve herself in a series of paternal seductions."[12] It requires a particularly rigid focus to maintain this view in the face of at least equally compelling, contrary evidence. True, James Stonehouse (the clergyman who was the sisters' neighbor in Park Street, Bristol), David Garrick (Covent Garden's actor-manager), Dr. Johnson ("Yes, Abyssinia's Johnson! Dictionary Johnson! Rambler's, Idler's, and Irene's Johnson!,"[13] as one of the sisters exulted), Horace Walpole (historian, Gothic novelist, and founder of Strawberry Hill Press), a whole bevy of bishops, and her indecisive suitor William Turner were attracted to the vivacious though self-possessed young woman. But this fact makes Hannah neither sycophantic nor coquettish. Older women, too, among them Frances Boscawen, Elizabeth Vesey, Elizabeth Montagu, Elizabeth Carter, and Eva Marie Garrick, established long friendships with her.[14] Looking down at her own tombstone in the Wrington churchyard on that summer afternoon prompted me to remember the role of sickbed and deathbed comforter—of women and men—that Hannah had performed so often. On the death of her husband, Eva Marie Garrick "ran into [Hannah's] arms."[15] It was More who saw Dr. Kennicott, the Hebrew scholar, "breathe his last."[16] When the Reverend John Newton's wife died, he opened his heart to Hannah More in a twelve-page letter, "assured of meeting from you with that sympathy and sensibility of which I hope I am not myself wholly destitute."[17] The recuperating Sir James Stonehouse requested all the Mores to visit, "for we have scarcely a friend in the world we can open our minds to, as we can to the sisterhood."[18]

The shadowy sisterhood, whose "insatiable curiosity"[19] about Hannah's London dinners and friends is fed in letters detailing the minutiae of her calendar but whose support and attentiveness are always taken for granted, is another problematic issue. Mary, Elizabeth, Sarah, and Martha—all, presumably, capable, shrewd "Bristol" women, who, as Hannah explained, did not "give something for nothing"[20]—were more than assiduous social secretaries deflecting unwanted visitors for their famous sister. The boarding school for young ladies, which Mary set up when she was nineteen years old and to which all the younger sisters contributed as tutors, teachers and administrators, was a hugely successful undertaking for more than three decades, moving from one prestigious Bristol address to another: from 6 Trinity Street, near the

College Green, to 43 Park Street, one of the first houses erected when Park Street was laid out, locations within walking distance of both Bristol Cathedral and the Theatre Royal, established in 1766. The waggish middle child, Sally, regaled Johnson, who eventually visited Park Street, with the history of their private venture school: "how we were born with more desires than guineas, . . . how we found a great house with nothing in it; and how it was like to remain so, till, looking into our knowledge boxes, we happened to find a little *larning*, a good thing when land is gone, or rather none; and so at last, by giving a little of this little *larning* to those who had less, we got a good store of gold in return."[21]

With funds raised through subscription and such patrons as Mrs. Edward Gwatkin, a Cornwall heiress, Norborne Berkeley and his sister, the Dowager Duchess of Beaufort, and the widow of Admiral Boscawen, the Mores' school, opening after Easter in 1758, offered instruction in French, reading, writing, arithmetic, and needlework. The advertisement at 11 March 1758 announced: "Young Ladies boarded on reasonable terms."[22] In sensible accord with Locke's views that dancing "gives *graceful Motions* all the life, . . . a becoming Confidence, . . . [and] cannot be learn'd too early,"[23] the sisters soon hired a dancing master. Mary was the principal; Betty, the housekeeper; Sally, Hannah, and Martha were pupils who quickly graduated to teachers. Their curriculum reflects the essential practicality of the sisters' upbringing. Mary had been a weekly boarder at a French school and had taught her sisters on the weekends. The girls' general fluency in French had been helped by Jacob's inviting paroled French officers, prisoners during the Seven Years War, to their Fishponds home. Hannah's exceptional proficiency led to her continuing study of Latin, Italian, and Spanish. Although they hired visiting masters, the sisters provided the mainstay of the curriculum. Keen on furnishing the mind of a young woman with more than what Swift had complained of, "a set of Phrases learn't by Rote," and on overcoming the inability "to hold her Tongue a Minute; / While all she prates has nothing in it,"[24] Hannah was especially proud of the addition of Addison's *Spectator* to the school's library. She must have been heartened by the *Spectator*'s lament about the "accomplished" girl, whose parents strive "to make her an agreeable person" and thus contribute to "our present numerous race of coquettes."[25] Praising the More sisters as "women of admirable sense and unaffected behaviour," Mrs. Montagu preferred their school "to any that [she had] seen for girls whether very young or misses in their teens."[26]

Unlike Anna Laetitia Barbauld who, having decided that a woman learns only "from conversation with father or brother or friend,"[27] limited herself to the instruction of the young gentlemen at her husband's school,

Hannah and her sisters clearly filled a need for the aspiring yet discriminating mercantile class. The establishment and heyday of their school coincided with Bristol's "golden age": in the eighteenth century the city's population grew threefold, and manufactories increased along with shipping. However, developments in education did not keep pace with commercial and industrial growth. The cathedral school "suffered from lack of money," and Bristol Grammar School declined so remarkably under a long-lived headmaster that "by the early nineteenth century it did not have a single pupil."[28] Unlike laxities in the public sphere, the Mores shrewdly hit on a winning formula and enrollment.

In many ways the sisters' school was a stepping stone for Hannah's career. Johnson was not the only powerful mentor welcomed to Park Street. She celebrated the electoral victory of their member of Parliament, Edmund Burke, in 1774, with verse and the presentation of a ceremonial cockade. "The decade's outstanding defender of the gentry," Burke played a great role in the formation of More's own antirevolutionary ideas, particularly in his exposure of "Jacobinical utopianism."[29] His *Reflections on the Revolution in France* (1790) used sustained rhetorical power to uphold the monarchical status quo. Yet, just as she disagreed with Johnson about the value of Milton's shorter poems and the suitability of Fielding's picaresque narratives, she also called Burke to account for his "unhandsome paragraph" on a mutual friend, Dr. Josiah Tucker, dean of Gloucester, who had been one of her earliest spiritual advisers. In More's absolutist judgment—and despite her own obsessive concern with these demarcations—the private and the public, "the man and the politician," should not be "different things." "I do not see," she wrote home to her sisters, "why a person should not be bound to speak truth in the House of Commons as much as in his own house."[30]

Among the influential parents and guardians Hannah met were William Powell, the actor-manger of the new Theatre Royal, for whom she wrote a prologue for his benefit performance of *Hamlet*, Amos Cottle, the bookseller and poet, and William Turner of Belmont, guardian of two cousins at the Park Street school. An invited guest of the cousins, she frequently visited the estate of this bachelor, twenty years her senior, in the village of Wraxall, south of Bristol, and ultimately accepted his proposal of marriage. Turner postponed the wedding three times over six years; finally and without Hannah's knowledge, Dr. James Stonehouse intervened, with the result that Turner settled an annuity of £200 on Hannah and bequeathed her £1,000. They remained friends—although two decades separated the third postponement and their next meeting—and neither married. The effect of these canceled marriage plans is unclear. No evidence remains that she ever wrote anything on the topic or confided in any of her sisters or older women friends. Speculation about the grave or minor consequences of this disappointment and theorizing about the jilted bride or frustrated prude are quite empty. What is clear is that she determined not to marry. Although her correspondence with John Langhorne, the translator of Plutarch who called her "a classic,"[31] was charming, he was a married and somewhat desultory man. Hannah never considered as a serious suitor the eccentric Scot James Burnet, Lord Monboddo, who did propose and whose proto-evolutionary theories of man were mocked by Johnson. Freeing her from teaching, the annuity also gave her the independence to concentrate on study and writing; she faithfully sent a copy of every published work to Mr. Turner. By not becoming the mistress of Belmont, Hannah became a writer. This result seems to me less a decision by default than one by sheer determination. For the well-read, alert, and ambitious Hannah, the prospect of suspending her "legal existence" as a wife "incorporated and consolidated into that of the husband, under whose wing, protection and cover she performs everything,"[32] as Blackstone had interpreted marriage in 1758, must have appeared less and less attractive.

Searching for a hidden or repressed sexual persona in the letters is as futile as attempting full-bodied sketches of the older sisters. Apart from Hannah herself, the most developed character is the youngest, Martha, Hannah's favorite, nicknamed Patty. Her *Mendip Annals* is an invaluable trove of information about the thirteen Sunday and day schools she and Hannah established and supervised in neighboring villages; in her account, spanning the period from the start of the Cheddar school in 1789 to the "malevolence" and "violent explosion, long pent up,"[33] at Blagdon in 1800, quotidian irritations and setbacks jostle with the reformer's zeal and otherworldly preoccupation the sisters shared.

On the basis of their earnings the sisters were able to retire and to build and maintain a commodious house in fashionable Pulteney Street in Bath, where they lived throughout the winters of the 1790s. Although Hannah made no bones about hating Bath and considering it "an exile,"[34] Barley Wood offered all the sisters a full, busy decade of uninterrupted, communal, country living. Yet ironies abound in this tale of sisters together. Despite her passion for gardening and protest that she could not "afford to buy" books because she had "spent all [her] money on trees,"[35] Hannah hardly settled into the role of puttering country matron. Major volumes on such topics as royal education, Christian morals, practical piety, and the character and writings of Saint Paul, many first editions of which were either "bespoken while in press" or "sold the first day,"[36] plus a staggeringly popular novel were the products of her first dozen years at Barley Wood. Despite the salubrious spot, however,

Hannah's health continued to be fragile. Details of the garden, of her desire for a meditative retirement, and of her older sisters' failing strength make many of her letters from the second decade of her residence at Barley Wood into "the annals of an hospital."[37] One postscript squeezed in upside down, above her salutation to Lady Olivia Sparrow, reads: "Respect of sisters. P. in declining state. We have ten thousand Roses."[38] The most frail and protected, Hannah outlived all her sisters as well as, by her own reckoning,[39] the fifteen physicians who had attended her and every contemporary, both from her "youthful" and "second" sets.[40] Her long life perplexed and ultimately fatigued her, as, confined to the "Bastile"[41] of her second floor bedroom and apartment for the last seven and a half years of her residence at Barley Wood, she realized that "this old crazy building is a long time in breaking up" and "this poor crazy tenement . . . encounters many shocks."[42] The quick succession of her sisters' deaths (Mary in 1815 at seventy-five; Elizabeth in 1816 at seventy-six; Sarah in 1817 at seventy-four; and Patty, in 1819 at sixty-nine) brought an abrupt close to their fifty years together. Hannah tried to palliate their agonies and assisted at all their deathbeds, being most inconsolable at the loss of Patty whom she mourned as her "chief earthly comfort, companion, counsellor, and fellow-labourer."[43]

A recurring theme of her Barley Wood correspondence is the need of time: "I have had too many cares and interruptions, and too little leisure and repose for age and sickness—too much of Martha—too little of Mary."[44] But despite her complaints about the burdens of afternoon levees and mountains of letters ("There is hardly a city in North America in which I do not have a correspondent,"[45] she lamented to Sir William Weller Pepys), Hannah made herself available to guests for a variety of reasons. She offered one string of crisply logical explanations. "If my visitors are young, I hope I may perhaps be enabled to do them some good; if old, I hope to receive some good from them. If they come from far, I cannot refuse to see them after they have incurred (though so little worth it) so much trouble and possibly expence to visit me; and if they live near, I could not be so ungracious and so unkind as to shut out my neighbours."[46] Another explanation is that she thrived on company and conversation, especially with like-minded people who managed to combine high spirits and seriousness in a blend similar to her own. As she disclosed to Zachary Macaulay, "I feel myself particularly drawn and attached to those who feel anxious and alive in the same sort of pursuits in which I myself am engaged."[47] William Roberts's efforts to shield her notwithstanding, her letters are full of candid glimpses of a woman who was "certainly happier . . . but . . . not one bit better"[48] in her rural retreat, who admitted her own "natural bias . . . on the side of levity and gaiety,"[49] and who realized that in her "uncommonly prosperous and happy" life she "carried too much sail."[50] Prosperity never led to extravagance: having an urn to Locke was one thing but, despite the imploration of the Bishop of Bath and Wells, buying "at any price . . . the little miserable cottage where Locke was born" was another. As she confided to Wilberforce, "it is not worth anything."[51] An immensely loyal friend, interested in generations of kindred spirits, Hannah found it as appropriate that Wilberforce brought his bride to the hermitage of her Cowslip Green cottage on their honeymoon as that their son, a newlywed twenty-five years later, repeated the visit to the solitary More sister at Barley Wood. She rejoiced in Millicent Sparrow's declaration to her mother's friend, "to you I know I may speak openly," as much as she admired the "angelic" Marianne Thornton, whose loss of both parents in one year made the girl in Hannah's eyes "an example of heroic piety."[52] Her letters to Marianne Thornton show a genuine, maternal fondness, even when Hannah's advanced age and failing eyesight reversed the roles of sympathetic supporter and dependant; one of the most affecting of these letters—incomplete and uncharacteristically scrawled in thick brownish marks indicating that it was written with a stick and not with her usual fine-nib, black-ink pen—gently requests a diversion of the younger woman (young enough to be her granddaughter): "Do, that is a dear?, write to me one of your entertaining letters now and then."[53]

But the figure of Hannah More, as perceived by those who never met her or who reprehended her ideas, remains a troubling issue. A walk the next day along Lower North Street, in Cheddar, brought me to Hannah More Cottage, the converted ox barn that Hannah, in the face of initial hostility and resentment, had boldly rented for seven years. In a corner of the main room, roughly the size of a small classroom today (8 x 12 m), are the remains of a late eighteenth-century tea service of plain dark brown, probably used by the hired schoolmistress, and an oak gate-legged table stamped by the Cheddar Female Club 1792. Propped up in an opposite corner is More's walking stick, a slender rod of about five feet, which must have contributed to an imperious air as this small, short woman strode in to inspect on a summer Sunday or led troops of hundreds of children and carts laden with roast beef, pudding, and casks of cider onto the hills, facing the Tor of Glastonbury or the Quantocks or the mountains of Wales, for the annual Mendip Feasts. In looking over the three sets of belongings, those of the Hannah More Trust, the Red Cross, and the Evergreens (old-age pensioners), I thought of the paradoxical cachet and curiosity of her name. Surrounded by this dusty, unused memorabilia, the Evergreens hold tea meetings and card parties, and the Red Cross convenes monthly sessions with a chiropodist. Across the street Hannah More Close is the location of an assisted housing project. The large tithe barn at Nailsea, a later location of one of her schools, now serves as an activities center for mentally handicapped adults, although at Hannah More Infants School in the same village there is no trace of information about its namesake. Throughout Somersetshire far fewer citizens than I had expected recognized the name. Two hospitable local historians, Daphne Outhwaite and Dulcie Dibley, from Cheddar, cast their vote decidedly against Hannah's approving of the current use of Barley Wood; but, though debates about her reaction to addiction may be anachronistic, their verdict does not include the exceptions and reversals for which More was famous. However much she resists translation to the present, the evidence of her genuine helpfulness to those in dire straits and her sensible interventions to improve the lot of women and children, in particular, suggests that—in the implausible scenario of Hannah in the 1990s—her notorious severity *might* be melted by the desire to help and, of course, convert.

More's clubs and schools, which, even when her health was "broken and infirm,"[54] she faithfully attended, exemplified her Evangelical conviction that "the parish should be a scene of ceaseless effort to win the souls of all, . . . [to] make real religion available to everyone."[55] In her eighties she was still managing the rents of her schools and contributing to the clothing of her pupils. With their assets in three parishes alone leaving "poor people possessed of nearly two thousand pounds" in 1825, her Female Clubs united their members "for some good purpose, and from their honest industry [to] lay by a trifle for the hour of need."[56] Through small (three half-pence) weekly contributions, women created a fund to help with the expenses of sickness (during which three shillings and sixpence would be allowed each week for four weeks), childbirth (with ten shillings sixpence at a married woman's lying-in), and death (sixpence toward each member's funeral). When, in 1818, the wives of the unemployed miners at Shipham and Rowberrow were unable to pay their dues, Hannah and Patty "by begging, borrowing and giving . . . cleared off their debts."[57] A year earlier, when the brass trade had collapsed in the depression of the aftermath of the Napoleonic wars and there was no call for the *lapis calaminaris* from which it was made, Hannah and Patty not only assisted the unemployed miners "individually to the utmost of our power," but Hannah and a neighbor also "commenced merchants, and purchase[d] a certain quantity of their commodity weekly, which [was] deposited in a warehouse till better times return[ed], and both their minds and bodies [were] improved by having employment as well as bread." A similarly charitable foresight led her to intervene on behalf of the poor of Shipham who "cannot buy a loaf of bread"; as she disclosed to John Harford, "I sent out and bought their own potatoes while they were tolerably cheap, and have had them buried in a pit, that they may have them for seed."[58] During an outbreak of typhus fever, in Wrington in 1822, More sent "the almost daily dole . . . through the apothecary,"[59] who attended her and her neighbors; effectively quarantined, she pinned a little bag of money to her curtain, and the apothecary acted as the go-between. Though originally intended for the children of laborers and farmers, and then extended to the parents who received instruction in the evening, the Mendip schools, "a model for the development of voluntary schools throughout the country,"[60] were another concrete way in which the More sisters became "humble instruments of usefulness."[61] With attempts to introduce small profitable manufactories as well as the rudiments of religion, Hannah More saw herself contributing to plain, practical Christianity and economic security.

An insistent pragmatism characterized all More's projects. Her school-mistresses often took the place of absent or derelict clergy; she furnished them with a little money so that they could dispense medicine and relief along with spiritual advice in their visitations. "They soon gained [the villagers'] confidence, read and prayed to them, and in all respects did just what a good clergyman does in other parishes."[62] Her Mendip Feasts became spectacular events—not just because of the ceremonial pageantry but because of the model frugality of "having fed about nine hundred people for less than a *fine* dinner for twenty costs."[63] More shrewdly calculated the benefits and insights gained from their various schools and societies, which by 1796 consisted of "about sixteen or seventeen hundred"[64] souls. Her greatest success came from "the most profligate places," while she sensed failure "with your *pretty good kind of people*, who do not see how they can be better."[65] In her estimate the outstanding benefit of the project was "the removal of that great gulf which has divided the rich and the poor in these country parishes, by making them meet together."[66]

But this rose of meliorism had some prickly thorns. In her own day, with detractors motivated by envy and fear of her power, More was accused of "teaching the poor without a license," a charge that so unsettled her that she confessed to Wilberforce, "Indeed, it seems just now particularly wrong in me to attempt to teach others, who am myself so disgraced, traduced, and vilified."[67] Today with our heightened awareness of "the inevitably political instrumentality of campaigns for 'moral' reform of the poor,"[68] we demystify More's benevolence by deconstructing its discourse of subalternism. Hence the enterprise of the Sunday schools, which More looked back on as an attempt "to steer the middle way between the scylla of brutal ignorance and the charybdis of a literary education,"[69] is now widely assumed to have been a narrow exercise of knowing and keeping one's place, teaching the laboring poor "piety, self-abnegation, and gratitude towards their betters."[70]

Visiting the snug Somerset villages, which in More's day were so depressed and lacking in any provision for the education of the poor and where her memory as an Evangelical do-gooder lives on mainly in the names of a few streets and schools, had the effect of intensifying the range of ambivalent responses to this writer and activist. Her life of service makes her an easy target for exaggeration and derision. Though some detractors would relish the comparison, Hannah More does not forecast Dickens's satirized Mrs. Pardiggle, who proudly proclaims: "'I am a School lady, I am a Distributing lady, I am on the local Linen Box Committee and many general Committees, and my canvassing alone is very extensive—perhaps no one's more so.'"[71] Too aware of her own weaknesses to be such a figure of ridicule, More seems to me to be reflecting on—if not preoccupied with—her own fallibility throughout her long career. The desire "not willingly [to] appear better than I am,"[72] the fear "that strangers will think me good,"[73] and the admission that "I feel myself so every way unfit to presume to set up for a teacher of others, that I wished to keep myself in the back-ground"[74] are refrains in her correspondence, symptomatic, I suggest, not of false modesty or coyness but of intelligent candor. She is equally removed from Wilkie Collins's viciously satirical portrayal of an Evangelical busybody, Miss Clack, who exhorts "young friends and fellow-sinners":

> Beware of presuming to exercise your poor carnal reason. Oh, be morally tidy! Let your faith be as your stockings, and your stockings as your faith. Both ever spotless, and both ready to put on at a moment's notice!
> I beg a thousand pardons. I have fallen insensibly into my Sunday-school style.[75]

Despite her moments of hilarity and natural high spirits, and intimate knowledge of the Sunday-school style, More was constantly examining and, as she confessed to Wilberforce, doubting her own motives: "I suppose my natural temper comes in; doubt and fear being my governing principles in common life. My very desire after that perfection, for which I trust I am labouring, proceeds too much from impatience and self-love. My right actions have but poor motives. I want the satisfactions and complacencies of a perfect state before I have got rid of the corruptions of a depraved nature."[76]

Just as Hannah's candor complicates easy conclusions about her benevolence and personality, her allegiance to hierarchy and belief in meliorism, for which she is most often excoriated today, should be assessed in light of the conventions of her age. Seeing Hannah within eighteenth-century traditions does not diminish her individuality, but it makes her less of an oddity.

Although she was no sustained ironist, her adroit handling of clergymen, publishers, and lawyers suggests an aptitude as subtle and aware as that of the "respectable woman" who "dared not to be nice,"[77] Jane Collier. In disagreeing with Samuel Richardson (who later published Collier's *Essay on the Art of Ingeniously Tormenting* [1753] and "dramatic fable" *The Cry* [1754], both jointly written with Sarah Fielding) on the matter of his proposed changes to Sarah Fielding's *The Governess*, she argued skillfully against spelling out the specific nature of Mrs. Teachum's "severe punishments." Collier's shrewd awareness of the needs of Fielding's "little readers," who should think Mrs. Teachum's punishment "to be the same that they themselves had suffered when they deserved it," does not blind her to the expectations of "elder readers" who, if they deduce "that Miss Fielding is against corporeal severities, . . . will say at once that they are sure her notions of education cannot be worth reading, as she has already shewn herself an enemy to what they call proper discipline."[78] By defending the correctness of a female author and daring to explore the creative possibilities of hints rather than full-fledged explanations with such an acknowledged arbiter as Richardson, Collier illustrates the limited yet effectual space for maneuvring within a pervasively patriarchal culture. Likely no one except the radical atheist William Godwin would have got away with the proposals in his *Enquiry Concerning Political Justice* (1793) for philosophical anarchy and objection to all constraints—governments and family being foremost—on the operation of pure reason.

In a world of such minimal opportunities, women writers' adherence to meliorism would seem a logical stratagem; this cognate belief also permitted a range of expressive platforms—for Mary Astell, Mary Chudleigh, and Jane Collier, as well as Catharine Macaulay and Mary Wollstonecraft. Although their suggested improvements led in many different directions, they shared the tenet of the integral value of education; this practical schooling for life that was invariably calibrated to class linked many diverse institutions: Bathsua Makin's girls' school at Tottenham High Cross, Astell's proposed collegiate community of ladies as well as her charity school, Sarah Scott's experiment in the pious female community celebrated by the male narrator of her *Description of Millenium Hall*, Wollstonecraft's establishment, with Fanny Blood, at Newington Green, and Sarah Trimmer's Sunday schools at Brentford. The diverse enterprises, and classes catered for, at Scott's "assured asylum against every evil"[79] make Millenium Hall an exceptional example of the radiating power of female education and philanthropy. "One of a band of eighteenth century pioneers,"[80] Sarah (Robinson) Scott was the sister of Elizabeth Montagu, More's champion. The gentleman traveler is affected by his hospitable welcome in "so uncommon a society"—with ladies and young girls reading, translating, drawing, painting, carving, engraving, and practising musical instruments in the Hall itself, older women in neat cottages teaching knitting and spinning to preschoolers, and the harmonious society of "those poor creatures who are rendered miserable from some natural deficiency or redundancy"—that he is moved to consider "a scheme to imitate them on a smaller scale."[81] The salient characteristic of this woman-centred commune is the interconnectedness of meliorism; acts of charity and service set similar gestures in motion. As one of the old women, who had been saved from starvation and sheltered in this community, relates, "The ladies settled all these matters at first, and told us, that as they, to please God, assisted us, we must in order to please him serve others; and that to make us happy they would put us in a way, poor as we are, to do good to many."[82] A utopia formed by female agency, *Millenium Hall* celebrates a "feminized, Christian economy . . . to redress the wrongs of women."[83]

Believing in a virtuous formation to enable women, in particular, to live productively and well, all these women writers and activists would have sympathized immediately with Frances Burney's characterization in *Camilla* of the studious though undervalued Eugenia Tyrold, "born to be a practical philosopher," since for her "in its purest proportions, moral beauty preserved its first energy."[84] Conversely Burney's grotesque tutor Dr. Orkborne, with his "ample hoards of erudition" and "total want of skill and penetration to know how or where they might turn to any account,"[85] would have impressed this critical coterie as dangerously pedantic.

More was a meliorist who believed passionately, forthrightly in the curative powers of education as an antidote to both the immorality of the upper ranks and the feckless improvidence of the lower orders. She did not mince words, yet she could excite and galvanize, indict and affect her readers. Her form of moral beauty and unswerving fidelity, though easily mocked, command attention. Ill-suited for frivolity or farce, lacking any successors (sanguineal, ideological, or literary), and captured only partially in the paintings of Reynolds, Opie, Bird, Clint, and Pickersgill, she remains a difficult but not impossible figure to sketch—even though, as E.M. Forster concluded, she was herself probably more of an underliner than a sketcher.[86] The determined set of the jaw and lustrous black eyes of an attractive woman who knew her own mind and was neat and plain in her dress, without jewels, meet the viewer in Frances Reynolds's full-faced, pensive young Hannah, in John Opie's powdered star of the Blues, in E. Bird's pouty, fussily bowed matron, in Mr. Slater's sweet but possibly enigmatic smiler, in Mr. Clint's solemn, even dyspeptic subject, and in the "corrugated visage" of H. W. Pickersgill's silver and blue, ancient but purposive, fairy godmother.[87] Although More shrank from this exposure, expressing "such a repugnance to having [her] picture taken,"[88] comparing a portrait session to sitting "down to a tooth-drawer,"[89] and mounting "earnest remonstrances and positive refusals" about what she considered "a cruel vexation, . . . morally and physically,"[90] the portraits do provide a certain physical reality. Even more revealing are the figurative labels contemporaries used to describe her power: for Dr. Johnson she was a Hannibal of poets; for the chief supporter of her Sunday schools, William Wilberforce, she was Britomart; and for her adversary at Blagdon, the Reverend Thomas Bere, she was "Scipio in petticoats."[91] Recognizing the backhandedness of Johnson's compliment to the young woman who read so voraciously, defended her favorites with such spirit, and scarcely brooked opposition, along with the petulance of Bere's attack, I find Wilberforce's tag the most appropriate and revealing. There are parallels and, of course, huge contrasts between More and Spenser's "martiall mayd."[92] Britomart is both a champion and a lover. In pursuit of her destined mate, Artegall, this armed knight unseats Guyon, relieves Redcrosse, escapes Malecasta's advances, wins a tournament for the Knights of Maidenhead, and dethrones her antitype, Radigund. Love is her duty; as Pamela Joseph Benson explains, "she is never assigned or asks for a masculine role, however successful she may be in the masculine realm of combat."[93] Exemplar of chastity, friendship, and justice, Britomart is also vulnerable, being caught "unwares"[94] in receiving wounds from Gardante, Busirane, and Artegall himself. Although her progeny with Artegall is prophesied, their union, less and less likely, remains unconsummated by the end of Book V. The Georgian version stamps a resolute temperament and awareness onto the original design. Without an Artegall and evidently[95] not mourning the loss of Mr. Turner, the later Britomart devoted herself more and more exclusively to championing the reform of manners along strict, at times idiosyncratic, Christian lines. Though she may have applauded the return to male rule in the city of Radegone, she moved in a direction quite different from that of the increasingly nuanced Spenserian maid. While Britomart, poignantly human in her anguish over Artegall, simply leaves Spenser's poem, Hannah More, in her pious preachments and ecclesiastical entourages, appears to leave ordinary, passionate, sexual humanity behind. The work to which "Saint Hannah," who was "so good and so bad,"[96] devoted most of her energies also distances her the most from sympathetic understanding. Despite the comparative degree that her surname teasingly invites, More is without parallel.

Although she sought—in youth as in old age—meditative quiet and release from the bustle, More was an active, sociable being, with a life-long dread of procrastination. Contemporaries clearly prized her energetic, public-

More, a painting by Frances
Reynolds (Georgian House, Bristol).

More, a drawing by Mr. Slater
(1813) (Bristol Museum and Art
Gallery).

More, a picture by E. Bird of Bristol, in the possession
of Messrs. Cadell and Davies (Bristol Museum and Art
Gallery).

More, a painting by Mr. Clint
(The Pierpont Morgan Library,
New York).

More, a painting by H. W. Pickersgill (Bristol Museum and Art Gallery).

spirited intelligence. In London, a regular at Mrs. Vesey's Tuesday get-togethers, she was also a favored guest at the all-male sour crout parties and at Mr. Cole's "select society" of lawyers, professors, and bishops.[97] Praised by Dr. Burney for the "force of sentiment and language . . . not equalled since . . . our great and pious moralist, Johnson,"[98] and remembered by the Dissenting clergyman, Dr. William Jay, for her "electrical wit,"[99] her writing was hailed as "a loud call to the world"[100] and her life as "a public benefit and a public blessing."[101]

While More preferred to publish anonymously, her notorious male critics, "Sappho Search," "Peter Pindar," and "The Reverend Sir Archibald MacSarcasm," in attacking both her writing and her image, all hid behind pseudonyms. As "Sappho Search," the perpetual curate of Butley, John Black, took jovial aim in versified form at More's *Strictures*, finding the basis of "all the pomp of her stile" in common fare and purloined ideas:

> To some will seem most abundantly plain,
> That a *pot*, not *alembic*, is Hannah More's brain.
> 'Tis *porridge*, not *spirit*, in which Hannah deals,
> And she puffs that ten thousand partake of her meals.
> But, while wholesome soup for the times she prepares,
> Ingredients to steal she unblushingly dares.[102]

Yet, quivering, he almost swallowed his criticism in the conclusion: "But no timid hare, or poor stag, is Miss More— / With a fierce thund'ring tusk, she may prove a wild Boar."[103] John Wolcot, alias "Peter Pindar," mounted another versified assault both against her eulogist, Bishop Porteus, whom he dismissed as "a very pigmy in the realms of Taste," and against the "humming Native of a Bristol pool" herself:

> Twice can't I read *her* labours for my blood,
> So *simply* mawkish, so *sublimely* sad!
> I own Miss Hannah's life is *very good*,
> But then her verse and prose are *very bad*.[104]

In addressing More directly he strove for an early psychoanalytical explanation of her discontent with some poets.

> Somewhat has wounded thee, 'tis very plain!
> Revenge, I fear, lies rankling in thine heart;
> Then say thy cause of anger and disdain—
> Why on poor POETS hast thou been so tart.[105]

Her most ferocious adversary, also colluding with her Blagdon antagonists, was "MacSarcasm," William Shaw. In his full-length study, MacSarcasm fulminated for more than two hundred pages, reviewing and denouncing all of her work, directing that some of it—*Strictures*, in particular—be burned, characterizing More as a plagiary, a virago, and a devil, and perorating intemperately on the "malicious disposition of her heart to calumniate, to injure and ruin others, under a robe of religious sanctity."[106]

Though more measured, two later critics, Macaulay and de Quincey, whom the kindly aunt at Barley Wood had made much of when they were younger, finally leveled negative judgments. An older and wiser Macaulay, cut off from the promised inheritance of More's library, allowed that "she was a very kind friend . . . from childhood, [who] called out [his] literary tastes [and] . . . was really a second mother," but refused to review her *Works* or *Life* since this universally unsatisfying exercise would involve "straining [his] conscience in her favour."[107] De Quincey's recollections of his mother's neighbor were more pugnacious, perhaps because he was deemed wayward and as a twenty-four-year-old fresh from Oxford had refused to light votive candles to the sixty-four-year-old grande dame. Admitting that their acquaintance rested on "a solid foundation of mutual dislike," and exhibiting some pride in his own Spenserian role of "a perfect Talus or iron man, as to equity, and as to logic," he delivered judgment on More as "a clever woman . . . a little spoiled by flattery" and "a woman of worldly mind . . . involuntarily laying too much stress on rank, public honours and, above all, on public opinion and . . . [being] conscious of this infirmity, . . . [having] struggled meritoriously against it."[108]

The earliest biographies by a clergyman and two laymen, in some instances cloyingly hagiographic, can be just as misleading as MacSarcasm's vitriol and de Quincey's testiness. Through abridging her letters and sermonizing in his commentary, William Roberts may actually have done a disservice to More's "pure and prudent application of popular talents"; however, he was performing what he saw as the biographer's duty: "to make her Christian Morality speak again to the people of this land, to restore a walking faith to its due preference above a talking faith."[109] Another official biographer, the curate of Wrington who was also her elegist, the Reverend Henry Thompson, elevated More as "the fearless and eloquent prophetess, . . . the Cassandra, who, however discredited, ridiculed, opposed, calumniated, still is found unmoved in her high vocation—the inculcation of THE TRUTH."[110] The most revealing of the trio, Thomas Taylor, insists on her status as "one of the most useful writers of the past age" by letting "her own works praise her" (Proverbs 31.33); tracing "the steady growth of her Christian character,"[111] Taylor illuminates the blending of firmness and conciliation in her public activities. Of the Mendip reformer, he observes: "making allowances for the mortification of, at least, implied censure, which she knew her exertions cast on clerical supineness, she carefully endeavoured to avoid giving offence to the vicar or curate of the parishes in which her schools were established."[112] In addition to the anonymity of the publication of her two volumes on the education of a princess, Taylor remarks, More astutely dedicated them to the bishop who had been appointed the royal tutor, a move "well calculated to conciliate the bishop for any undue intrusion upon the duties of his office, or any imputations on his incapacity to discharge them aright, of which it might perhaps otherwise have been chargeable."[113] On only one occasion, the result of More's "amiable disposition" and "incaution" in trusting her servants, does he find her "in some degree, censurable."[114]

More was certainly the darling of most female Victorian biographers. Mrs. Elwood's *Memoirs*, though admitting that More's "principles partook . . . of the austerity of the old puritanical doctrines,"[115] celebrated her intelligence and accomplishments. Helen Cross Knight's study presented Hannah More as "one of the most complete models of christian character" whose "integrity of moral consciousness" was her "hidden strength."[116] While Clara Lucas Balfour praised the "elasticity" of her temperament, Catherine J. Hamilton ventured to develop More's resemblance to Harriet Martineau (1802–1876): "Both were free from romance, and had an earnest desire for freedom and independence; . . . both were able to lead a happy, contented, useful, single life, in a quiet country retreat. Many gulfs, of course, yawn between them. Harriet Martineau believed in nothing but herself and Mr. Atkinson; while Hannah More was full of faith, and was the oracle of the extreme Evangelical party."[117] While support of abolitionism and education for the working class link these writers, contrasts are actually stronger than similarities here. No single man in Hannah More's life exerted an influence comparable to that of the mesmerist and amateur scientific theorist, George Henry Atkinson, with whom Martineau corresponded and whom she regarded as a "mentor" and "prophet"[118] in her acceptance of reverend agnosticism.

In the generations immediately after her death, More's reputation was waning. Her exclusiveness, in religion as well as social circle, exercised George Eliot, who made no secret of her hearty dislike of "that most disagreeable of all monsters, a blue stocking monster—a monster that can only exist in a false state of society."[119] Charlotte Yonge's contribution to the Famous Women Series of books put the case for the other side; in a carefully detailed examination, astute and sympathetic, of the life and works of a forerunner, whose reputation for " 'goodness' " had already caused her to be forgotten,

Yonge defended More as "no narrow-minded woman absorbed in village gossip" but as "a real influence on the tone of education in all classes of English women."[120]

The steady trickle of essays[121] that followed characterized More as a woman of strength and moral conviction. She became a quaint curio to be dusted and displayed periodically. In this pious persiflage no one imitated the outspoken critique of Augustine Birrell, who brazenly proclaimed Hannah More "one of the most detestable writers that ever held a pen" and pictured her floundering "like a huge conger-eel in an ocean of dingy morality."[122] Impenitent, he defended burying the nineteen volumes of her works "in full calf" in the garden: " 'Out of sight out of mind,' said I cheerfully stamping them down."[123] Without Birrell's overstatement these studies also lack any astute understatement, such as E.M. Forster provided in his subtly shaded biography of his great-aunt, who was Henry Thornton's eldest daughter and Hannah More's friend. Although Forster realized that the exhortations of the Clapham sect "will not travel," he suggested that their affectionate gaiety "can still be heard by those who sit quiet" and indicated that patient unraveling could expose common humanity: "The twentieth-century observer has to remind himself that inside all this cocoonery of words there was love, there was pain."[124]

Yet it is More's texts, the words themselves, that are the biggest impediment. When book-length studies[125] do not simply synopsize, they discount her writing as "verbose and repetitive, . . . unread and unreadable"[126] and the writer herself as "always didactic, always moralistic, and practically always conventional."[127] Feminist criticism has been understandably and rightly severe about More's dedication to the doctrine of the two spheres and her solemn discourses on submission. In contrast to the revolutionary women novelists (Mary Wollstonecraft, Mary Hays, Helen Maria Williams, Elizabeth Inchbald, and Charlotte Smith), More is the touchstone of conservatism.[128] The "diffidence" of the heroine of her novel is censured for being "so compelete as almost to amount to contented self-erasure."[129] As the patron of Ann Yearsley she is charged with using bourgeois privilege to engage in "character assassination."[130] As a Tory Abolitionist, More is depicted reaffirming "evangelical gendered class values and their relation to racial subjugation."[131] But many readers also highlight the inherent doubleness of More's attitude, the surprising parallels with revolutionary contemporaries, and the contradictions in her life and writing. "Such alternative (but not mutually exclusive) domestic ideologies as More's model of Evangelical femininity and Wollstonecraft's rational womanhood," claims Mitzi Myers, "are parallel, even symbiotic, female responses to political upheavals, attempts to take advantage of national unease to re-pattern domestic life through new schematic images of social order."[132] Further, More's insistence on "the reformist responsibilities inherent in Evangelical female ideology" helps explain the "virulence" of her Blagdon enemies who castigated her "for both cunning femininity and masculine feminism."[133] For Mary Poovey More is one example of the phenomenon of "double consciousness" in women who "thought of them-selves as textbook Proper Ladies even as they boldly crossed the border of that limited domain."[134] Leonore Davidoff and Catherine Hall clarify More's "contradictory messages" in confining women "to the sphere of the private and the domestic" yet in arguing for the central importance of their influence "in nurturing morality in an amoral world."[135]

Without picturing More as rejoicing in her chains or dismissing her combination of "a good heart and an inadequate methodology" as the "liberal lie in action,"[136] I plan to pursue the doubleness and contradictions, the declarations and outright misgivings of her largely neglected or superficially mined works—from the determined experiments of the earliest plays to the poignantly revealing essays on practical piety, Christian morals, and Saint Paul. I shall use "works" to include More's published writing, philanthropic activities, and voluminous correspondence. Her ambivalence between expres-sive interiority and social purposiveness, refusal to be bullied by clergymen, lawyers, or publishers, assumption of the hortatory role oblivious of restric-tions of gender, and resoluteness in swimming against the current sustain my fascination (not entirely unproblematic) with this singular woman's oratorical and debating genius. More's ironic observations of the literati in her poetry, the ventriloqual storytelling of her tracts, ballads, and dialogues, her stun-ningly popular response to the novel of sensibility, her contemporizing of Saint Paul, and her blurring of the distinctions between private and public in the letters locate her as a forceful voice in her own day and one who, from the point of view of plain justice, deserves a more nuanced treatment today. Even when she was the object of prolonged persecution, More herself pleaded for an inclusive, comprehensive assessment of any writer. "For it is not so much from an insulated passage," she argued, "as from the general tenour and spirit of his writings, that an author's principles may be deduced."[137]

Without venerating or trivializing More I believe she is altogether more complex and conflicted than most detracting comments or piecemeal excerpts indicate. Barbara Newman's cautions about the "three besetting sins [of] . . . the temptations to idealize, . . . to pity, and . . . to blame" and "an exaggerated notion of the solidarity of women [that] may deny the otherness and diversity of the past"[138] are as instructive for dealing with medieval celibates as with Hannah More. In some ways More had actually experienced all of these temptations before her death. An emphatic foe of card playing, she must have found it particularly galling that her reputation was used to market a game of "amusement with instruction," *Hannah More's Cards of Wisdom*. This tiny (60 x 85 cm) curiosity, housed in the Bristol Public Library, consists of twenty-five question and twenty-five answer cards, all offering some sententious but inauthentic More-ish nugget about such "party" topics as "the most effectual method to conquer weakness" and "the difference between an acquaintance and a friend." The directions point out that one of the players should "officiate as Mrs. More," but add, with faltering bluffness, that "if the choice falls on a Gentleman, he need not be ashamed of so distinguished a title."[139] An additional irony is the unwitting hint of true Morean spirit in the answer provided to ways of accepting compliments: "as trifles to be felt, as little by those who hear them, as they are in fact by those who speak them."[140] Shortly before the bedroom-bound More was forced to sell and leave Barley Wood, "driven like Eve out of paradise" by the unknown extravagances of her eight "pampered minions,"[141] she confided to John Harford, an older brother of the buyer, that she had to rely on the "intervention" of Zachary Macaulay to settle her affairs with Cadell. Describing the son of her original publisher as "a hard man" and "narrowly watchful of his own interests," she vented frustration with a characteristic blend of humility and shrewdness. "My poor works have been so long published, and, I am thankful to say, have had so much wider circulation than many far better books, that I have now £400 to receive, but he pays me by such small, shabby instalments that I may be dead before I receive it!"[142] The four-storied narrow row house overlooking the Avon Gorge, at 4 Windsor Terrace, in the Bristol subdivision of Clifton, where More spent the last five years of her life, may have been "an elegant and convenient residence"[143] in the 1830s. Although the wrought iron balconies are solidly in place and the grimy Corinthian capitols intact, the only distinguishing feature of Number 4 is a small, blue-lettered oval plaque, erected by the Clifton and Hotwells Improvement Society, declaring

Hannah More
1745–1833
Authoress
lived here
1829–33.

It's likely the fate of such signs to be precarious, important for a moment and then overlooked. More's lot has been the same.

❀ 2 ❀
The "Complicated Temptation"
of the Theater

Hannah More wrote five separate dramatic works, whose influence and portents this chapter will explore. A popular teacher in her sisters' school, she composed the pastoral drama, *The Search after Happiness*, first published in 1773 and running through thirteen editions, for performance by their female students. Having made a present of the proceeds to her sister Patty, More expressed some surprise that more than ten thousand copies had been sold by the time of the ninth edition, in 1787.[1] Her free translation of Pietro Metastasio's *Attilio Regolo: The Inflexible Captive*, premiered at the Theatre Royal in Bath on May 6, 1775, and played at Exeter a few days later. Under the tutelage and patronage of the recently retired actor-manager David Garrick, her second tragedy, *Percy*, was her London debut. Opening December 10, 1777, it filled the Theatre Royal in Covent Garden for an exceptional twenty-one-night run; a first edition of four thousand sold out in a fortnight, and when *Percy* was remounted in Bristol in September 1778, a crowd threatened to storm the building to secure seats. Her final tragedy, *The Fatal Falsehood* (originally called *The Bridal Day*), lasted only four nights, in April 1779, with More being distracted and, according to her sister's testimony, "indifferent about the matter,"[2] due mainly to Garrick's death in January and to a lesser extent to Hannah Cowley's stinging public charge of plagiarism. More's final plays, *Sacred Dramas* (1782), based on biblical texts and aimed at young readers, were not intended for performance.

Although she admitted being "diverted with the conjectures which are formed of [her] principles, from the Dramas"[3] (referring specifically to the biblical vignettes), More's plays appeared to cause real friction with her principles. It is clear that she grew to distrust her own passion for the stage because of the theater's corporeality, its physical directness. And yet, in the very act of renouncing this "complicated temptation," the attention More lavished on the lure itself betrayed her unwillingness to be cut off entirely from "doctrines, not simply expressed, as those of the Sunday are, in the naked form of axioms, principles, and precepts, but realized, embodied, made alive, furnished with organs, clothed, decorated, brought into sprightly discourse, into interesting action; enforced with all the energy of passion, adorned with all the graces of language, and exhibited with every aid of emphatical delivery, every attraction of appropriate gesture."[4] Despite her reluctant conclusion about the incompatibility of the stage with "the more correct and considerate Christian" character, she remained hopeful that "something of concert and congruity" would continue to link her to a like-minded readership. Her plea for an "intellectual commerce" between writer and reader relies on the reader's enabling allegiance.

Between him who writes and him who reads there must be "a kind of coalition of interests, something of a partnership, however unequal the capital, in mental property; a sort of joint stock of tastes and ideas."[5] But, just as there were no hints of the autonomy of reader response from More prefacing her collected works in 1801, so there is scant evidence of shared interests among her few readers today.

Was "Garrick's Sappho"[6] ever a playwright at all? Were her London successes "a kind of slum adventure,"[7] or the result of the attentiveness of the Bluestockings toward their protégée? Allan Cunningham's backward glance at "The Literature of the Last Fifty Years," published in *The Athenaeum* in the year of her death, is cautious in its estimate. "Of Hannah More it is not easy to speak," he begins ominously. Despite the admission that "she has some-times aided the influence of religious feelings by dramatic details," he stops short of praise, allowing that "she has never succeeded in communicating that life or variety which brings popularity."[8] Scarcely five years later, her elegist and second official biographer, the Reverend Henry Thompson, remarked equivocally that her plays—then nearly a half-century old—were being excluded from the stage on account of "improvements and declensions of publick taste"; in spite of his disapproval of the keenness about the frigid unities promoted by Garrick, Thompson did concede that all More's stage work was "sufficiently dramatick."[9] Most of the comments on her plays either endorse or question this sufficiency. Garrick's own biographer prognosticated More's "rising genius in tragedy,"[10] while the mid-Victorian literary ency-clopedist, Robert Chambers, maintained in both versions of his entry on More that she showed real promise, judging "that the authoress might have excelled as a dramatic writer, had she devoted herself to that difficult species of composition" and later emphasizing that "the venerable Mrs. Hannah More might have been remembered as a playwright had she settled down seriously to dramatic work."[11] Augustine Birrell, predictably, harumphed that her three tragedies "were not damned as they deserved to be."[12] Most readers register some dissatisfaction with the far-fetched motivation of her melodramatic, pseudo-romantic tragedies, while M.G. Jones forecloses the project of examining the plays by deeming them "entirely lacking in dramatic quality."[13] As always, More remains fair game for ridicule, even as a playwright. A "historical novel of the eighteenth century," Ciji Ware's *Wicked Company*, casts Hannah in the role that most recent criticism assigns her: sententious killjoy. In contrast to Ware's fictitious playwright, the hotheaded and much sought after Sophie McGann, who is also tutored by David Garrick, the real-life More sits—edgy and prim—on the sidelines of the novel's racy Covent Garden and Drury Lane action. Obsequious in the extreme, Ware's "self-satisfied Miss More" speaks "sanctimoniously," "self-importantly," "dolefully"; although Sophie takes "pleasure at Hannah's look of envy," she does recognize "the schoolmistress from Bristol" as "her fiercest competitor for the Garricks' affections."[14] Aside from being narrow and incomplete, Ware's treatment of Hannah More as a character and a playwright is also misleading. Although More is clearly out of place in the lurid world of this novel, she herself was very levelheaded in acknowledging the need for action, disorder, and irrationality on stage so as to grip viewers. "If any body were to write a play about good sort of quiet, reasonable, orderly, prosperous people," she observed to Mr. Pepys, "the audience would not be able to sit out the first act; they would long for the relief of a little distress, and languish for the refreshment of a little misery."[15] The female characters of her plays, in fact, have a strength, determination, and reserve quite different from the amorous entanglements that construct and constrain Sophie McGann. But despite their virtue and protestations of heroic self-control, the daughters, wives, and widows of More's plays are not mere cardboard cutouts; some succeed as poised, close-to-omniscient instructors, while the tragic circumstances of others force them to abandon noble resolve and accept emotional collapse. In addition, More does not stand by indifferently empowering and upbraiding her female characters; rather, with intelligent sympathy she invests in these women, voicing their assurances and their doubts. As a playwright More is a curious amalgam of passionate intensity and moral purposiveness, an "incorrigible best-seller"[16] genuinely attracted to the theater but seeing it through her specially tinted lenses of the stage's reformative mission.

Changing and Fixed Strictures on the Education of Girls

More's first publication, *The Search after Happiness: A Pastoral Drama*,[17] is a sober piece of juvenilia; its history of editions and revisions also shows her dedication to the idea of the stage as an agent of improvement. Although not published until she was twenty-eight, More wrote it, as her preface attests, when she was eighteen, for recitation by the "young ladies" at her sisters' school in Bristol. Attending thoughtfully to the counsel of the widow Urania, the "fond maternal friend" (12), the all-female cast conducts its own benediction devoted to the ideal of sequestered happiness. To its credit *The Search after Happiness* slips through the nets of most labels: a pastoral that makes the settings of "a grove," "a cottage," and "a rural entertainment" the mere spots from which the notion of happiness is addressed and interrogated; a didactic piece, using converts rather than genuine searchers, that nevertheless succeeds in conveying the process of learning. As a consciousness-raising exercise, it seems to have had its effect too. Although there were several gaffes and some laughable miscasting in the performance of *Search* that Mary Russell Mitford recalls from her school days, Mitford herself discovered that the play "was only too good for me," a mildly ironic point illustrated by the alumnae scene with which she concludes: "Whenever a happy chance throws two or three of us together, the English teacher and her favourite play are sure to be amongst the first, the gayest, and the tenderest of our school-day recollections."[18]

The view of learning that *Search* presents indicates a striking maturity on the part of the teenage playwright. Of course we have no way of knowing if, ten years after the fact, More actually changed or polished the original manuscript, especially since the publication history of this play shows a number of major revisions before its inclusion in the collected works in 1801, which was the play's thirteenth edition. The changes to the first and second edition, both published in 1773, are significant; it was this second edition that went through six successive but unchanged editions, with Bristol and London publishers, until 1785. Only with the ninth and eleventh editions, in 1787 and 1796, did More again revise the text "with additions." The revisions point out the meticulousness with which More scrutinized this youthful exercise and the decided shift in her interests, from dramaturgical effectiveness to moral and theological precision. Not only does the play, then, inaugurate More's career but it also signals her major preoccupations.

Initially an anonymous publication, *A Search after Happiness* was subtitled *A Pastoral, in Three Dialogues*. With a lock-step punctiliousness, the three exchanges relate the reasons for the search, the young ladies' confessions of past attempts, and Urania's advice. The searchers, Euphelia, Florissa, Pastorella, and Laurinda, explain their follies: Euphelia's sharing of her hours "betwixt the Park and the Play" (9), Florissa's pining for "passion, sentiment, and stile" along with "abstruser studies" (11), Pastorella's love of "pernicious novels" that made "fiction [her] nature, and romance [her] law" (12), and Laurinda's malleability in being "Too indolent to think, too weak to chuse /

Too soft to blame, too gentle to refuse" (14). Without missing a beat and with only a minor reordering, Urania responds in turn to Euphelia, Pastorella, Florissa, and Laurinda. Urania's last words praise the young shepherdess Florella who has escorted the searchers, because "Her thoughts are rational, her virtue pure; / —A virtuous mind is Happiness secure!" (23).

In the same year, More's emendations to the second edition—with a switch to the definite article in the title—underscore her desire to sharpen emphases and give dramaturgical bulk to the exchanges. Since she has several similar-sounding names (with a searcher called Florissa, one of Urania's daughters called Flora, and the young shepherdess herself) More changed Florissa to Cleora and Flora to Sylvia. Florella and Urania's daughters now supply extensive songs to link scenes and highlight developments. Urania's advice to the confessing quartet is reordered so that the final admonition is reserved for Cleora and her aspirations for "abstruser studies." Urania's praise of Florella in this considerably longer text takes a bold step in linking her rational thoughts to religion:

> Reason in her to pure religion tends,
> Subservient only to the noblest ends;
> True piety's the magnet of her soul
> Which upwards point, immortal bliss the pole. (36)

The additions to the ninth and eleventh editions mainly concern the praise of Florella. Steering clear of the pure religion of reason, Urania now focuses her eulogy on ingenuousness:

> No dark disguise about her heart in thrown,
> Tis virtue's int'rest fully to be known;
> Her nat'ral sweetness ev'ry heart obtains,
> What Art and Affectation miss, she gains. (1787: 40)

More retains the epilogue, inserted in the third edition in 1774, in which one young lady admits reluctantly "These bagatelles we must relinquish now / And good matronic Gentlewomen grow." The epilogue cites the joining of female virtue and sense in "moral CARTER," "faultless AIKIN," "accomplish'd MONTAGU," "polish'd BROOKES," and "fair MACAULAY" (1774: 44).[19] Still included is Urania's discourse on woman's "real good" and "true interests"; her gaze is earth-bound as, for matronic gentlewomen-in-the-making, she advises compliant yet ultimately powerful obedience: "By yielding she obtains the noblest sway / And reigns securely, when she seems t'obey" (1787: 41). As if to moderate this counsel, however, by extending her earlier stress on women's

"Angel-kindness" and "virtuous thirst of doing good" (1773b: 38), Urania now pontificates with an eschatological apostrophe to "Heav'n's minist'ring Angel":

> But know, the awful all disclosing day,
> The long arrear of secret worth shall pay.
> Applauding Saints shall hear with fond regard,
> And He, who witness'd here, shall there reward. (1787: 42)

By the time of the collected works edition in 1801 the changes are marked, assertive, and severe. The epilogue with its admission of a love of versified bagatelles is chopped. Gone too is Urania's advice about yielding to gain supremacy. In place of Euphelia's observation on Urania's teaching, "With double grace she pleads Discretion's cause," she now relates, more correctly according to the tastes of the playwright, her pleading of "Religion's cause" (1801: 328). The most arresting revisions occur in the preface and prologue, which had been unchanged since the second edition. The preface had shown traces of diffidence—"sensible [the play] has many imperfections" and "almost ashamed to alledge" that the circulation of "imperfect, . . . mutilated copies" had prompted this publication. No such admissions appear in the later preface. Contrasts between the two prologues are even more pointed. The 1773 text is short, ingenuous, and direct. The speaker introduces herself "with trembling diffidence, with modest fear" and assures her listeners "No deep laid Plot adorns our humble page, / But scenes adapted to our sex and age" (ix). The author's aim, she contends, is simplicity itself: "To make Amusement and Instruction friends." Although this author shies away from "critic **man**" of whom "she could not stand the test," she begs indulgence of a female audience: "Ladies protect her—do not be satyric, / Spare censure, she expects not panegyric." Whether she expected praise or not, the author of the later prologue certainly did not apologize for "a Drama void of wit and free from love." Now an accomplished swimmer against the current—with the anti-Jacobin sentiments of *Village Politics* and her Cheap Repository project being widely disseminated and her reputation as an acerbic critic of aristocratic and middle-class neglect of moral responsibility well established through *Thoughts on the Importance of the Manners of the Great*, *An Estimate of the Religion of the Fashionable World*, and *Strictures on the Modern System of Female Education*—she presents her work as a deliberate contrast to available, popular fare. More offers a play that will frustrate prurient interests and refuse to connive at libertinism,

> Where no soft Juliet sighs, and weeps and starts,
> No fierce Roxana takes by storm your hearts;

> No comic ridicule, no tragic swagger,
> Not one elopement, not one bowl or dagger!
> No husband wrong'd who trusted and believ'd,
> No father cheated, and no friend deceiv'd;
> No libertine chambermaid that rake had bribed:
> Nor give we, to reward the rover's life,
> The ample portion and the beauteous wife. (275)

Vowing not to "transplant these noxious scenes / . . . to misses in their teens" (276), the author, though she calls herself "timid," "aims at simple truth and common sense." Clearly the biggest gap separating the green playwright from the established author collecting her works for republication is the public, authoritative persona of the older More.

What unites them is just as noteworthy: "in a modish age" a single-minded concern for female education that prefers "plain virtue to the boast of art" (277). This central, unifying concern reformulates in a distinctive way Locke's assertion that "'tis Vertue then, direct Vertue, which is the hard and valuable part to be aimed at in Education; and not a forward Pertness, or any little Arts of Shifting."[20] Urania fills all the requirements of Locke's tutor, who "should know the World well; The Ways, the Humors, the Follies, the Cheats, the Faults of the Age he is fallen into, and particularly of the country he lives in,"[21] with several notable exceptions. Sought after by the girls themselves instead of being retained by their parents, this tutor is female, equally intent in her aim to "pull off the Mask," but more benign and gentle than the Lockean model in tempering instruction "with the constant Marks of Tenderness and good Will."[22] More's pastoral interlude reflects a knowledge of real girls and their delusions, the kind of experiential sifting Richardson's virtuously rewarded Pamela recommended. In the episodic conduct book, volume II of *Pamela* (1740), the young wife is asked for a critical précis of "Mr. Locke's Treatise on Education," and discerning "some few things which . . . want clearing up," she proposes to arrive at an accurate judgment of Locke by testing his claim against her observations of real children: "now reading a chapter in the *child*, and now one in the *book*."[23] The firsthand experience of the Park Street school likely provided a rich source for characterization, just as Sarah Fielding's memories of Mrs. Mary Rookes' Boarding School in the Close of New Sarum, attended by the four Fielding sisters, helped her depiction of pupils at the little female academy. Urania is as alert as Fielding's Mrs. Teachum to her charges' willful follies and every bit as resolute in correcting them.

In all versions of the pastoral More retained her teenage reworking of *The Seasons* to stress both firmness of purpose and a largely female readership;

her epigraph adjusts Thomson's address to the "delightful task" shared by "the Father's Lustre, and the Mother's Bloom"[24] "to fix [not 'plant,' as Thomson had put it] / The gen'rous Purpose in the *Female* [not Thomson's 'glowing'] breast." Through all its variations the play figures learning as unfolding self-awareness, as a necessary blend of venturesomeness and tractability. The searchers are mainly adolescents, "represented by young Ladies from eight to fifteen years old." Their confessions or declarations of "the various methods . . . essay'd / To court, and win the bright celestial maid" (14) of happiness are already tinged with judgments about the wastefulness, indolence, and wrongheadedness of these earlier attempts. Because, in seeking both confirmation of these judgments and guidance from Urania to direct their "ductile youth" (18), they appear to be compliant good children and sound like commonsensical grownups, they hardly conform to the eighteenth-century adolescents who, "like bad children . . . often rejected the wisdom of their elders, and . . . disconcertingly manifested quite adult powers of resistance."[25] Are we to conclude that More's zealous questers, seeking out a maternal preceptor who "makes every thing a lesson to the heart," are unreal goody-goodies? I do not think so. The girls' eagerness and Urania's approval of their "candor," pity of their "foibles," and love of their "merits" (22) recall the tradition of being virtuously and tenderly bred, a tradition that stretches back at least as far as such Renaissance manuals as Elizabeth Grymeston's *Miscelanae* (1604), Dorothy Leigh's *The Mothers Blessing* (1616), and Elizabeth Joceline's *The Mothers Legacie, to Her Unborne Childe* (1624). Fearing her own death in childbirth, Joceline wrote "what [she] understood might serve for a foundation to a better learning," while Leigh advised that "what disposition so ever they bee of gentlenesse will soonest bring them to vertue, for frowardnesse and curtnesse doth harden the heart of a Child, and maketh him weary of vertue."[26] In "A True Relation of My Birth, Breeding, and Life," Margaret Cavendish, the Duchess of Newcastle, illustrates the effects of these directives through the recollections of her upbringing in the 1630s: "instead of threats, reason was used to persuade us, and instead of lashes, the deformities of vice was discovered, and the graces and virtues were presented unto us."[27] These strategies are precisely the ones More uses to great advantage in *Search*.

Among the most overt devices to fasten attention on her instructional aim is the reliance on rhyming couplets. There is no sing-song cant here, but strictly channeled, utilitarian axioms. With caesural breaks and chiastic constructions, the couplets themselves emblematize the contrasts between art and nature, outside and inside, riches and wisdom, society and solitude, and acclaim and serenity. But the pithiness does not become simply predictable because More continually interjects into this monitored discourse of instruction the imagery of cultivation and nurturance. Hence, the concept of learning that emerges is a deliberate blending of binary oppositions and organic growth; such hybridization neatly conveys an understanding of learning itself as a combination of trial and error with amenability to instruction. Cleora opens the play with a carefully crafted farewell to the world she has known; showing how thoroughly (some would say prematurely and unnaturally) programmed she is to renounce and start anew, she moves away

> From the gay misery of the thoughtless great,
> The walks of folly, the disease of state;
>
> . . . .
>
> Where pleasure never comes without alloy,
> And art but thinly paints fallacious joy;
> Where languor loads the day, excess the night,
> And dull satiety succeeds delight. (1)

Pastorella, "la jeune fille au romanticisme excessif,"[28] leavens the censoriousness somewhat by observing excitedly, "How this description with the scene agrees!" (2). Such congruency furnishes the basis for Euphelia's elevation of nature and the internal over art and the external.

> Here simple nature strikes the enraptur'd eye
> With charms, which wealth and art but ill supply;
> The genuine graces, which *without* we find,
> Display the beauty of the owner's *mind*. (2)

It might strike the reader's ear that these would-be rustics are merely prating. But one way of modifying their baleful sense of assurance about all that they have done wrong is to picture the means of improvement as indeterminate and in flux. Florella's song of bucolic busy-ness accentuates the link between cultivating physical and mental gardens.

> V.
> Our water is drawn from the clearest of springs,
> And our food, nor disease, nor satiety brings;
> And our mornings are chearful, our labours are blest,
> Our ev'nings are pleasant, our nights crown'd with rest.
>
> VI.
> From our culture yon' garden its ornament finds
> And we catch at some hint for improving our minds;
> To live to some purpose we constantly try,
> And we mark by our actions the days as they fly. (23)

Her mentor has no doubt been Urania, whose adage "If *Good* we plant not, *Vice* will fill the mind, / And weeds despoil the space for flow'rs design'd" (33), results naturally and logically from her view of the mind as a fertile garden:

> Know then, that life's chief happiness and woe,
> From good, or evil Education flow
> And hence our future dispositions rise,
> The vice we practice, or the good we prize.
> When pliant nature any form receives,
> That precept teaches, or example gives,
> The yielding mind with virtue shou'd be grac'd,
> For first impressions seldom are effac'd. (29)

But the play's own first impressions, its mixed messages about the nature-nurture binary, remain troubling. A strict and contrastive pedagogy, already active before the interlude begins and borrowed from the tradition established by Bunyan, Janeway, and Watts of the spiritually precocious child-spokesperson, has resulted in the girls' withering self-criticism. In recasting her frivolous pursuits, Euphelia asks rhetorically, "Without reflection whence could rise content?" (14). Cleora's acuteness leads to an unflattering assessment about her admiration of Locke and Boyle as a desire for glory, since she "sigh'd for their fame, but fear'd to share their toil" (18). Pastorella characterizes herself as "A victim to imagination's sway" in the same breath as she admits the perverse grip of novels and fiction: "still I found them false—and still believ'd" (19). Laurinda's indolence has been infantilizing, for she was "In size a woman, but in soul a child" (21). Does it make dramaturgic sense to use the searchers as the mouthpiece for the playwright's didactic aims? In a curious way the declamations suit this oratorio-like play.

Equally appropriate is the zeal with which the girls seek and listen to their "faultless model, . . . whose virtues fire / [Their] virgin hearts to *be* what [they] *admire*" (5). With a name borrowed from Sidneian pastoral romance, Urania blends the features of both the royal foundling reduced to poor shepherdess of the Old Arcadia and "Heavenly Beauty inspiring Heavenly Love, the Muse of Christian Poetry"[29] of the New Arcadia. Although it is less likely that More would have been familiar with *The Countess of Mongomeries Urania* (1621) by Sidney's niece Mary Wroth, the eponymous heroine of this jigsaw-puzzle narrative is also a shepherdess who, as well as being the friend and counsellor of the perpetually distressed Pamphilia, is revealed to be the sister of the inconstant Amphilanthus. At the outset the counsel of More's Urania, "plain, well-meant, imperfect yet sincere" (29), is ostensibly the product of her own life history: "what time has taught me, and experience shewn" (25). But when this "antient shepherdess" tailors her advice to each aspirant, she also universalizes with equivocal observations on woman's learning and place. In what sounds like an antieducational manifesto, Urania proclaims that "Science for *female* minds was never made" since "*learning* suits not our less vig'rous powers" (34)—an ambivalent position, at best, to be embedded in a play that closes by praising a female classicist and translator, a female Shakespeare critic, and a female historian. However, it is a tame version of the separate spheres argument More developed in *Essays on Various Subjects, principally designed for Young Ladies* (1777), especially in "Thoughts on the Cultivation of the Heart and Temper in the Education of Daughters." Although she never permitted this "juvenile" work to be reprinted, arguing that she handled the topic more fully in *Strictures*, her attitude in these pieces—likely composed close to the time of the major revisions to the second edition of *Search*—is nothing short of retrograde. Perhaps More herself realized the severity of her *ex-cathedra* pronouncements. For instance, although she promoted the power of the domestic sphere, where women are to "employ their lives" not simply "adorn their leisure," she also advocated that girls' "bold, independent, enterprising spirit" be "suppressed" in order to attain an alarming state of submission where "girls should be taught to give up their opinions betimes, and not pertinaciously to carry on a dispute, even if they should know themselves to be in the right."[30] By comparison Urania sounds almost progressive and egalitarian! But she has been cut from the same bolt. In place of the renown and roughness of learning Urania employs the criteria of utility and self-reformation:

> You might be *dazzling*, but not truly *bright*,
> A pompous glare, but not an useful light;
> . . . .
> Accomplishments by Heaven were first design'd
> Less to adorn, than to amend the mind. (35)

Forceful personal conviction characterizes her tribute to the angel in the house.

> So *Woman*, born to dignify retreat,
> Unknown to flourish, and unseen be great,
> To give domestic life its sweetest charm,
> With softness polish, and with virtue warm,
> Fearful of Fame, unwilling to be known,
> Shou'd seek but Heaven's applauses, and her own. (38)

Withdrawal and ambition (albeit repressed and embryonic) exist side by side in this portrait. Though More was not ironizing, how can her readers—particularly those trying to give her the benefit of the doubt, since a coalition of interests seems impossible—make sense of such utterances and of the junior playwright who used this discourse of domesticity as her way out of its restrictions and constraints?

The simplest solution is to dismiss the play as inconsistent or reactionary or both. Yet it would be unjust to reject this seminal work or consider it insignificant. When it first appeared, the pastoral was attributed only to "a young Lady"; but she was soon identified. "On Seeing Miss H. More in the title page of the 2d Edition of the Search after Happiness: A Ballad" by W. Buller, sewn into a late eighteenth-century Commonplace Book, warns "bachelors . . . briskly pursuing the sweet Hannah More" against plans for an easy conquest: "When to this Damsel, a wooing you go, / Pray be not dismay'd if she answer you no."[31] Buller also alerts readers and spectators to a protean slipperiness about this witty damsel.

> And since this same prudence deals much in disguise,
> O trust not her words, but examine her eyes,
> Tis there you may learn what you wish to explore,
> And the sentiments learn of the sweet Hannah More.

More seems to have become more elusive and paradox-ridden than ever. Despite the repressiveness of her methodology and principles, she energetically devoted her life to the education of all classes. Even though she came to see the stage in a way that is anathema to all actors, as teaching the theme of "self-conquest,"[32] she loved the theater at one time, regularly trooping her sisters' pupils from their school at the foot of Park Street the short distance to the Theatre Royal.

More's perpetual struggle between "bright intellect" and "stern Puritanism"[33] illuminates both the real promise and the tension of her playwrighting. In *Search* Florella's directive "to wean from earth" (27) captures the play's thesis about learning and living, growth and nurturance in all its complexity. Though rooted in the earth, learning and growth must ultimately be directed elsewhere. Troping this disengagement as a way of accustoming oneself to doing without the mother's milk suggests that Hannah More had a grasp of both worlds of sense and spirit. She understood and genuinely sympathized with the young searchers' so-called follies; she also felt the keen attraction of virtue transcending mundane realities. *The Search after Happiness* provided her the platform to function as dramatic and spiritual mother, choreographing a quest and indicating its full extent.

Experiments in Emotions: The Tragedies

Beyond her correspondence with the Garricks about early drafts of *Percy*, there is no evidence of More's revising the three tragedies.[34] Gloomier and fuller than the oratorio of *Search*, they emphasize feeling and introspection over dialogue and action. These stunning successes in the late 1770s perplex us more than two hundred years later. Their awkwardness, convolutions, and overstrained emotional reactions are not to modern (and especially postmodern) tastes. In More's period, however, women writing for the stage—among them Frances Brooke, Elizabeth Griffith, Frances Sheridan, Hannah Cowley, Amelia Opie, Elizabeth Inchbald, and Harriet Lee—were not at all uncommon. In fact, they "seemed to be about to come into their own as dramatists."[35] Brooke's ballad-opera *Rosina* was a triumph in 1782. Although Frances Burney's early comedy *The Witlings* and her three later tragic plays and lengthy fragmentary sketch of a fourth are full of private allegories, these unpublished, unperformed plays were immensely important to her development as a writer and, as Margaret Anne Doody observes, indicate that Burney "might have made a career as a dramatist."[36]

Although More, like Burney in this respect, was not launching a career in the theater, she was experimenting with forms, characters, and vocabularies, an exercise that would eventually direct her to the genres and styles where she was most at ease and productive. Her tragic heroines, Attilia, Elwina, and Emmelina, are full of high-sounding purpose, but they live in worlds hostile to their virtue. Although Attilia, the daughter of the Roman warrior Regulus, held captive in Carthage, dares to tell the consul, Manlius, what must be done to secure her father's release ("A woman shall inform you" [320], she asserts), she soon sinks "down the dread precipice of deep despair" (333). Filial obedience results in Elwina's marriage to the pathologically jealous Douglas, while her true lover, Percy, pines in the wings. The misfortunes of Elwina and, specifically, the ways in which her words are discredited or disproved chart the tragic decline. She pledges to bear Douglas's "fearful indignation" (202) by adopting "manly force."

> Thou melting heart be firm as adamant;
> Ye shatter'd nerves be strung with manly force,
> That I may conquer all my sex's weakness,
> And live as free from terror as from guilt. (202)

In short order Elwina accepts the poison Douglas insists she consume, should he (Douglas) be overcome by Percy in their duel, as "my kind dismission from a world of sorrow, / My cup of bliss, my passport to the skies" (217). On being told that Orlando, her romantic interest, has refused her, Emmelina reacts with extraordinary self-possession: "See, I am calm; I do not shed a tear; / The warrior weeps, the woman is a hero" (276). Her father is moved to beg her pardon.

> Forgive me if I thought thee fond and weak.
> I have a Roman matron for my daughter,
> And not a feeble girl. (276)

But Emmelina, too, follows the pattern of noble resolve and emotional collapse so characteristic of More's tragic heroines. She goes as far as to justify Orlando's rejection ("He could not choose but love whom Rivers lov'd" [286]); as disconsolate as Attilia at the return of her father and as distracted as Elwina by Douglas's bloody jealousy, Emmelina dies protesting that she is "not mad" but that "the afflicting angel has been with [her]" (303). More's masochistic-sounding heroines are caught in a bind: striving to overcome the prevailing assumptions about their weakness, they predictably fall prey to them.

Yet these women are considerably more than pawns to the powerful men who surround and often lecture them. At the very least their strong personalities provoke responses from fathers, husbands, and lovers; their feelings, ambivalent sign of potency and vulnerablity, demand attention. Attilia's father speaks openly of "the weakness of her sex" (348) and the softness of her soul; highmindedly he refuses all liberation attempts, returning to Carthage with this punctilious observation for his daughter during their last exchange: "Passion—which is thy tyrant—is my slave" (374). However enfeebled Attilia, who faints as her father sails away, may appear, More's version of Metastasio's opera, in which he sought "to delineate the character of a Roman hero of consummate virtue, according to the Pagan idea, not only in principle, but practice,"[37] colors the original significantly. There is more dramatic business, more expansiveness, and more tugging at the heartstrings in her five-act play.[38] While it allows Regulus to succeed as a philosopher-hero, More's translation also stresses the girlish rashness and inexperience of Attilia. Unlike the rhymed bromides about "that unshaken mind" and "a pattern . . . / Of one who knows not guilt or fear" prattled by the heroine in John Hoole's faithful English translation of the three-act Regulus,[39] More's Attilia resigns herself—an attitude her creator was always ready to endorse—to the hand of Providence.

> Teach me to yield to your divine command,
> And meekly bow to your correcting hand;

> Contented to resign, or pleas'd receive,
> What wisdom may withhold, or mercy give. (345)

Though spotlighting the emotional fragility of Attilia, More also cashes in, dramaturgically, on the curious power of feeling. She adds a scene between Manlius and Attilia, in which the Consul admits "The softness of thy sorrow is contagious" (362). More builds on the love business between Attilia and the tribune Licinius, with Regulus cushioning the blow of his departure by telling his daughter, "I give thee to his [Licinius's] wishes; I do more— / I give thee to his virtues" (374). She constructs a much longer farewell than the Italian original. After saying goodbye for more than one hundred lines, Regulus, according to More's stage directions, "fixes his eye steadily on [Attilia] for some time, and then departs to the ships" (381).

More wants Elwina, who has been compared to Iphigenia and Bérénice,[40] to be both the affective heart of the tragedy and the clear-voiced moralist at its close. Having capitulated to her father's tearful request to marry a man she does not love, this daughter tries to vindicate her obedience to the recently returned and incredulous Percy by explaining "the cruel tyranny of tenderness":

> Hast thou e'er seen a father's flowing tears,
> And known that thou couldst wipe those tears away?
> If thou hast felt, and hast resisted these,
> Then thou mayst curse my weakness; but if not,
> Thou canst not pity, for thou canst not judge. (198)

The skill with which Elwina makes so-called weakness the foil for callousness shows the stock that More put in this character; it might also explain such diverse critical responses as *The Monthly Review*'s endorsement of the "delicate" text and its "flowing and easy" language and Katharine Rogers's relatively recent dismissal of this "priggish tragedy."[41] More and Garrick corresponded over improvements to the fourth act, the last encounter between Percy and Elwina, and each planned initially to have the actor, Mrs. Barry (who played Elwina), deliver the epilogue. Both the original drafts and the published version, spoken by Mr. Lewes "in the character of a fine gentleman," emphasize the discrepancy between the polished age and the archaic virtues of "these ballad heroes." Although the epilogue is credited to Garrick, one of the earlier drafts is definitely in More's hand.[42] She may, in fact, have provided Garrick with an epilogue (her facility with couplets is unquestioned) that he edited slightly. The first and second sets of Garrick's alterations are noteworthy. In her version—at least, the version in her hand—More describes the age's beaux as calmly unperturbed:

> They never can be hurt, however exposed:
> Let then the vulgar virtues of this night
> Rest with their owners—for if brought to light
> They ne'er, this polish'd age, can profit, or delight.

While empowering Mrs. Barry to speak as a contemporary satirist, she alludes indirectly to the lost Horatian formula. Garrick sliced the final couplet to "Old vulgar virtues cannot be defended. / Let the dead rest—the living can't be mended," and, in the same way, the petulant fop in the published version sneers, in closing, "we living can't be mended." It is arguable that Garrick's changes pack more dramatic punch. Assigning the speech to a man—and not to the recently raving and poisoned heroine—blunts the moral effect. Obliterating the allusions to instruction, the offhandedness of the published epilogue opts for a raw contrast between then and now.

Moderation of feeling in *The Fatal Falsehood* is the precise trait that exonerates More from the charge of having plagiarized from Cowley's *Albina, Countess Raimond*. Although More expressed "the deepest regret" at being "compelled to take a step so repugnant to her own feeling" when defending herself in *The St. James's Chronicle*,[43] the greatest proof of the insubstantiality of Cowley's accusation lies in the texts of the two plays themselves. *The Fatal Falsehood* concerns the passions of three men and two women. Rivers, Lord Guildford's son, loves and is betrothed to Julia, his father's ward. Rivers's friend, Orlando, an Italian count seeking refuge at Guildford Castle, is ostensibly the suitor of Guildford's daughter, but is really also in love with Julia. Bertrand, the villain of the piece, will stop at nothing to become Guildford's heir. The figure bent on revenge and destruction in Cowley's play is Editha, who admits "I think of nothing but my wrongs."[44] In her attempt to hold on to Edward as a lover, Editha vilifies his fiancée, the virtuous widow Albina, and to this end enlists the aid of Albina's feckless but lusting brother-in-law. At the eleventh hour, Edward and Albina are reunited, as are Rivers and Julia in More's play. But the differences in plot, characterization, and language are vast. Cowley charges that "there is a scene between the Father and his Daughter, on her being rejected by Orlando, that bears the same resemblance, in the literal expression, to the scene between Westmoreland and Albina, in the fourth Act of the Play."[45] It is the literal expression that is so contrasting. When she hears the accusation of "vile licentiousness," Albina sinks into her father's arms, considers herself "forsaken! scorn'd! left like a

loath'd disease!" and prepares to "plunge . . . in the depths of madness";
Westmoreland remarks, "This keen, tumultuous sorrow misbecomes thee."[46]
Emmelina takes the news of Orlando's preference with a searing honesty, as
she insists "No flowers of rhetoric can change the fact, / No arts of speech can
varnish o'er my shame: / Orlando has refus'd me!" (277). The restraint of
More's heroine and the excesses of Cowley's keep them apart. In examining
the "strained" logic of the charge of plagiarism and the "meta-theater" of the
newspaper exchanges, "a mud hen wrestling match into which Cowley and
More had been reluctantly pressed," Ellen Donkin argues that David Garrick's
mentoring, which "took the form of creating a competitive daughter syn-
drome," was the true source of the tension between the women.[47] Compelling
though her argument is, it does not go far enough in stressing the uniqueness
of More's ruminative, speechifying, and largely static dramas.

Infusing "a gen'rous warmth": Sacred Dramas

Despite Garrick's suggestions "to counter a tendency in her work to create
cantos with a downward inflection rather than acts and scenes with a rising
inflection,"[48] these are exactly the features More chose to concentrate on in
Sacred Dramas: Chiefly Intended for Young Persons. With an ardour comparable
to her earlier effort to scour *Search* of libertines and rakes, ridicule and
swagger, More deliberately excises intrigue and strives for usefulness. In
aspiring rather "after Moral Instruction than the purity of Dramatic Composition," she explains the difference between stage business and the task she has
set for herself. "There, all that is tender, and all that is terrible in the passions,
find a proper place. But I write for the Young, in whom it will be always time
enough to have the passions awakened; I write for a class of Readers, to whom
it is not easy to accommodate one's subject, so as to be at once useful and
interesting."[49] Although she returns to the oratorical mode of *Search* and
even reverts to rhyming couplets for the final vignette of Hezekiah's reflections, the biblical plays also show the results of her experience of the London
stage. Her own fear that "the word *Sacred* in the title is a damper to the
dramas"[50] could not have been too inhibiting, for More displays considerable
dramaturgic sophistication in her treatment of individual character's torments, in the invention of character, personality, or situation to round out
particular episodes, and in the adroit blocking of action so as to underscore
contrasts.

Curiously, when More stops writing for performance, her plays acquire
the most unambiguous dramatic force. Why is it, when she commits herself
to "Correct th' irregular, reform the wrong, / Exalt the low, and brighten the

obscure" (6), that she also writes about feelings in the least clotted, most sympathetic way? Her familiarity with the source of these plays and absolute adherence to a biblical faith and ethic may have provided a certain liberation. Removed from the factionalism and broad jesting of Covent Garden, from the tasks of adapting secular material, and from concerns over performability, she may have felt free to invent characters and probe emotional complexities. Although More invoked assistance from the prophet's fire, David's harp, and Milton's inspiration, in her design "to infuse / A gen'rous warmth, to rouse a holy zeal" (6), she also relied on native shrewdness and a developed sense of the stage even for these closet dramas.

Her fabrications afford both names and credible motivations. Moses's mother, identified only by the patronym "a daughter of Levi" (Exodus 2.1), is here called Jochebed (as disclosed in Exodus 6.20). More develops an effective contrast between the anxious Jochebed, who acknowledges that "A mother's fondness frames a thousand fears," and her assured daughter, Miriam, who knows that Moses is safe:

> Joc.   Come and lament with me thy brother's loss.
> Mir.   Come and adore with me the God of Jacob!
> Joc.   Miriam!—the child is dead!
> Mir.   He lives! he lives!
> Joc.   Impossible!—Oh, do not mock my grief;
>   See'st thou that empty vessel?
> Mir.   From that vessel
>   Th' Egyptian Princess took him.
> Joc.   Pharoah's daughter?
>   Then still he will be slain: a bloodier death
>   Will terminate his woes.
> Mir.   His life is safe!
>   For know she means to rear him as her own. (23)

When Cadell's rights to her text, which she had sold, expired in 1814, More came to his rescue since "several booksellers were taking undue advantage of this, and were publishing editions of *The Sacred Dramas*, to *his* no little injury";[51] she wrote an additional scene for *Moses in the Bulrushes*, in which Miriam functions as a prophet with knowledge extending to the New Testament. A prescient Christian, this Levite proclaims that

> Moses, though great, is but the type of ONE
> Far greater; ONE predestin'd to redeem
> Not Israel only, but the human race. (33)

Usually More's identification of sketchy or nonexistent biblical characters furthers dramaturgic contrast. David's two brother's in the Israelite camp, the scornfully jealous Eliab and the more compassionate Abner, supply one model of the division separating the shepherd boy's singular accomplishment and King Saul's jealous misery. Appropriately David's public defeat of Goliath, who had taunted him as "light boy," "stripling orator," and "insect warrior," is sandwiched between lengthy private monologues in which Saul admits his corrosive, venomous jealousy, as mortal as the blow to the Philistine giant:

> O Jealousy,
> Thou ugliest fiend of hell! thy deadly venom
> Preys on my vitals, turns the healthful hue
> Of my fresh cheek to haggard sallowness,
> And drinks my spirit up! (75)

In *Belshazzar*, More identifies the "queen" (Daniel 5.10) as Nitocris and elevates her "prudent counsels" above the sacrilegious feasting of the court. The other truthsayer in the piece, Daniel, supplies an encomium that chimes in neatly with Urania's discourse of utility and More's own shunning of fashionable gatherings.

> To-night a thousand nobles fill his hall,
> Princes, and all the dames who grace the court:
> All but his virtuous mother, sage Nitocris:
> Ah! how unlike the impious king, her son!
> She never mingles in the midnight fray,
> Nor crowns the guilty banquet with her presence.
> The royal fair is rich in every virtue
> Which can adorn the queen, or grace the woman.
> But for the wisdom of her prudent counsels
> This wretched empire had been long undone. (91)

Not only does the invention of Araspes, as the catechumen eager for Daniel's tutelage, provide a motive for the prophet's orations, but the invention of the schemers at Darius's court, Pharnaces and Soranus (reminiscent of Pandemonium councillors), also furnishes a grisly contrast to Daniel's message of salvation, as they inherit the punishment they had designed for Daniel. According to Araspes' report, "the hungry lions, greedy for their prey, / Devour'd the wretched princes ere they reach'd / The bottom of the den" (153). As speedily as More dispatches the antagonists, she lavishes additional detail, involving some faintly humorous ventriloquism, on the discovery of Daniel.

Dar.   O Daniel! servant of the living God!
       He whom thou hast serv'd so long, and lov'd so well,
       From the devouring lion's famish'd jaw,
       Can He deliver thee?
Dan.   (*from the bottom of the den*).
               He can—he Has!
Dar.   Methought I heard him speak!
Aras.   Oh! wondrous force
       Of strong imagination! were thy voice
       Loud as the trumpet's blast, it could not wake him
       From that eternal sleep!
Dan.   (*in the den*).
               Hail! king Darius!
       The God I serve has shut the lion's mouth,
       To vindicate my innocence.
Dar.   He speaks!
       He lives!
Aras.   Tis no illusion: 'tis the sound
       Of his known voice.
Dar.   Where are my servants? Haste,
       Fly, swift as lightning, free him from the den. (150)

Reflections of King Hezekiah, in His Sickness (based on Isaiah 38.9–22 and 2 Kings 20.1–11) shows More's creative determination in adjusting and extending biblical accounts. Hezekiah, king of Judah, is an uneven figure: on one hand, as a leader and reformer, he appears to have enjoyed Yahweh's favor by being given an additional fifteen years of life; on the other, after his recovery from sickness, he succumbed to pride, a fault for which Isaiah rebuked him (Isaiah 39.5–7), and after the siege of Jerusalem, he capitulated and paid tribute to the Assyrian king. Making Hezekiah the philosopher-king of escahatology, More concentrates on the period of sickness as a time to ponder final things. While she does not whitewash Hezekiah, his name and the general features of the story of a long-lived, successful, and finally remorseful monarch are the springboard for her versified inspection of "the soul on earth [as] an immortal guest, / Compell'd to starve at an unreal feast" (161). Although Hezekiah apparently conducts this examination of conscience, his rhetorical questions relate to the issues of purposive, directed existence that absorbed More.

          Did my fix'd soul the impious wit detest?
          Did my firm virtue scorn the unhallow'd jest;
          The sneer profane, and the poor ridicule

> Of shallow Infidelity's dull school?
> Did I still live as born one day to die,
> And view th' eternal world with constant eye? (159)

We might wonder how much of this can—or ever could—be understood by the intended young readers. Ultimately also, we must ask what kind of a playwright More was. Why was she so at ease when disciplining subjects "with the stiffest theological backboard?"[52] What connections exist between More's bleak tragedies and instructive pastoral and biblical dramas? Were her plays dramas at all, or choreographed philosophical disquisitions? Did they capitalize on the performative or, perversely, eschew it? More was serious, practical, and devout. However unfashionable or restricting, these are the constants of her life. She also had an expressive, ebullient temperament, and it seems to me quite natural that she would attempt to blend entertainment and instruction through the mimetic, engaging mode of drama. Critical opinion almost invariably laments that the penchant for instruction overcame or outran any talent to entertain. Her own publisher, Thomas Cadell, observed toward the end of her celebrity at Covent Garden that she was "too good a Christian for an author"; although More often disagreed with Cadell, she judged this remark to be "very good advice."[53] But Cadell's assessment does not tell the whole story. True, More's writing for the theater—of costumed actors and of impressionable schoolgirls—launched her faith-directed career. But it was also an initial gathering point, a node of creative and experimental energies, for an ambitious, capable young woman.

It is really not such a mystery, after all, that More wrote for the theater. As a child she had filled precious quires with letters to imagined depraved sorts and, what is equally astonishing but also reflective of her early sense of the curative nature of art, return epistles from these now-penitent beneficiaries of her reforming zeal.[54] Surely a young author who arrived in London with her own translation of an Italian opera in her pocket was drawn by more than the prospect of visiting bookshops and meeting bishops. Writing at "midnight" to the stage-struck visitor from Bristol, Mrs. Boscawen, though herself "almost asleep," recognizes the close-to-narcotic effect of Garrick's performance: "Yr head is still aching for King Lear!"[55] A little treasure among the Garrick papers at the Folger is an autograph poem of More's appearing above a medallion portrait of the actor; in her tribute she admits

> Tis he who gives my breast a thousand pains,
> Can make me feel each passion that he feigns;
> Enrage, compose, with more than magic art,
> With pity, and with terror, tear my heart;

More's autograph poem appeared above this medallion portrait of David Garrick (Folger Shakespeare Library).

And snatch me o'er the earth, or thro' the air,
To Thebes, to Athens, when he wills, and where.[56]

At the *conversazione*, where More gained ready but not undiscriminating acceptance, Milton was not the only poet she defended. In one letter home she describes taking up cudgels of sorts in defense of Shakespeare's "language of passion."[57] After confessing impishly to her correspondent, Mrs. Gwatkin, that she would love "to take a peep at Voltaire," she is also curious about her friend's reactions to "the diversions of Paris." "How do you like the Comédie," she asks.[58] More's interest in the theater, long banished in her scheme of entertainments, still percolates through many of her later letters to Mrs. Garrick. Three decades after Mrs. Boscawen's friendly note, More writes to the Adelphi inquiring after poor "weak" Mrs. Boscawen, but also asking, "Do you go to the Play?"[59]

Her curiosity is not prurient, nor is her enthusiasm disingenuous. However, from the very beginning there are flaws and fears in her view of the moral uplift and chastening that the theater might provide. To be appropriately moral and high-toned, expression must be governed by religious principles. Restriction and abridgement inform her notion of channeled, utilitarian entertainment; the idea of government, containment, control is strong and insistent throughout More's writings. In the so-called *volte-face* of the preface for the 1801 edition, More credited her realization of that "delusive and groundless hope, that the stage, under certain regulations, might be converted into a school of virtue," as effecting "a revolution in the sentiments of the Author" (125–26). Yet she desperately wanted the genre of tragedy to be "one of the noblest efforts of the human mind," to the extent that she carried on a personal debate about those elements of the drama—mind and heart, understanding and feeling—which most attracted and implicated her. This declaration from an idealist, who could be and had been moved, is full of the conflicts between intention and effect that continued to preoccupy her:

> I am not even now about to deny, that of all public amusements it is the most interesting, the most intellectual, and the most accommodated to the tastes and capacities of a rational being; nay, that it is almost the only one which has *mind* for its object; the only one which has the combined advantage of addressing itself to the imagination, the judgment, and the heart; that it is the only public diversion which calls out the higher energies of the understanding in the composition, and awakens the most lively and natural feelings of the heart in the representation. (127)

Although her semi-emotional argument yields very strong opinions, like the rejection of medieval mysteries and moralities as "obsolete rubbish, compounded of ignorance and superstition" (129), her evaluation of the stage and its potential for goodness is levelheaded. "For, unfortunately, this Utopian good cannot be produced," she argues, "until not only the Stage itself has undergone a complete purification, but until the audience shall be purified also" (128). More judges the theater by exceedingly strict standards, yet in its very circumscribed orbit, her argument is also logical. Because she sees the Christian called to "unostentatious . . . habitual self-denial" (133), it makes sense for her to contend that the periodic sprinkling of religion or "the finest sentiments of piety" in tragedies is not enough. In highly coloured, paratactic language she presents such medicinal doses of religion as inadequate to stop the deeply intrusive force of evil.

> But the single grains of this counteracting principle scattered up and down the piece, do not extend their antiseptic property in a sufficient degree to preserve from corruption the body of a work, the general spirit and leading tempers of which . . . are evidently not drawn from that meek religion, the very essence of which consists in 'casting down high images:' while, on the other hand, the leaven of the predominating evil secretly works and insinuates itself, till the whole mass becomes impregnated by the pervading principle. (136)

Did More retreat in fear of succumbing to such a complicated temptation? Although her success may have surprised her, the lure of the stage—however embodied, forceful, and emphatic—probably did not engross her. Perhaps she sensed that her own fascination with ideas and debate, with a mental rather than a physical life, was better suited to expression in prose and poetry. Narrative may have beckoned as a mode more indulgent of observations about the interior life.

Did her heroines and their victories and defeats forecast things to come? It is not incidental that the most effective teachers, in *Search* and, with the exception of Daniel, in *Sacred Dramas*, are women, nor that the greatest sufferers in the tragedies are also women. In contrast to the serenity of Urania, the prophecy of Miriam, and the sagacity of Nitocris, did More set up Attilia, Elwina, and Emmelina for a fall? Impassioned conviction stamps all More's work, and the heroines, whether unruffled or doomed, are no exception. While More loved the intellectual life and was excited by virtuous ideals, she knew acutely the difficulties of realizing noble aims in a dull and often hostile reality. The tragic heroines do not enjoy the luxury of a protective, removed pastoral bower, nor can they rely on the buffer of absolute faith. Vulnerable and isolated, patronized and vilified, Attilia, Elwina, and Emmelina struggle poignantly. Capable of representing both triumphalist pedagogy and crushing emotional torments, More passed an instructive apprenticeship in the theater.

❀ 3 ❀
Poetics of Beneficence:
Practice and Patronage

Hannah More and William Blake were writing poetry at the same time; yet they appear to live in totally different worlds. In contrast to the prophecies and visions of Blake exploring woman's socio-sexual dilemma and the more general corruption of human potentiality, the intellectual matrix of More's couplets is still deeply influenced by Augustan poetics and ethical considerations. Throughout her poetry she accents or underscores the Augustan humanist enterprise, which Paul Fussell has characterized as "deducing a stable ethics from the actual nature of man tenderly but no less rigorously considered,"[1] with a distinctive biblical consciousness of peccant fallibility. More's poems offer a characteristic "moral workout" in which human beings operate as "social and public creature[s] only because [they are] too frail and incomplete to exist by [themselves]."[2] Whether in iambic tetrameter or pentameter, the couplet was as deeply congenial for More's serio-comic or satiric purposes as it had been for the Augustans, who, as Margaret Anne Doody observes, "were so taken with the couplet, it answered their desires and expectations so fully, that they had a hard time getting away from it."[3] Although More was accomplished in writing in many voices to accommodate a high and low readership, "the problem of the audience for poetry," such a "formative part in the Romantics' manner of address and . . . consciously 'democratic' cast of many of their themes and stylistic innovations,"[4] is not a prominent issue in her poems. More contentedly wrote for exclusive, discrete audiences, public or private. Poetry was largely a medium of instructive communication to which she resorted—in reworked ballads, biblical synopses, and even spontaneous versification on a dead pig—over the entire span of her writing career.

More's attraction to poetry was longer lasting and more firmly fixed than her approach-avoidance response to the theater. But just as she viewed the theater through specially tinted lenses, so her poetry was essentially a medium of teaching and information rather than exploration, rehearsing noble ideals and frequent shortcomings more often than expressing states of being or perception. In her quest of "the kindred mind, . . . the large soul which takes in human kind," she treated the subject of the emotions with a matter-of-fact utilitarianism.

> As FEELING tends to good or leans to ill,
> It gives fresh force to vice or principle;
> Tis not a gift peculiar to the good,
> Tis often but the virtue of the blood:
> And what would seem compassion's moral flow,
> Is but a circulation swift or slow:
> But to divert it to its proper course,
> There wisdom's pow'r appears, there reason's force.[5]

A diverter of courses and a force of reason, More continued to search for "the flash of intellect" meeting "congenial fires," and remained pragmatic enough to assert that "sparks electric only strike / On souls electrical alike."[6] In promoting opportunities for congenial flashes and electrical sparks, her design was to polish "intellectual ore" and utilize "education's moral mint."[7] A generation after the publication of her poetry in adult circles, this purposiveness made her a staple of moralizing anthologists for the young. Snippets of her verse enjoyed an extended life in such collections as Elizabeth Hall's *The Poetical Monitor: Consisting of Pieces Select and Original, for the Improvement of the Young in Virtue and Piety* (1796), Lucy Aikin's *Poetry for Children* (1801), Eleanor Fenn's *The Family Miscellany, in Prose and Verse; Designed to Supply Lessons for Children of Various Ages* (1805), Elizabeth Mant's *The Parent's Poetical Anthology: Being a Selection of English Poems, Primarily Designed to Assist in Forming Taste and the Sentiments of Young Readers* (1814), and Emma Price's *The Moral Muse; A Present for Young Ladies* (1830).[8]

But, as well as providing recyclable lessons, More realized that the genre required personal identification, and so her own criteria were clear and pressing: "I must have *men* and *women*, with whom I can have sentiments, affections, and interests in common: I don't care how romantic the story, or how exalted the character, provided it be still *probable* adventure, and *possible* perfection.[9] Her poetry—from ballads and romances to a polemic on the slave trade—supplied pictures of fashion that themselves reflected with satiric pointedness the professional and upper-class culture of the late eighteenth century. In its urging of "reason, virtue, and caution" and its "call, not for sensibility but for sense, not for erotic passion but for rational love, a love based on understanding, compatibility, equality and mutual respect,"[10] her poetry also conformed to the general characteristics of feminine Romanticism.

For such a conscientious advocate of the doctrine of the separate spheres as More, however, equality was a moot issue. Her politics of domestic responsibility clearly privileged the virtuous, rational, albeit isolated girl or wife who instructed or reformed the impetuous, volatile suitor or husband. The feminine subjectivity More thereby constructed was uniquely empowered but also uniquely vulnerable. For all of their quiet zeal as household managers and more vocal dedication to censorious judgments of the fashionable set, More's women were often the victims of loutish men and the butts of modish ridicule.

As with the chart of her heroines' fortunes, reading More's poetry on the whole demands a certain juggling skill. Shunning Romantic stylistic innovations, she does not participate in the culture of radical Dissent or in the millennarian transformation of political life heralded in France. She appears to have at least one foot in the Augustan world yet to endorse the sensible, rational, respectful tenets of feminine Romanticism. Her repeated use of the humility topos, waving off the verse as occasional, idle, and trifling, must be balanced against the exclusivity of her calls to the "happy virtuous few"[11] and careful assessment of what the market tolerates and pays. Her first "venture to try what is [her] real value, by writing a slight poem and offering it to Cadell,"[12] resulted in a very handsome offer in which the publisher, himself a shrewd judge of the market, agreed to match Goldsmith's payment for "The Deserted Village." Though showered with praise, More studied "like a dragon," reading "four or five hours every day," and interpreted the favourable reviews as having "so much flattery that [she] might . . . choke [her]self on [her] own pap."[13] Yet, with what purports to be first-hand knowledge, she also felt the stings of mockery: "th' unfeeling jeer, / The civil, grave, ironic sneer; / The laugh, which more than censure wounds, / Which more than argument, confounds."[14] She basked in Johnson's adulation, happy to relate the "honour" he did her of adding a stanza to "Sir Eldred of the Bower," "amused" to discover that Johnson's portrait in Pembroke College bears a motto from her own "Sensibility," and savoring the mixture of fun and earnest in his "jokes" about the danger of mentioning poetry in her presence: "it is talking of the art of war before Hannibal."[15] Like the double edge of Johnson's remarks, referring to an accomplished as well as to a commanding critic, More kept her own counsel about the great man, even daring—though in the confidence of a private letter—to censure the inadequacy of *Irene*: its "deficiency in what relates to the passions and affections."[16]

How does More herself fare with passions and affections? A cautious, at times fatalistic, observer, narrator, and commentator, More painstakingly lists the factors leading to attraction but steers clear of any headlong abandonment to passion: no disorienting *coup de foudre* here! Her début quarto, in 1776, consists of two love laments: "The Bleeding Rock; or, The Metamorphosis of a Nymph into a Stone," a legend fancifully explaining the red spots of sandstone in the rock in Failand (which becomes "Fairy Land"), a hamlet about six miles from Bristol, and "Sir Eldred of the Bower," a retelling of the ballad of Gil Morice. Remarkably comfortable with couplets and alternate-rhyme quatrains, More constructs purposive narratives, where a didactic intent hovers over the love story. Both poems feature virtuous women done to death by rash men. Although More alerts the reader ominously at the outset of "The Bleeding Rock" that "*Beauty* but serves destruction to insure, / And *sense*, to feel the pang it cannot cure" (395), she also recounts a nicely nuanced tale of the nymph Ianthe, "too unsuspecting not to be deceiv'd," and her "vain" and "selfish" seducer Polydore, "rich in large domains, / In smiling pastures, and in flow'ry plains" (396–97). Adroitly the narrator connects the "exterior charm" of Polydore's "smiling pastures" with the "fictitious mark" of his postures: "The sigh elaborate, the fraudful tear, / The joy dissembled, and the well-feign'd fear" (396). Although it activates Polydore's remorse, the rejected Ianthe's Ovidian[17] metamorphosis into stone does not entirely fulfill her wish for "some form where love can have no part / No human weakness reach [her] guarded heart" (398). The location of the action is close to the Belmont estate of More's dilatory suitor, William Turner, and hence, the legend has been construed as a reflection of her own situation. It is unlikely that "The Bleeding Rock" is a "protest"[18] poem about ill treatment during her on-again, off-again engagement to Turner. If she made no mention of the circumstance—however tragic or liberating for her it may have been—in her private letters, it seems implausible that she would have worn her heart on her sleeve in a public poem.

More is just as interested in the men's pangs of conscience as in the women's dejection. In fact the women in these early poems lead their irresponsible suitors to a realization of guilt and sorrow. Just as Polydore is "appall'd" and "smitten" by Ianthe's metamorphosis, so Sir Eldred learns from his dying bride, Birtha, that the stranger he has stabbed is Birtha's own brother.[19] Exhortations to self-control, which Sir Eldred clearly lacks, and praise of virginal modesty, which the "embower'd" Birtha personifies, interlace throughout the ballad. As the reader learns at the beginning, despite Eldred's "kind" heart and "fond affections," he can be quickly brought to the edge:

> Yet if the passions storm'd his soul,
> By jealousy led on;
> The fierce resentment scorn'd control,
> And bore his virtues down. (366)

The observations of the concluding quatrains about "erring man" and his "passions uncontroll'd" being the cause of his own "deadliest wounds" reinforce grimly the lessons of the four deaths. As the "peerless" Birtha's "goodness heard, and grace beheld" initially subdue Eldred, they also compound his sorrow at having mistrusted and lost so rare a prize. Birtha's ballad-perfect charms had even prompted the narrator to compare her to present-day public beauties.

> Unlike the dames of modern days,
> Who *general* homage claim;
> Who court the *universal* gaze,
> And pant for *public* fame.
>
> *Then* beauty but on merit smil'd,
> Nor were her chaste smiles sold;
> No venal father gave his child
> For grandeur or for gold. (379–80)

More is fond of allusions that run forward and backward in time. While Birtha, for whom "not a shrub or plant was there / But did some moral yield" (370), reflects the tenets of a Evangelical upbringing, the reaction of her father, "good old Ardolph," to the sight of his slaughtered children recalls that of an Old Testament judge:

> The father saw—so Jephtha stood,
> So turn'd his woe-fraught eye,
> When the dear, destin'd child he view'd,
> His zeal had doom'd to die. (383)

As the vow of the Israelite chieftain showed his insecure faith, so the connection here indicates that Ardolph's earlier reliance on the "nymph celestial," Religion, who comforted him at the death of his wife by teaching "this rebel heart . . . Submission to its God" (378), has now been dealt a mortal blow.

When More's poetry abandons the prop of narrative to concentrate instead on such abstract ideas as the vulnerable, feeling heart ("Sensibility"), the luxury of benevolence ("Inscription in a beautiful Retreat called the Fairy Bower"), and the essence of conversation ("The Bas Bleu), the predictable restrictions are securely in place: a domestic site and a religious bias. Her epistle to Mrs. Boscawen, published along with *Sacred Dramas* in 1782, is a strenuous attempt to define sensibility by contrast and example. Unlike those "insulated souls" who "n'er feel the pow'r / Of gen'rous sympathy's ecstatic hour" and the author who, "scorning life's low duties to attend, / Writes odes on friendship, while he cheats his friend," the poem celebrates and apostrophizes

> Sweet SENSIBILITY! thou keen delight!
> Unprompted moral! sudden sense of right!
> Perception exquisite! fair virtue's seed!
> Thou hasty conscience! reason's blushing morn!
> Instinctive kindness e'er reflection's born! (173)

But instinct is not entirely unreflective and unguided, since the epistle presses the logic of the conclusion that "if RELIGION's bias rule the soul, / Then SENSIBILITY exalts the whole" (176). A similar level of abstraction and exclusivity informs "Fairy Bower," tipped into the seventh edition of *The Search after Happiness* in 1778. Along with banishing "Mortals! form'd of grosser clay" the poet commands:

> Folly's minion, Fashion's fool,
> Mad Ambition's restless tool,
> Slave of passion, slave of power,
> Fly, ah! fly this tranquil bower. (46)

The gaze claims to be sympathetic, but the option is blunt and peremptory: "Learn to pity others' wants, / Or avoid these hallow'd haunts" (46).

Disarming honesty and playfulness[20] set "The Bas Bleu" apart from the other philosophical divagations.

> I shall not stop to dwell on these,
> But be as epic as I please,
> And plunge at once *in medias res*.
> To prove the privilege I plead,
> I'll quote some Greek I cannot read. (292)

Although Sylvia Harcstark Myers has judged its celebration of Mrs. Vesey's conversation parties, where guests chose their own circles, to be "somewhat misleading" and "rather superficial,"[21] when seen within the context of More's own artistic development[22] rather than the established Bluestocking network, her poem is a confident, spirited exercise. Her opposition to the "rage for polish, ton, and graces" is as animated as her support for "Vesey's plastic genius" (297). But More's whimsy is strictly functional; her panoramic sweep of the guests exaggerates not to ridicule but to challenge:

> Here sober Duchesses are seen,
> Chaste Wits, and Critics void of spleen;
> Physicians, fraught with real science,
> And Whigs and Tories in alliance;
> Poets, fulfilling Christian duties,
> Just Lawyers, reasonable Beauties;
> Bishops who preach, and Peers who pay,
> And Countesses who seldom play;
> Learn'd Antiquaries, who, from college,
> Reject the rust, and bring the knowledge;
> And, hear it, *age*, believe it, *youth*,—
> Polemics, really seeking truth. (298)

More definitely favors the ethical highground; yet unlike those critics who picture her condescending from the mountaintop of her exalted wit, I see More continually exhorting readers about the way things ought to or might be. With care and determination she develops whole image clusters, such as this example of the mining, minting, and circulating of the currency of the mind, to reinforce the invitation to her vantage point.

> Our intellectual ore must shine,
> Nor slumber idly in the mine.
> Let education's moral mint
> The noblest images imprint;
> Let taste her curious touchstone hold,
> To try if standard be the gold;
> But 'tis thy commerce, Conversation,
> Must give it use by circulation;
> That noblest commerce of mankind,
> Whose precious merchandize is MIND! (301)

As in so much of her work, More participates in and distances herself from her age—appealing to a mercantilism, but that of the mind, and sharing a vision that is both hortatory and obligating.

From the vantage of her Cowslip Green cottage, the glance she casts at the fashionable world in "Florio: A Tale for Fine Gentlemen and Fine Ladies," an Horatian commentary on city and country manners, is similarly knowledgeable and censorious. But this return to narrative shows both the effect of the confident forcefulness acquired from the earlier meditations on feeling and conversation and the cast of her mind as she was preparing *Thoughts on the Importance of the Manners of the Great to General Society*, a typically Augustan satiric reflection on the unsatisfactoriness of the present. The poem illustrates the essay's contention, that "the mischief arises not from our living in the world, but from the world living in us; occupying our hearts and monopolising our affections,"[23] through the subjectivity of its hero, a modishly educated yet likable idler needing to be reclaimed.

> His mornings were not spent in vice,
> Twas lounging, sauntering, eating ice;
> Walk up and down St. James's Street,
> Full fifty times the youth you'd meet;
> He hated cards, detested drinking,
> But stroll'd to shun the toil of thinking;
> 'Twas *doing nothing* was his curse,
> Is there a vice can plague us worse? (320)

As a narrator-instructor, More writes with the expectation that the reader is likeminded, relishing her send-up of Florio's being *au courant*—

> He read *Compendiums, Extracts, Beauties,*
> *Abrégés, Dictionnaires, Receuils,*
> *Mercures, Journaux, Extraits,* and *Feuilles*:
> No work in substance now is follow'd,
> The Chemic Extract only's swallow'd. (320)—

as well as disapproving of the "free-thinking sneer" and "little sceptic prattle" (322) of his erstwhile friend, Bellario, a supposed satirical portrait of Hume or Gibbon.[24] Bellario's foil is the unequivocally conservative country squire, a "cheerful knight of good estate," Sir Gilbert; warm-hearted, bounteous, and beloved, this bluff anti-Jacobin lives according to "old-fashion'd State"—a state that, picturesquely, avoids any mention of changes in the agrarian economy, the process of enclosure and rural unemployment.

> He dreaded nought like alteration.
> Improvement still was innovation;
> He said, when any change was brewing,
> Reform was a fine name for ruin. (327)

However stodgy or even ludicrous Gilbert may seem to the reader, the narrator, loyal to his sympathies, privileges the country life in a number of ways. Although the gallant is permitted to laugh at his poor friend's "pastoral shades and purling streams" and "at his present *brilliant* life" (336), the narrator rejoins with criticism of the sacrifice of reputations and feelings by this "flattering, fashionable tribe" and of the despotism of the hostess Flavia surrounded by her fawning "little senate" (338). Flavia's opposite is Sir Gilbert's daughter, Celia, as ideal as Birtha or Ianthe. The contrasts pile up: the venom of London repartees from which "scars indelible remain" (339) and the "reasonable reading" (344) of *The Idler* that Florio discovers in Sir Gilbert's library; the "factitious charms . . . [of] *bon-ton* grimace" and "Celia's powers of face" (342). The marriages of the two friends supply the most vivid opposites. Immediately before the ceremony that "would tack the slight and slippery band, / Which, in loose bondage, would ensnare / Bellario bright and Flavia fair" (345), Florio leaves the city for the country, while on the very wedding day of Florio and "pious" Celia, Bellario sues for divorce.

More never shies away from lessons in her poetry; in fact, she delights in such purposiveness, whether it masquerades cheerfully or snaps the reader to sharp attention. Sensible cheer prevails in "The Puppet Show: A Tale" and "An Heroic Epistle to Miss Sally Horne." Without apology or demurral she points the moral of the "preposterous peer" who buys a puppet to enjoy its "sense" and "wit" at home. Curiously, he buys Punch (not Judy), but More does not linger over the issue of its gender in condemning—in the spirit of the animadversions to be developed witheringly in *Strictures*—the selection of a "dumb idol."

> The moral of the tale I sing,
> To modern matches home I bring.
> Ye youths, in quest of wives who go
> To every crowded puppet-show;
> If, from these scenes, you choose for life
> A dancing, singing, dressing, wife;
> O marvel not, at home to find
> An empty figure void of mind;
> Stript of her scenery and garnish,
> A thing of paint, and paste, and varnish. (389)

When, in the guise of Goody Two Shoes, More pens a verse letter on the blank pages of Mother Bunch's Tales to the three-year-old daughter of the president of Magdalen College, her topic is mock-humorous: the superiority of these tales to most histories. The address to a child—unless young Sally Horne, a future pupil at the Park Street school, was a real prodigy—is a sham, for More's discourse on the "morality of fictions," where the good are both rewarded and enriched, and the "profligate learning" of fairy tale justice, which "mend[s] the heart," is deeply serious. To support the crucial discerning of Mother Bunch, More tosses off such axioms as "Till Hercules to cleanse was able, / No doubt they *shut* th' Augean stable."

Although the Epistle questioned the veracity of historical knowledge, which may be "as doubtful" and "as vain" as the tale of Jack the Giant Killer, More herself was quite prepared to stretch authenticity in both the phoney futurism of "Bishop Bonner's Ghost" and the abolitionist propaganda of "Slavery." Irony literally drips from the words the "good Old Papist" author, writing in 1900, puts in the mouth of the Marian bishop. Bonner resents the intrusion of the "Reformer['s] . . . innovating hand" and the absence of "that holy gloom which hid / Fair truth from vulgar ken" (309). His complaints about what has been lost serve to criticize the authoritarianism of Papistry at the same time as they entrust ordinary folk with real theological acumen.

> The tangled mazes of the schools,
>   Which spread so thick before;
> Which knaves entwin'd to puzzle fools,
>   Shall catch mankind no more.
>
> . . . .
>
> For knowledge flew, like magic spell,
>   By typographic art:
> Oh, shame! a peasant now can tell
>   If priests the truth impart.

Such overstatement did not go unnoticed by Anna Barbauld, whose Noncon-formist rejoinder defends the bishops while satirizing the ghost's making "a stir with notions so ungrounded"; Barbauld also hints at a certain righteous-ness and dustiness within the Establishment:

> Well warned from what abroad occurs,
>   We keep all tight at home,
> Nor brush one cobweb from St. Paul's
>   For fear we shake the dome.[25]

The ultimate discrediting of the author More impersonates, who is also the porte-parole for Bonner, takes the form of a final note dismissing the "*pre-tended* Traffic of the Human Species" as merely one of "the exaggerations of History . . . to blacken the memory of former ages" (312). Though More discounted the poem as a "trifle" she "would never have printed," she was "delighted" with Walpole's "magnificent" printing of "the little brown Bon-ner: it is so new and so old, and so whimsical, and so unique!"[26]

She was less sanguine about "Slavery," admitting that it was "too short," "too much hurried" and "very imperfect."[27] Composed in almost a fortnight so as to "come out at the particular moment when the discussion comes on in parliament,"[28] its sentimental abolitionist argument was designed to present the views of the recently formed Anti-Slavery Society and to support the bill proposed by her friend, the Evangelical businessman and member of Parliament for Yorkshire, William Wilberforce. More's allegiance to this public figure, who had declared that "God Almighty has placed before me two great Objects—the Suppression of the Slave Trade and the Reformation of Manners,"[29] is straightforward, and so is her loyalty to the antislavery cause, to which she bequeathed the second largest sum in her will.[30] However, it is not the sense of haste but the conflictedness of attitudes within the poem that accounts for critical opposition to it today. Moira Ferguson designates More's attempt to reform society as a "decisive though atypical female intervention"; but she also reads the text as emanating from "the authorized European" voice and casting slaves "into a mode of radical alterity."[31]

Informing her appeal to parliamentarians with the received bourgeois and hegemonic view of the black, More deliberately juxtaposes concepts of sameness and difference, closeness and distance. All people share "th' immortal principle within" (111), "the fond vital links of Nature" (113), "His sacred image which they bear" (114), and "Nature's plain appeal" to the heart, since "all mankind can feel" (115). But considerations of "the casual colour of a skin" (111) emphasize that More's is a view from the outside: "with firm, though erring zeal" (111), "dark and savage, ignorant and blind" (114), Africans hold her attention as reclaimable, tractable souls. Her criticism is leveled at the slaver; whether motivated by "lust of gold or lust of conquest," the "WHITE SAVAGE" along with more particularized conquerors (Cortez, Columbus, Cartouche, and Caesar) is subject to More's indictment: "The means may differ, but the end's the same; / Conquest is pillage with a nobler name." (118). Liberty is the encasing concept of her propagandistic argument; figured at the outset as "bright intellectual Sun!, . . . *sober* Goddess!" and carefully distinguished from "mad Liberty, . . . that unlicens'd monster of the crowd" (109–10), the idea of liberty also clinches More's appeal to bourgeois, conservative patriots.

> Shall Britain, where the soul of Freedom reigns,
> Forge chains for others she herself disdains?
> Forbid it, Heaven! O let the nations know
> The liberty she tastes she will bestow;
> Not to herself the glorious gift confin'd,
> She spreads the blessing wide as human kind;
> And scorning narrow views of time and place,
> Bids all be free in earth's extended space. (119)

Appearing at almost the same time as More's poem, Sarah Trimmer's "Anecdotes of Negroes," a regular segment in her monthly *Family Magazine*, idealized the black in ways similar to More's treatment of the slave Quashi, who commits suicide rather than retaliate against his master in self-defence. After narrating the account of a freed slave who repeatedly comes to the rescue of his former master, Trimmer engages and implicates the reader with the rhetorical question, "will any man pretend to look down with contempt on one capable of such generosity, merely because the colour of his skin is black?"[32] Another "anecdote," as condemnatory of the white slaver as More, extends the criticism to include the incendiary, vengeful black crowd; Trimmer presents an idealized black servant defusing the situation and defending his master: "The *Europeans*, who have carried away our countrymen, are savages, replied the generous *Cudjoe*; kill them whenever you meet with them; but the white man who lodges with me is a good man, he is my friend; my house is his castle; I am his soldier and will defend him."[33] Another echo of More's argument about human commonality and specific national shame is voiced by the African "Mungo" in Trimmer's excerpt from the epilogue to "an opera called the *Padlock*." Speaking ostensibly from the inside, the first-person voice interrogates the shibboleths of both freedom and national pride.

> Vain, vain, that glorious privilege to me,
> I am a *slave* where all things else are *free*.
> Yet was I born, as you are, no man's slave,
> An heir to all that liberal nature gave;
> My mind can reason and my limbs can move
> The same as yours; like yours my heart can love;
> Alike my body food and sleep sustain,
> And e'en, like yours, feels pleasure, want and pain.
>
> . . . .
>
> I speak to *Britons*—*Britons*, then, behold,
> A man by *Britons* snar'd, and *seiz'd*, and *sold*.
> And yet no *British* statute damns the deed,
> Nor do the more than murd'rous villains bleed.[34]

The form of female abolitionist discourse used by More and Trimmer found a ready public, as the *Critical Review's* endorsement of "the amiable sensibility of the female breast" and "the pure medium of virtuous pity" makes clear.[35] In examining the "morally and spiritually schematized framework"[36] of More's poem, in particular, Moira Ferguson points to at least three additional and problematizing indicators of contemporary response to abolitionism.[37] Jacobin and Dissenting voices, such as those of Helen Maria Williams and Anna Laetitia Barbauld, follow and diverge from More's pattern by confronting her "attack on workers between the lines." As the white female subject speaking for the African, More was actually contributing to the accentuation of racial difference, "an unconscious strategy of encirclement." Most provocatively, Ferguson speculates that the poem contains its own— conscious or unconscious—reflection on white British gender politics, in which female abolitionists might "interlace worries about themselves as subjects with concerns about colonized others." This is the ticklish point, the one that the evidence of the text itself—however teased or manipulated— simply does not yield. Not only does Liberty defeat pale Oppression, but the activities of Faith and Freedom are so closely allied that, in the closing prayerful petition, the illumined freed also become the converted. I am suggesting that More was neither rejoicing in her chains nor acting as the blithe agent of the patriarchy. She was as aware of the support of slavery by the Church of England and George III as of the widespread belief in women's powerlessness and instances of their emotional and sexual degradation. Her female abolitionist voice has compelling strength and determination. She exposes and indicts greed and covetousness. While the pathos and sentiment of her characterization of the black may indeed have contributed to a theory of radical otherness, her intention—despite the inadequate methodology— was reformative: to extend the benefits of freedom and, what she viewed as the necessary corollary, Christian conversion to Africans and to galvanize women to advance this social program.

As the bequests of her will indicate, abolitionism was a continuing cause for More's support. In 1817, at the request of her friend Sir Alexander Johnston, chief justice of Ceylon, she composed a rhymed dialogue, "The Twelfth of August; or, the Feast of Freedom," to commemorate the dissolution of domestic slavery for all children in Ceylon born after 12 August 1816. The commencement of this "AEra of Liberty" was an anglophilic and missionary triumph in More's opinion; coinciding with "the birth-day of His Royal Highness the Prince Regent," the feast allowed for the association of freedom with "reverence for the Crown under the protection of which that blessing was received" (26). Her mouthpiece in the dialogue, Silva (later changed to "Sabat"), explains the link between productivity and devotion:

> Then let our masters gladly find
> A FREEMAN works the faster;
> Who serves his God with heart and mind,
> Will better serve his master. (30)

The concluding Cingalese chorus is a tidy advertisement for the British and
Foreign Bible Society.

> O give us Silva's Holy Book,
> With transport we will read;
> There we shall see where'er we look,
> God's Freeman's free indeed! (31)

Despite what strikes the contemporary reader as the limitations of her
colonializing, imperialistic, orthodox blending of affairs of church and state,
the influence of More's work in her own day spread far and wide. Her most
prized present from Johnston was one of her *Sacred Dramas* translated into
Cingalese and written on palm leaves encased in an ornamental wooden box.
"[Johnston] tells me," she wrote to Miss Buchanan, "all my dramas are now
translating as well as my other writings in the Cyngalese and Tamul languages
which are to be circulated throughout India."[38] Charles Wesley, Esq., set *The
Feast of Freedom* to music in the 1820s, with the benefits of the sale of the
sheet music, as More outlined to one of its deputized sellers, the Reverend
Charles Ogilvie, going to "the benefit of the poor Irish."[39] In 1828 More's
friends actually had a piano moved up the stairs and into her bedroom at
Barley Wood so that she could enjoy a private performance.

Poetry remained an intensely purposive, religious medium for More—
whether in the verse and ballads aimed at inculcating lessons for the Cheap
Repository project (to be considered separately) or, almost three decades later,
in the "*Catalogue Raisonné* of the *names* of the *books* of the Bible."[40] Even
though More, sick and feeble, realized that such "poetical embellishment" was
otiose, she nevertheless devoted herself to packing a real surplus of admonitions
into the tortured verse, as in this homiletic treatment of the original Passover:

> Saved by the heaven-appointed blood,
> Israel alone uninjured stood;
> Then, when the Paschal lamb they shared,
> Th' *Atoning Antitype* appeared.
> The speaking emblem shadowed forth
> The sacrifice of countless worth.
> Loins girt, feet shod, staff in hand,
> May *we* too seek the promised land;
> But bear in mind it must be *won*
> Before possession's entered on. (195)

But everything was not as lugubrious. Versifying could also be an
amusement for More in her late seventies and into her eighties. Her gift of a

pair of garters with an accompanying poem to Sir Thomas Acland shows her reverting to the sprightliness of the "Bas Blancs"; although she did not emerge from public battles and critical reviews unscathed, she could now afford to indulge in a gamboling but still witty distance from the fray.

> Not even Reviewers here can find a botch,
> British, nor Quarterly, nor scalping Scotch;
> The deep logician, though he sought amain
> To find false reasoning, here may seek in vain.
> Quibbling grammarians may this work inspect,
> Yet in no bungling Syntax spy defect,
> Its geometric characters complete,
> The parallels run on, but never meet.
>
> . . . .
>
> Though some its want of ornament may blame,
> Utility, not splendour, was my aim.
> Not ostentation I—for still I ween,
> Its worth is rather to be *felt* than seen.

She often thanked Dr. Carrick, her last physician, and his wife for their attentiveness in verse letters. Jousting with her well publicized aversion to card playing, she presented a pair of card racks to Mrs. Carrick along with this note:

> The love of the donor gives worth to the Present
> Tho' the last is but trifling, the first is most pleasant.
> *My* cards are for *Visits*, not *gambling* I trow;
> The gift in itself is just nothing I know.
> Not Clubs, Spades, or Diamonds can here have a part,
> Tho' these are excluded, it comes with a *Heart*.[41]

Her "sublime and affecting MONODY . . . *spoken* Extempore on seeing the body of a large fat pig dragged up the Hill to the House for dissection" shows More's continuing playful delight in rhymed observations; from her own "sty" she held forth with mock gravity on Piggy's value and duty.

> The saddest sight that e'er was seen
> Was Piggy rolling up the Green!
> Tho' dragged, he still would roll alone,
> Downward, like Sisyphus's stone,
> This Pig, as good as e'er was sold,
> Was worth—not quite—his weight in gold.

. . . .
Those *Men* who dancing lives have led,
Are worse than nothing when they are dead;
While Piggy's goodness ne'er appears
Till, closed his eyes and stopped his ears.
If *hang'd*, or *kept*, as some contended,
In either case he's still sus-pended.
Tho' feeding spoilt his shape and beauty,
Yet feeding was in *him* a duty:
In spite of this reproof, or that,
Twas his sole merit to grow fat,
No need of sorrow or repentance
Death was to him no awful sentence.
How many a Gourmand proud & big
Might envy thy last Hours O Pig.[42]

Whether jocular or ruminative, whimsical or earnest, More's verse was an entirely consistent expression of her temperament. Its intrinsic utility, its serviceableness in conveying biblically attested maxims and conservative moral paradigms established More as an acute, astringent observer, particularly of the middle and upper ranks, a skilled rhymster, and a social thinker whose reformist impulses shaped her utilitarian rather than aesthetic views of the literary medium. Relying on the resonances of the authoritative voice as opposed to the gropings and imaginings of the embryonic soul, the lessons her poems conveyed were to be construed as precepts for life. Top-down, controlling, distanced, and even dispassionate, this axiomatic quality may account for the relatively brief and limited popularity of her poems. These same characteristics also continue to fuel the debate over More's treatment of the poet she discovered and attempted to rescue and promote.

"Lactilla" and "Stella": More as Patron[43]

The friendship between Ann Yearsley, the Bristol milkwoman, whose first volume of poetry was published in 1785, and Hannah More, poet, essayist, and retired playwright, whose subscription campaign to print Yearsley's work netted over £500, lasted scarcely a year. Some reviewers of their exchanges during 1784 and 1785 would balk at the term friendship to describe More's active intervention as what Robert Southey called "a most efficient as well as kind patroness" and "first benefactress" in the life of this "uneducated" poet with "no strain of her own whereby to be remembered."[44] A century and a half after Southey, Moira Ferguson goes as far as to mold Yearsley's "refusal to be coerced or intimidated" into a model "of the kind of resistance that workers [later] would muster against . . . 'oppressor bosses' "; Ferguson lionizes Yearsley's "defiance of patriarchal attitudes" and "zesty self-confidence" in the face of More's "condescension" toward and "ultimate abandonment" of her "cultural find, a laboring woman who independently composed poems but who was not to be allowed any financial (and by extension social) independence."[45] Elizabeth Kowaleski-Wallace opens her study of patriarchal complicity in More and Maria Edgeworth with the unexamined claim that "all published accounts suggest More treated Yearsley badly."[46] In inquiring into "the mutual ideological tensions of class expectation and antagonism," Donna Landry poses a fundamental question about Yearsley's freedom and agency: "How is the laboring poet to make use of the offer of sisterly alliance without sacrificing her dignity and independence, confronted by middle-class propertied confidence, self-righteousness, fear of insurrection, and the authority of 'educated' speech?"[47] Landry judges ultimately that the strain between More's "middle-class fear of social mobility" and Yearsley's "laboring-class" attempt "to control the context of her own production" was too great.[48] The politics of class also informs Mary Waldron's study of Yearsley, but the distance between patron and newly discovered poet is considerably less. Because Waldron pictures Yearsley "identifying herself chiefly with the bourgeois rather than the proletarian," she explains Yearsley's "touchy pride" at being "wrongly categorized and stripped of any claim to respectability."[49]

The reaction to the Yearsley-More quarrel by their contemporaries and our own is not solely the result of differing cultural norms. Clearly such changes—especially a common revulsion at tokenization and paternalism—play a part, but they do not explain the whole metamorphosis in attitudes. Before we leap to conclusions about More's bossiness or Yearsley's victimization, we should be aware of the scrupulous concern to protect and provide for Yearsley's family that More's plans show.[50] Such arrangements, then, are not extraneous details, but are entirely relevant to a judicious reconstruction of this alliance gone awry. Instead of emphasizing merely the divide between then and now, I propose to reconsider the particulars of the quarrel and of opinions of both these women before and after their disagreement erupted. For it seems to me a matter of justice to attempt to understand the contexts and personalities of both combatants. It robs us of a richness and complexity about each artist to edge More's now-unfashionable patronage out of the picture in order to give prominence to Yearsley, whose recognition, while not undue, also involves the risks of "tokenizing . . . through selective canonization of [her] 'exceptional' plebeian texts."[51] In sifting through the skewed and distorting rhetoric of the champions of both sides, it is as important to recognize Yearsley's expressions of gratitude as it is to note her corrosive anger; similarly, More's zeal and tirelessness in Yearsley's cause must be remembered as well as her miscalculations and intransigence.

Understandably Yearsley is a figure more talked about than actually talking before the dispute arose. From the time More found out about the poetical milkwoman, either from her cook or from the other reported rescuer of the Yearsleys, Mr. Vaughan, her eagerness to help this woman was triggered as much by the desperate situation as by Yearsley's poetical inclinations. More literally flung herself into the campaign to save the woman who, in the third trimester of a pregnancy, was found starving along with her four surviving children, unemployed husband, and dying mother. It is misleading, in my view, to interpret More's concern as the mere product of an "easily aroused and uncritical enthusiasm"[52] or her "uncomprehending aestheticization of poverty."[53] Horace Walpole was a friend who knew her well; although he moved in a largely secular world, he did recognize that More was "not only the most beneficent, but the most benevolent of human Beings."[54] This greeting begins one of Walpole's last letters; unfinished and written in a very faltering hand, it conveys his admiration of More's constantly active charity with a candor that we have no reason to doubt. "As a cripple to [his] couch," Walpole feels compelled to express his "infinite gratitude" for More's inquiry after his health. "Yes, though forever busied in planning and exercising services and charities for individuals or for whole bodies of people," Walpole scribbles, "you do leave a cranny empty into which you can slip a kindness." The diametric opposite of Walpole's thankfulness is the attack, well after the fact, of "Archibald MacSarcasm," who clings to the ludicrous fiction of More's jealousy of Yearsley to reduce the would-be benefactor "to the situation of a barbarous Goth and Vandal, or a common thief."[55] From the outset, then, I support placing due emphasis on More's genuine and benevolent concern to rescue Yearsley.

As well as her own artistic intuition, More used her knowledge of the London literati, her tutelage during Garrick's editing of her plays, and her close acquaintance with the Bluestocking circle and their proclivities to judge the amazing potential of this unschooled woman's work and to devise a subscription for its publication. Yearsley's welfare became the topic of most of More's letters for a full year. Thanks to More's introduction, Yearsley was invited to visit the Duchess of Beaufort, the Duchess of Rutland, Lady Spencer, and Mrs. Montagu. In addition to a gift of a set of books of poetry sent by the Duchess of Devonshire,[56] the Duchess Dowager of Portland gave her £20; Mrs. Montagu, £22. According to More, Yearsley "was inexpressibly affected at [this] generous bounty, and . . . you would have thought her silence and her tears as touching as the most elaborate expressions that ever flowed from the rattling tongue of saucy and audacious Eloquence."[57]

Aside from her practical gifts, More's visits to Yearsley offered strength and encouragement to this woman struggling with the daily demands of her family and the new and no doubt daunting prospects of seeing her work in print. She gave Yearsley copies of Ossian, Dryden, and Ovid, "hired for her a *little* maid, to help feed her pigs, and nurse the little ones, while she herself sells the milk, and . . . desired her to put one or two of her children out to learn to read; the idea of bringing them up in ignorance being to her [Yearsley, that is] more terrible than their being hungry."[58] More signed each of the broadsheets announcing the campaign; the notice[59] was a straightforward bill of undertaking which read:

> PROPOSALS
> for
> Printing by Subscription
> (Price Five Shillings)
> A VOLUME OF POEMS,
> by
> Ann Yearsley, a Milkwoman of Bristol.
> The poems to be delivered to the Subscribers in the Spring.
> The money to be paid at the time of subscribing.
> Receiv'd _____ 1785, of _____
> for _____ Copies of Ann Yearsley's Poems.
> H. More [signature]

Although the response was brisk and promising, More often had to buoy up Yearsley's spirits. "One day I found her in a state of despondency," she confides to Mary Hamilton, in November 1784.[60] "I expostulated on the sinfulness of it; soon after she sent me a long poem," in the closing lines of which she addresses her patron as "the Fount of Light, / Which pierc'd old Chaos to his depth profound, / While all his native horrors stood reveal'd." More did not have to share Yearsley's tragedies to be able to respond with compassionate practicality to her needs.

> The more I see of this heaven-taught genius the more I am charmed and astonished with her. It is with grief I perceive that her bitter sorrows have tinged her soul with melancholy. The terrible circumstance of seeing a beloved mother die of hunger is ever before her eyes, and her verses continually allude to it. My present plan is, if Heaven blesses my endeavours, to put her into a small farm; she implores not to be put into any employment which must make her mix with the world, and rob her

of her beloved Solitude. I have no wish to make her an idler or a useless being; she has duties to fill, the smallest of which is of more importance in the eyes of Heaven than the best couplet that ever Dryden made.

Is it condescension or common sense to plan to relieve the milkwoman in a way that also safeguards her role as mother of a large family? Similar admissions from More, like her remark to Mrs. Montagu of being "*utterly* against taking her out of her station," prompt Moira Ferguson to comment on More's "even more obvious . . . condescension toward Yearsley that was to influence imminent events."[61] Committing her energy, determination, and sympathy to Yearsley's support, More did not see herself as meddlesome: it was through her that any notice was taken of Yearsley at all. Most early readers of Yearsley's work were decidedly more cautious than More. Walpole, though a subscriber, hesitated about the "gloomy" imagination of "this unhappy Female," and underscored for his friend, "She must remember that she is Lactilla, not Pastora, and is to tend real Cows, not Arcadian sheep." His letter echoes the concerns of More's associates and of Georgian philanthropists, in general: "Were I not persuaded by the samples you have sent me, Madam, that this Woman has talents, I should not advise her encouraging her propensity lest it should divert her from the care of her family, and after the novelty is over leave her worse than she was."[62] Although, for some, More's Christian purposiveness comes with too many strings attached, present-day judges of the quarrel (mainly critics of More's insensitivity) should also factor into their assessments the immense enthusiasm and positiveness More contributed to Yearsley's cause.

Despite the caution of her friends, More's zeal for the milkwoman knew no bounds. She broke one of her own strict Sabbatarian principles in writing to her publisher, who had also become Yearsley's first publisher, on a Sunday to set up the investment of the subscription money. At no time in her life did More ever dawdle; accordingly, the "particular favour" she asks of Cadell—"if you will desire your broker to purchase *immediately* as agreed in the 5 Per Cents and then it will be ready for me to accept on Tuesday morning the 14th, the only day I shall be in Town"—makes great sense. By using her considerable personal influence with wealthy donors, More collected an extraordinarily large sum on Yearsley's behalf, much greater than the standard doubling of the cost of printing and paper for subscription volumes. Placing the £350 realized from the campaign, after the payment of printing costs, in a five percent stock (an early guaranteed investment scheme) seems to More a defensible, long-term plan—safeguarding the money she had collected by indebting herself to so many influential donors—and she hopes that her

Sunday letter "will reach [Cadell] early enough in the day for the business to be done."[63] In the same month, shortly before the dispute was to break out, More provided Mrs. Montagu with a lengthy financial accounting, admitting her satisfaction "to see so magnificent a book" and explaining the details of the investment.

> I paid near fourscore pounds *all* expenses; have lodged £350 in the Five per Cents which will produce about £18 a year, and shall take her down about £20 to cloathe her family and furnish her house. As I wished to have the honour of your name to sanction my own, I have laid out the money in *your* name Madam and Mine, having first had an instrument drawn up by the Lawyer signed by Yearsley and his wife allowing us the controul of the money, and putting it out of the Husband's power to touch it.[64]

Open-hearted trust, conviction about doing the right thing, and shrewdness all mingle here. More's obliviousness of any imminent disagreement with the newly and handsomely published poet is as noteworthy as her desire to control the access of the husband, in particular, to the accumulated and invested money. These two attributes are evident throughout More's correspondence on Yearsley. While she presents her matter-of-fact judgment to Mrs. Montagu about the Yearsleys' predicament ("misfortune, six children, and the Poet's vice, want of oeconomy, have dissipated this *ample* patrimony"), in the same letter she also admits envying Yearsley's "entire self-possession" and "the state of her mind . . . when famine and death stared her in the face."[65] Her report of Yearsley's response is as ominous for subsequent events as any perceptions of condescension on More's part. "Don't envy me Ma'am she reply'd for I have great doubts as to my motives; I am afraid my mind is rather *hardened* than *subdued*."

The prefatory letter to the first edition of Yearsley's verses[66] charts the development of More's scrupulous concern for the milkmaid-poet's well-being. More recognized early on "the genuine spirit of Poetry," the "perfect" ear, and the "native fire" of Yearsley's work. On visiting Yearsley she has been impressed by the "perfect simplicity in her manners" and "the justness of her taste." Although she surmises that "the study of the sacred Scriptures has enlarged her imagination and ennobled her language," More does not want to tame these "wild wood notes": "I should be sorry to see . . . her rustic muse polished into elegance or laboured into correctness." A sensible meliorist, More will not be inhibited by the possibility of "unsettl[ing] the sobriety of her mind and . . . exciting her vanity" since "it would be cruel to imagine that we cannot mend her fortune without impairing her virtue." As to her own motives in amassing almost one thousand subscriptions, More disavows "the idle vanity of a discoverer" in this confession: "The ambition of bringing to light a genius buried in obscurity, operates much less powerfully on my mind, than the wish to rescue a meritorious woman from misery, for it is not fame, but bread, which I am anxious to secure to her."

Yearsley's poems themselves, from the first edition, also contribute to our knowledge of matters beforehand. Downcast and unlettered, she clings to the idea of being an outsider. Since "learning, Heaven's best gift, is lost to [her]," she presents herself "cheerless and pensive . . . like the poor beetle" and "far estrang'd / From social joy" ("Night. To Stella," lines 80–82, 161–62). She admits feeling excluded:

> The too gaudy Sun
> Shines not for me; no bed of Nature yields
> Her varied sweets; no music wakes the grove. (lines 168–70)

The dejection is temporized by the frequent invocations to Stella to assist her "too daring theme" (line 71) and guide her "wilder'd thought" (line 136). She concedes that the influence of this new friend has been instructive and beneficial.

> Stella, how strong thy gentle argument!
> By thee convinc'd, I scan the iron lore,
> The savage virtues of untutor'd minds:
> In thy mild rhetoric dwells a social love
> Beyond my wild conceptions, optics false!
> Thro which I falsely judg'd of polish'd life. (lines 201–6)

Although Lactilla does not conceal her own circumstances, in "Thoughts on the Author's Own Death" and "Clifton Hill," especially, she acknowledges— with an acumen comparable to the Renaissance courtier's—the benefactors she has discovered. Poems to Walpole, the Duchess Dowager of Portland, and about Mrs. Montagu show her keen sensitivity to this recently established network of support. "To Mr. Raikes, on His Benevolent Scheme for rescuing Poor Children from Vice and Misery, By Promoting Sunday Schools" endorses the reformer's zeal, whereby "Ignorance, Vice, and loud-mouthed Reprobation" (line 21) are transformed and "the ductile mind, / Pliant as wax, . . . wear[s] the mould you give" (lines 47–48). Lactilla was also a careful observer of and listener to her patron, astutely picking up on the topics of her conversation. More than a trace of cravenness affects Yearsley's tone in "To Stella, on a Visit to Mrs. Montagu," as she protests, "I neither ask, nor own th' immortal name / Of friend" (lines 2–3), yet obligingly positions herself to receive any leftover:

> But ah! shou'd either have a thought to spare,
> Slight, trivial, neither worth a smile or tear,
> Let it be mine. (lines 66–68)

When she defends the "more than needful awe" with which she views "the great," Yearsley's reply to Stella, "On her Accusing the Author of Flattery and of Ascribing to the Creature that Praise which is due only to the Creator," sums up the adroit ways her roughness was responding to More's nurturance.

> For mine's a stubborn and a savage will;
> No custom's, manners, or soft arts I boast,
> On my rough soul your nicest rules are lost;
> Yet shall unpolish'd gratitude be mine,
> While Stella deigns to nurse the spark divine. (lines 8–12)

Does the mode change to ingratitude, as Yearsley publicizes her disagreements with this patron and More nurses her own wounds in private letters? Although in broad outline the dispute appears to involve such a reversal, in fact, the problems inherent in the issues of class, control, and what we currently call ownership of intellectual property had likely been brewing for some time. Yearsley's hasty signing of the deed of trust, authorizing and empowering More and Montagu "to pay, apply, and dispose of all, and singular, such sum and sums of money as shall remain . . . together with the interest . . . in such a way and manner as they shall judge most for the benefit of, and advantage of, the said Ann Yearsley and her children,"[67] no doubt forced matters to a head in the various confrontations of July and August 1785. Although Moira Ferguson's discovery of Yearsley's unpublished poems reveals Yearsley's "self-discipline in holding them back from publication" and in insuring that "her private life becomes less a matter of public record,"[68] Yearsley's anger was definitely publicized. As there were complications and inconsistencies beforehand, even more discrepancies and expressions of shock occur once the rift is revealed and widens. I am suggesting that their dispute was not a sudden *volte-face*, but part of the very architectonics of their relationship.

With a bluntness that barely concealed her indignation, Yearsley disclaimed the repeated charge of ingratitude when, in the "Autobiographical Narrative to the Noble and Generous Subscribers, who so liberally patronized A Book of Poems, published under the auspices of Miss H. More," prefacing the fourth edition of *Poems on Several Occasions* (1786) and reproduced in the preface to her next volume, *Poems on Various Subjects* (1787), she presented her side of the affair. The precipitate signing of the deed, with no time to take a copy, made her feel "as a mother deemed unworthy the tuition or care of her family." The aptness of her poignant comparison is a reminder of the deliberateness of her account, written in self-defense after the rallying of More's sizable party. While Yearsley recalls consenting to "the capricious terms" and signing "in despair," she adds the pseudo-supplicatory note, "I vainly imagined, by this submission, I had secured my character from the imputation of ingratitude." Though she admits becoming "very obnoxious" to More, she quickly adjusts her opinion of this benefactor: "From elaborate commendation the elevated Stella descends to low scurrility, charging me with 'drunkenness,' 'gambling,' 'extravagance,' and terming me 'wretched,' 'base,' 'ungrateful,' 'spendthrift.'" She refutes the story of having dashed money in More's face. The consistent thread of Yearsley's "Narrative" is the quixotic nature of More's behavior, making "her wonderful transit from the zenith of praise to the centre of malicious detraction." Her poem addressed "To those who accuse the Author of Ingratitude" challenges the devotees of "noos'd opinion" and their "love of base detraction" to "scan the feelings of Lactilla's soul." The opening retort uses a tellingly recycled phrase:

> You, who thro' optics dim, so falsely view
> This wond'rous maze of things, and rend a part
> From the well-order'd whole, to fit your sense
> Low, groveling, and confin'd; say from what source
> Spring your all-wise opinions? Can you dare
> Pronounce from proof, who ne'er pursu'd event
> To its minutest cause?

Almost two years earlier her verse to Stella had recognized the inadequacy of her own "optics false"; now she excoriates Stella's supporters for their nearsightedness.

Yearsley adjusted many of her earlier perceptions. Just as she changed her view of the More coterie, so she reworked her "Address to Friendship" to apply to her subsequent patron, Frederick Hervey, the Earl of Bristol. References to Christianity, specifically to organized religion, become more pugnacious, too. Her historical play, *Earl Goodwin*, presents a "blindly zealous" Edward the Confessor, "the dupe of designing men," whose soul is bound by "these crafty priests."[69] While the prologue acknowledges that "*no witless patron* thunders in her cause," the epilogue parries criticism of the "Milky Dame's play" by particularizing and praising the domestic site of production.

Doom'd, while she wrote, to rear an infant brood,
Attend their cries, and labour for their food;
Thro' toilsome day no leisure she possest,
The Muses snatch'd the moments stolen from rest,
She fear'd this aim had prov'd above her flight.
But your applause turns tremor to delight,
Secure of that, no frowns can now wail,
Nor wanton critic overturn her *pail*.[70]

Predictably More's friends closed ranks against Yearsley. Mrs. Boscawen called her "that odious woman."[71] Mrs. Montagu, referring to "*l'ingrate*," lamented "that bestowing a gift on such wretches gives them power over one."[72] As they did earlier, More's reports of Yearsley have a ventriloqual aspect. In mid-July, while entertaining Yearsley at supper, "treating her with all imaginable tenderness," More tells Mrs. Montagu how speechless she was left by Yearsley's accusation "of a design to defraud her of the money."[73] On 12 August, she writes to Mrs. Garrick, relating her version of events at one of the next meetings with Yearsley, when More had surrendered all accounts "to be examined . . . by several Gentlemen" and given Yearsley eleven guineas.

> She dashed it at me, and said she never would take that or any thing else from me, for that I had added insult to the weight of imaginary obligations. The Gentlemen were quite petrified; she gave me the eye a hundred times. Poor Wretch! I pity her, or any body who has such a heart to carry about with them. All this is because I won't give her the money which is in the Stock V for the poor children.[74]

Although she forges ahead with the second edition and attempts to find employment for Yearsley's husband, More *does* have a blind spot about the money.

Yet More's observation is very far from being dismissive or offhand. The more Yearsley presses the charges of tyranny and fraud, the more grimly determined to resist she becomes. She doubts that Yearsley, who is reported to wear "very fine gauze bonnets, long lappets, gold pins," is "to be trusted with the poor children's money."[75] More's next letter to Montagu, written on 16 September,[76] is a double-barrelled statement of resistance; she transcribes a letter from Yearsley, whom she refuses to see, and then comments on it. "Poor yet proud," Yearsley taxes More with the charge that her "favours arose more from . . . vanity than generosity" and vows "to disown as obligation a proceeding which must render me and my children your poor dependents for ever." Indecorously and abruptly Yearsley intends to turn the tables: "as its necessary for *my* character to be wrecked to do justice to *yours,* I submit to it; in this it is your turn to be grateful." The very toughness of More's reaction and her resolve not to be bullied—refusing to sacrifice "a duty to a fear" and trying to dismiss the newspaper accounts by not taking "the least notice of any of *their* scurrilities"—indicate how deeply wounded and shocked by Yearsley's venom she was.

Although by October More has renounced all financial responsibilities, having "prevailed on a gentleman . . . to receive the trust," it takes her some time to come to terms with "such unprovoked malignity."[77] Significantly More does not mention Yearsley's name in the remainder of this letter, but their two distinct personalities and grievances clash in every sentence.

> She is going to bring out her Poems as she originally wrote them, before they were spoilt by me. She tells everybody my envy of her makes me miserable, and that I cannot bear her superiority. It is amazing how notorious she has contrived to make her own business. I have had near a hundred letters on the subject, and the Booksellers assure me that her behaviour had quite spoilt the sales of book, which would have been very great. . . . What a holiday to me when I have done with her and her business which has occupied near a whole year of my Life!

In November More is still involved, telling Mrs. Garrick that she cannot specify the date of her visit because she is "so harrassed and perplexed about Mrs. Yearsley's affairs which are not yet settled."[78] By late December, though she manages to insert a note about her Christmas plans, More is still preoccupied with Yearsley, reporting to Mrs. Montagu that "the poor wretch" hopes "to present the King a Petition against [More]" and charging that "she conceals above two hundred pounds of the money [More] paid her which amounted to considerably above £600."[79]

Yearsley and More went separate ways. Although vestigial references and allusions[80] occur in their work after 1786, all communication between them ceased. As Yearsley's transcribed letter put her case, "my feelings and gratitude is traduced,"[81] while More bore the "trial" and "vexation" of Yearsley's conduct because, as she maintained to Mrs. Carter, "my conscience tells me I ought not to give up my trust for these poor children, on account of their mother's wickedness."[82] Arbitration by the reader is a complicated issue, not only because the correspondence is itself so conflicted but also because some published opinions are so wide of the mark. Joseph Cottle's suggestion that had More known of Yearsley's desire to educate her sons and open up a circulating library she would "no doubt" have "instantly acced[ed] to so reasonable a request"[83] (either to give Yearsley more money or allow her to be an executor of the trust) is not convincing since it disregards the fixity of More's intentions. When opinions favor More, they usually do so by simplifying Yearsley. William Roberts dismisses the milkwoman as "equally a stranger to gratitude and prudence."[84] Early biographers take a similar line. Henry Thompson, reflecting on Yearsley's life as a morality play by negative example, regrets "her waywardness," which "wrested . . . the money from its prudent and legitimate guardians."[85] After discoursing on the fraud, "invariably more easily practised upon persons of an open, amiable, unsuspicious mind," Thomas Taylor concludes that More "too readily and too implicitly placed confidence in the milk-woman's pretensions to piety."[86] Class distinctions play a large part in Charlotte Yonge's retrospective glance at "ignorant distrust of the upper classes . . . in excitable, unbalanced temperaments."[87] Such pronouncements as "Lactilla was no great hand at poetry"[88] or Yearlsey's "signs of independence, . . . of overstepping [her] station in life," meant that "she was quickly dropped"[89] contribute little to our understanding of the dynamic between patron and client; however, the ways in which these problematic dicta have been expanded and contextualized by Donna Landry and Mary Waldron are very illuminating. Various explanations, favouring one side or the other, have been put forth. Though mainly concerned with Yearsley, J.M.S. Tompkins's able and detailed treatment of the quarrel makes the point that Yearsley "never forgave or attempted to understand Hannah More."[90] Rayner Unwin's attempt to dispense justice to both sides results in prevarication; "freedom came to the wrong person, and too late," he decides for Lactilla, whereas with More, "to be so much as questioned put that lady on her dignity, and made discussion impossible."[91]

An as-yet untried way of seeing these women is to concentrate on the features they actually shared. Both disliked "social unruliness" and were committed "to social order and the status quo."[92] Both also showed evidence of naïveté and extremity, despite the apparent paradox of such a combination. Patronage that cut across class lines was as new to the miserable but yearning Lactilla as it was to her eager benefactor, whose experience as Garrick's protégée had not entailed a vast cultural or economic gap. Each wanted desperately to believe the best of the other's motives and conduct, with the upshot of the quarrel being a schizophrenic denial of the earlier beatitude. Lactilla's untutored genius translates for More into the vexations of a poor wretch. Stella's genteel guidance becomes for Yearsley insupportable servitude. They were both absolutists, denying any hint of the worm. Stella was an all-radiant tutor, and Lactilla an enchanting warbler of native wood notes. Yet this benefactor, a published author with a string of literary contacts, also considered that she knew best about financial arrangements for an impoverished, unknown milkmaid. The proletarian poet, though without a dictionary and standard cultural accoutrements, knew the power of words to impale some and exculpate others. The frugal, responsible manager of her own resources, who was busily planning to build a cottage retreat with her royalties, extended this management to include the affairs of the reduced, improvident Yearsleys. The milkwoman, whose financial situation had been precarious for some time, saw the sales of her poetry as an income to which she was entitled.

Do the before and after attitudes cancel each other out? Was there ever any hope for the aspiring milkmaid and the benevolent ex-schoolmistress? Cynicism about the impossibility of their alliance and even surprise that it lasted as long as it did only take us to the limits of their bitter disagreement. The really saddening aspect of this predictable rupture is the lost promise it represents. What might have been and how each one's life could have been changed are admittedly speculations, but not necessarily saccharine ones. Rereading More's praise of Yearsley's "striking and original" language and her "morality [that] has not evaporated into sentiment"[93] lets us recall how impressive, perhaps instructive, More found the milkwoman to be. In her early encomiastic stage Lactilla realized that Stella made her "a convert: thou hast turn'd / My rusting powers to the bright strains of joy."[94] Intervention deemed intrusive and a conversion repudiated testify to the backfiring of these best-laid plans. They also remind us of the intricate linkage of praise (*laus*) and blame (*vituperatio*) on the coin of *encomium*.

❀ 4 ❀
"That which before us lies
in daily life":[1] Social Discourse

To attempt to compress more than three decades of More's essay writing in a single chapter may seem both trivializing and impossible. The authorial voice does become more resonant, moving from the neophyte's offer of "a few remarks on such circumstances as seemed to her susceptible of some improvement, and on such subjects as she imagined were particularly interesting to young ladies"[2] to the authoritative clarion call to "British ladies" and "what they themselves might be if all their talents and unrivalled opportunities were turned to the best account."[3] But many of the informing ideas—from *Essays on Various Subjects* (1777), *Thoughts on the Importance of the Manners of the Great to General Society* (1788), *An Estimate of the Religion of the Fashionable World* (1790), *Strictures on the Modern System of Female Education* (1799), and *Hints Towards Forming the Character of a Young Princess* (1805) to her only novel, which extends this discourse to the procedures of courtship, *Coelebs in Search of a Wife: Comprehending Observations on Domestic Habits and Manners, Religion and Morals* (1808)—remain the same. Addressing the privileged and the great, whom she labels in *Strictures* as "the higher class," and specifically the women of this class, More blends first-hand observation of and a judgmental distance from the events and practices discussed. The ratio of influential relations is direct: as "Reformation must begin with the great, . . . [whose] example is the fountain whence the vulgar draw their habits, actions, and characters,"[4] so women's influence is supremely suited "to raise the depressed tone of public morals, and to awaken the drowsy spirit of religious principle."[5] Whether from Cowslip Green, or Pulteney Street, or Barley Wood, she adopts a position comparable to Cowper's; like the poet, whose "natural" images and "original and philosophic" thinking "enchanted" her,[6] More prefers "through the loop-holes of retreat / To peep at such a world."[7] A cultural but not an ethnographic critic, she trains her sights on British women, whose character is "never [to] be determined by a comparison with the women of other nations."[8] Although More contends that she is "not sounding an alarm to female warriors . . . [or] a female polemic," and that she has no "desire to make scholastic ladies or female dialecticians" or any "wish to enthrone [women] in the professor's chair, to deliver oracles, harangues, and dissertations,"[9] she does not hesitate to display her own rhetorical skill and debating expertise. As acute in her suspicions of a woman's "deep and designing panegyrist"[10] as she is audacious in striking deliberately close to home where "certain faults . . . press too near our self-love to be even perceptible to us,"[11] More uses these lengthy prose works to develop, extend, and illustrate her ideology of the female station and influence.

She does much more than cast an occasional glance, for her intimate knowledge of fashionable Christianity becomes the most powerful weapon of her declarative, bold prose. Among the "worm[s] . . . feeding on the vitals of domestic virtue," this strict Sabbatarian points to such habits as the summoning of a hairdresser on Sunday, the "petty mischief" of card money, by which "part of the wages of the servant is to be paid by his furnishing the implements of diversion for the guests of the master," and "the daily and hourly lie of *Not at home*."[12] More bases her indictment of the great on the firm conviction that "an extempore Christian is a ridiculous character";[13] hence, she is empowered to puncture the hypocrisy behind "their terror, lest the character of piety should derogate from their reputation as men of sense,"[14] and the anomaly of their "encouraging so many admirable schemes for promoting religion among the children of the poor" but not "encouraging it in their own children and their servants also."[15] Her focus is unabashedly national, local, and domestic, since she charges those persons who "should gladly contribute to spread the light of Christianity in another hemisphere, actually obstruct the progress of it at home."[16] Like her attitude, her suggested remedies are not for the fainthearted; although she knows that "the houses and hearts of the more modish Christians" will be closed to her, she nevertheless endorses laying "the axe to the root oftener than the pruning knife to the branch."[17] Uncompromisingly she insists that the fundamental Christian tenets should not stand out "like the *appliquée* of the embroiderer" but should be "interwoven, . . . so as to have become a part of the stuff"; the climax of this lesson is the sheer brand of "knowledge that is *burnt in*, . . . seldom obtrusive, rarely impertinent."[18]

Undeterred by the eagerness of "fashionable Christians" to dismiss her as a "palpable enthusiast, the abettor of 'strange doctrines,' long ago consigned over by the liberals and the polite to bigots and fanatics,"[19] More meets this belittlement head-on. As she argues repeatedly, the central, albeit unpopular, tenet of human corruption, with its aim "to humble the sinner and exalt the Saviour,"[20] is not "a morose, unamiable, and gloomy idea."[21] Whether attempting to dissuade ladies from simpering frivolity or outlining the moral advantages of the study of history for the Princess of Wales, More keeps her central thesis always in view. While lecturing Princess Charlotte that "history furnishes a strong practical illustration of one of the fundamental doctrines of our religion, the corruption of human nature," she goes as far as to rescript events, with a seemingly naive emphasis on rectitude and purity of intention:

> How much more effectually, and immediately, might the Reformation have been promoted, had Henry, laying aside the blindness of prejudice, and subduing the turbulence of passion, been the zealous and consistent supporter of the Protestant cause; the virtuous husband of one virtuous wife, and the parent of children *all* educated in the sound principles of the Reformation!—Again, had the popes effectually reformed themselves, how might the unity of the church have been promoted; and even the schisms, which have arisen in Protestant communities, been diminished![22]

Is More's related stress on the need for women to be excellent and distinctive similarly oversimplified? It is expedient to dismiss her as reactionary and antifeminist; of the younger generation of Bluestockings, Sylvia Harcstark Myers rates More as "probably the most regressive in her attitudes towards the advancement of women."[23] Her conservative intransigence truly baffles. It *is* hard to figure out why in the earliest *Essays* she commits herself so totally to such a restricting view of the "bounds" "prescribed" by "nature, propriety, and custom."[24] Why, at a time when she herself is nursing literary ambitions, does she pronounce so thunderingly that "pretensions to that strength of intellect, which it is requisite to penetrate into the abstruser walks of literature, it is presumed [women] will readily relinquish?"[25] In reserving "the lofty Epic, the pointed Satire, and the more daring and successful flights of the Tragic Muse . . . for the bold adventurers of the other sex," is she deliberately minimizing her own dramatic success and silencing her quick, opinionated tongue about the foibles of fashionable life? She assumes that her belief in separate temperaments, aptitudes, and spheres for women and men is ordained and natural: "both shine from their native, distinct, unborrowed merits, not from those which are foreign, adventitious, and unnatural."[26] By exhorting her readers "to be good originals, rather than bad imitators, . . . excellent women, rather than indifferent men,"[27] she also consigns them to a static fate. In More's imprisoning, Catch-22 argument, women's vocations are limited—there will never be "one female logician" or chronologer—just as their personalities are determined. While men provide the sobering counterpoints, women will continue to "speak to shine or to please," to "admire what is brilliant," to "prefer an extemporaneous sally of wit, or a sparkling effusion of fancy, before the most accurate reasoning," and to "admire passionately."[28]

Although More temporized somewhat in her next major sally into this field, in *Strictures*, she never officially recanted anything. In fact, when a pirated version of *Essays* was circulating as late as 1810, a "vexed" More insisted that Cadell and Davies publish the following announcement which she had devised in the London papers, while she undertook to advertise it in the Bath and Bristol papers.

> Messrs Cadell and Davies desire to inform the Public that the new Edition of the Volume of Essays by Mrs. H. More lately advertised by Sharpe and Hailes is not only unauthorized by her, but against her consent. She having given public notice many years ago in the Preface to her twelve volumes that she had suppressed those Essays as a very juvenile work and having treated the same subjects more in detail in her Strictures on Education.

More was very adamant that the phrase "against her consent" be included because, as she crisply explained, "they asked it and I refused."[29] Whether embarrassment at the severity of this juvenile work also accounted for its suppression remains only a speculation.

One way of assessing the singularity of her views within the literary coterie of the day is to compare her *Essays* with Catharine Macaulay's slightly later *Letters on Education* (1790). "Fair Macaulay," whom More had praised in the epilogue to *The Search after Happiness*, was celebrated along with More in Richard Samuel's painting, "Nine Living Muses of Great Britain" (c. 1775). However, more than the allegiances of Whig and Tory separated these muses. Macaulay's *Letters* mounted a cogent argument for coeducation, exposing "the absurd notion that the education of females should be of an opposite kind to that of males." Rather than assenting to "much false speculation on the natural qualities of the female mind," Macaulay contends that women's vices and imperfections "are entirely the effects of situation and education."[30] Not only does she neatly parry Pope's dictum that *"a perfect woman's but a softer man"* with her own proposition, that *"a perfect man is a woman formed after a coarser mold,"* she also tosses out as irrational and absurd Rousseau's theory of the natural subjection of women: "it is pride and sensuality that speak in Rousseau, and, in this instance, has lowered the man of genius to the licentious pedant."[31] Although Macaulay starts from a position of equal abilities, unlike More's distinct talents, both argue against "bringing a young lady up with no higher idea of the end of education than to make her agreeable to a husband, and confining the necessary excellence for this happy acquisition to the mere graces of person."[32]

When it comes to animadverting on vanity and the popular notions of women's education, no one can rival More. Her unparalleled position becomes clear in a comparison with an earlier work that, at first glance, might seem the originating model: *Strictures on Female Education; Chiefly As It Relates to the Heart* (1787) by John Bennett, a Manchester curate. Bennett's thesis of paternalistic proprietorship could not be further from More's galvanizing rhetoric. In contrast to More's calls for responsible action, Bennett advises the model of quiescent objectification. "Considering females as a species of treasure," he writes, "a man will wish to become the sole, exclusive proprietor of one or more of them, as of any other object."[33] Quite content with consigning women to the role of pleasing charmers, "the fairest *ornaments* . . ., the embellishers of society, and the sweeteners of life,"[34] which More was inveighing against, Bennett denied women's capacity to pursue the firmness, depth and complexity of ideas in argument. In light of More's vastly superior essay and its aims to lead women "to think, to compare, to combine, to methodize," Bennett's most egregious claim is surely that women "cannot, like the men, arrange, combine, abstract, pursue and diversify a long strain of ideas."[35]

The excellence More calls for involves gradual and virtuous, just and sober cultivation. It is "an experimental thing which is to grow gradually out of observation and practice."[36] As it requires tractability in the pupil, it also relies on discrimination in the teacher to "appreciate the individual character of each pupil, in order to appropriate her management."[37] Cultivation and management, though emphasizing divergent ideas of development, intermingle throughout More's prose. The teacher and the gardener need a similar astuteness, for "the cultivator of the human mind must, like the gardener, study diversities of soil, or he may plant diligently and water faithfully with little fruit."[38] Secure on her moral highground, More casts a withering glance at the "merely ornamental" life of the young lady of her day, which "resembles that of an actress; the morning is all rehearsal, and the evening is all performance."[39] Complacent, patronizing remarks on women's literary projects by male so-called panegyrists also warrant some cutting ripostes. To arm the author who "will have to encounter the mortifying circumstance of having her sex always taken into account, and her highest exertions . . . received with the qualified approbation *that it is really extraordinary for a woman*," More adroitly turns the tables by exposing this condescension for the ridiculous banter it is.

> Men of learning, who are naturally disposed to estimate works in proportion as they appear to be the result of art, study, and institution,

are inclined to consider even the happier performances of the other sex as the spontaneous productions of a fruitful but shallow soil, and to give them the same kind of praise which we bestow on certain salads, which often draw from us a sort of wondering commendation, not, indeed, as being worth much in themselves, but because, by the lightness of the earth, and a happy knack of the gardener, these indifferent cresses spring up in a night, and therefore we are ready to wonder they are no worse.[40]

However, the fact that More was promoting "the enlargement of the female understanding" as a "means to put an end to those petty and absurd contentions for equality" and to accommodate woman to a "more accurate" view "of the station she was born to fill" at the same time as she was petitioning that a woman "be more reasonably educated and . . . the native growth of [her] mind . . . cease to be stinted and cramped"[41] raises the fundamental issue of the liberation or imprisonment of women in her schemes for their education. Questions about More's distance from or affinity with the contemporary open advocate of rights for women, Mary Wollstonecraft, also require closer attention.

Educating Women to Save the Nation and Serve the State: More and Wollstonecraft

Only seven years separate the publications of Wollstonecraft's *Vindication of the Rights of Woman: With Strictures on Political and Moral Subjects* from More's *Strictures on the Modern System of Female Education, With a View of the Principles and Conduct Prevalent Among Women of Rank and Fortune*.[42] Yet "seventy times seven" (Matthew 18.21) differences appear to keep them apart and, unlike the Matthean injunction, unreconciled. With its dedication to Talleyrand, open talk of abused rights, and disdain for the inhibiting influence of the "pestiferous purple" (99), the *Vindication* was predictably well received in the *Analytical Review* but savaged in the *Anti-Jacobin Review*. With its citations of Burke and Wilberforce, quarreling with notions of rights and prefectibility, and upholding of religion as the force that "spiritualizes the social affections" (439), More's two-volume *Strictures*, which went through seven editions in 1799, won surprisingly temperate kudos among the Anti-Jacobin coterie in spite of its systematic battery of her Mendip village schools. Hailing the "manly praise" of country in her "detached observations on the present practice," the *Anti-Jacobin* reviewer (Theobald J. Boucher) entreated More "to continue her labours . . . on the style of education that prevails among the daughters of those who, if not of rank, are yet of great importance in the social scale, that is, the gentry of the kingdom; the daughters of mercantile men; of officers of the army, whose fortunes and views are limited;

and (though last not least) the daughters of clergymen."[43] Experienced teachers and established public figures—with Wollstonecraft moving in independent, liberal, radical, and reformist circles and More being championed by Bluestockings and Evangelical activists—both nevertheless envisioned transforming the state by modeling governance on a domestic arrangement. Wollstonecraft would have no quarrel with More's call to women "to exert themselves, with a patriotism at once firm and feminine, for the general good" (4), and her contentions "that private principle is the only solid basis of public virtue" (40), that "education is but an initiation into that life of trial to which we are introduced on our entrance into this world" (128), and that "the chief end to be proposed, in cultivating the understandings of women, is to qualify them for the practical purposes of life" (216).

My aim is not to obliterate the obvious and easily exaggerated differences between the caricatured hyena and old bishop. In fact, More's distinction from Wollstonecraft, whose work she vowed never to read, is virtually a critical commonplace. As early as the verse epistles of "Sappho Search" the idea of More's envy of Wollstonecraft was entertained.

> On poor Mary's errors, she's coldly severe,
> Nor drops o'er her wrongs, or her grave, one soft tear.
> In vigorous expression, and passion's true tone,
> Perhaps she was piqued to be greatly outshone.[44]

Although plaudits abounded from More's friends, lay and clerical, with Mrs. Carter predicting that *Strictures* would be universally admired, Dr. Burney praising its forceful language, and Mrs. Barbauld considering it a necessity for every drawing room, the author was assailed—and from within the Establishment, too—for daring to animadvert on the masculine topics of religion and order. The minister of Christ's Church, Bath, her friend the Reverend Charles Daubeny, published a fifty-six-page letter chastizing her "want of precision in language," which could lead "ignorant Christians" to "downright enthusiasm," in her presumed misinterpretation of the connection between faith and works.[45] Daubeny himself misread More; despite his sputters about remaining "secure from the imputation of being unnecessarily scrupulous on this subject,"[46] More declined to respond and *Strictures* continued to sell. In contrast to the prurient sensationalism surrounding Wollstonecraft's liaisons with Imlay and Godwin is the utter silence, even in More's at times chatty letters, shrouding the circumstances of her canceled wedding. Wollstonecraft traveled quite widely, living in France for over two years and, after the publication of *Vindication*, as Imlay's "best friend and wife," a kind of business agent, visiting Sweden, Norway, and Denmark. Though elected to the Académie Royale des Belles Lettres de Rouen and carrying on a grateful correspondence in French with her electors,[47] More never journeyed to France; yet it was she, knowing intimately the route between Bristol and London and the country lanes of the Mendips, who commented on the similar roles of the moralist and the geographer. Events across the channel affected the lives and works of both reformers. The seizure of the Bastille and strong feminist direction of revolutionary projects steeled Wollstonecraft's resolve to write about the need to establish equality, to confound ranks, and to free women. "This moment of alarm and peril," as More referred to her own era at the opening of *Strictures*, reinforced the urgency of her appeal to firm and feminine patriotism.

Matters of expression, authority, and restraint keep Wollstonecraft and More apart, but the underlying issues of the excellence, capacities, and duties of their sex bind them as cultural reformers and warriors. Intensely focused on a woman's sphere and adept at speaking in a hortatory, public voice, each author addresses her audience—middle-class for Wollstonecraft and aristocratic for More—in an appropriately idiosyncratic style. Wollstonecraft eschews polish and elegance in favor of usefulness and persuasion, relying on "significant" (147) words to pack the requisite punch. She exhorts women to lay aside coquettish art and feigned delicacy, with an expressivness that runs all the way from normative assertion to rhetorical question and climactic exclamation. Notice how adroitly she pits the insinuating strategies of securing affection against the longed-for goal of respect.

> To gain the affections of a virtuous man, is affectation necessary? Nature has given woman a weaker frame than man; but, to ensure her husband's affections, must a wife, who, by the exercise of her mind and body whilst she was discharging the duties of a daughter, wife, and mother, has allowed her constitution to retain its natural strength, and her nerves a healthy tone,—is she, I say, to condescend to use art, and feign a sickly delicacy, in order to secure her husband's affection? Weakness may excite tenderness, and gratify the arrogant pride of man, but the lordly caresses of a protector will not gratify a noble mind that pants for and deserves to be respected. Fondness is a poor substitute for friendship! (112)

The link between domestic virtue and marital friendship supplies the conclusion that Wollstonecraft presents as an indisputable fact: "besides, the woman who strengthens her body and exercises her mind will, by managing her family and practising various virtues, become the friend, and not the humble dependent of her husband" (113). Aware of the "horse-laugh" that the noted exception "where love animates the behaviour" may excite, she decides not to "stifle" the observation that "with a lover," a woman is "always a woman," that is, with "his authority and her sex . . . stand[ing] between them and rational converse" (146–47). Despite her announced wish that women "may every day grow more and more masculine . . . which raises females on the scale of animal being, when they are comprehensively termed mankind" (introduction), Wollstonecraft's praise of the historian Catharine Macaulay stops short of calling hers "a masculine understanding." Although she was quick to decode the meaning of "masculine understanding" as the ability to reason abstractly, she refused to compliment Macaulay in this manner, which would exclude all other women. What Wollstonecraft does admire about Macaulay's style seems to be the very features she strove to exemplify and incorporate in her own writing: "Possessing more penetration than sagacity, more understanding than fancy, she writes with sober energy and argumentative closeness; yet sympathy and benevolence give an interest to her sentiments, and that vital heat to arguments, which forces the reader to weigh them" (206–7).

Contemporary reviewers weighed and considered More's long but controlled sentences, finding them as powerful as those of Addison. "Sappho Search" quipped, "These rich *babes of grace*, Hannah knows how to dandle; / And the bright tools of rhetoric, with cunning to handle."[48] No mention of the disorientations of love interrupts the orderly, though often digressive, march of her argument. A nonwhimsical toughness stamps More's talk of "right minded women," the "practical purposes of life," and "bounden duties" (41–42). In Nancy Cott's judgment, "More's work perfected the transformation of woman's image from sexual to moral being."[49] Her hard stand on coquettishness—before and during marriage—removes her directives from Dr. Gregory's cat-and-mouse advice to his daughters "never to discover to him the full extent of your love"; both reformers would have balked at the "case," cited in Gregory's *A Father's Legacy* (1774), "where a woman may coquet justifiably to the utmost verge which her conscience will allow."[50] More's friendship[51] with the Reverend Thomas Gisborne, whose *Enquiry into the Duties of the Female Sex* preceded *Strictures* by two years, notwithstanding, she took a much less conciliatory stand on "the ornamental acquisitions" of female education, which Gisborne had valued as contributing "to preserve the mind in a state of placid cheerfulness."[52] This innocuousness is too removed from activity for such an advocate of precision, exactitude, and a realistic eliciting of truth as More, who challenges at the same time as she upbraids and admonishes her readers.

A lady studies, not that she may qualify herself to become an orator or a pleader; not that she may learn to debate, but to act. She is to read the best books, not so much to enable her to talk of them, as to bring the improvement which they furnish, to the rectification of her principles and the formation of her habits. The great uses of study to woman are to enable her to regulate her own mind, and to be instrumental to the good of others. (216)

As "a female crusader" with an "explicitly conservative message," More was, as Mitzi Myers reminds us, "infinitely more successful than Wollstonecraft" in inoculating "everyday routine with aggressive virtue"; Myers sees More's text "rhythmically alternating the systole of ingratiating genuflection and the diastole of combative assertion."[53] Concerned to train up neither "Amazons nor Circassians" but rational and accountable Christians, More forces her reader to confront the inevitable though rhetorical question, "should we not carefully cultivate intellect?" (52).

The especial power of a woman's mind, though figured differently by each author and working under quite different constraints, is the basic tenet that unites Wollstonecraft and More. Education is a discipline for life. Wollstonecraft and More write with passion about the education of women, in particular, and the preeminence of influence in the domestic sphere because each topic has been so sadly trivialized. Whether in the breathless, impulsive hurry of Wollstonecraft, or in the measured periodicity of More, these manifestos promote fundamental changes in attitude, which Wollstonecraft designates a reformulation of social order and which More envisions as a needed seriousness.

Wollstonecraft spends a lot of time detailing how women's potential has been wasted in a "disorderly, . . . random . . . [and] instinctive kind of education" (104), sacrificing "strength and usefulness to beauty" (79) and ensuring "a state of perpetual childhood" (81) in "gentle, domestic brutes" (101). Finding no amiability in weakness or in "romantic wavering feelings" (169), she writes to rouse her audience to consciousness and indignation about being "educated for dependence" (135), "immured in their families groping in the dark" (87), and "legally prostituted" (151), as "the mind is left to rust" (171), the "delusive flattery" (194) of being called an angel is tolerated, and woman's "reason, her misty reason! is employed rather to burnish than snap her chains" (202). Quarreling with the "false hypothesis" (93) of Rousseau's state of nature, as well as with Milton's description of "our first frail mother" (100) and "Moses' poetical story" to justify man's exertions of "strength to subjugate his companion" (109), she directs attention to the consequences of this wayward, purblind miseducation of women. "They both acquire manners before morals, and a knowledge of life before they have from reflection any acquaintance with the grand ideal outline of human nature" (106). The stimulation and exercise of the understanding in "a proper education" that "store[s] their mind with knowledge" (285) are crucial because they encourage "rational fellowship instead of slavish obedience" (263), "mutual duties" (283) replacing "cattish affection" (295) in "more observant daughters, more affectionate sisters, more faithful wives, more reasonable mothers" (263). In championing her sex, Wollstonecraft situates potentially informed, modest, steadied women in the domestic, albeit nonornamental sphere. As a means of making "their private virtue a public benefit," she argues that "honest, independent women" be encouraged "to fill respectable stations" (262) and be allowed entry to the professions, medicine in particular. Unfortunately a sustained treatment of women's legal and political rights, the topic for a projected second part, never materialized.[54]

Although More's regret and huffiness about the "disdain of control" and "revolutionary spirit" that result in fulminations on "rights" (109) announces a different sense of legal entitlement, *Strictures* does convey an astute, astringent plea for women to be taught "that human life is a true history, many passages of which will be dull, obscure, and uninteresting, some perhaps tragical" (124). Her animadversions on human nature support the claim that women should be happy to be free of—and not disposed to envy—"the distinctions of public life and high offices, . . . the responsibility attached to them, and the mortification of being dismissed from them" (241). She wants women to be strong but sheltered, capable but strictly domestic managers. Conducting an argument as self-serving as the general conviction and righteous corrective of her preface to the tragedies, More holds forth in a professional voice while she warns against exciting "in women an uneasy jealousy that their talents are neither awarded with public honours nor emoluments in life" (241). But she is also as dismissive as Wollstonecraft about the "frenzy of accomplishments," the intoxication of flattery, and the mere "talent for conversation" that is usually the "precursor" and not "the result of instruction" (130); like her contemporary, she has "no wish to bring back the frantic reign of chivalry nor to reinstate women in that fantastic empire in which they then sat enthroned in the hearts, or rather in the imaginations of men" (13). While the "complicated drug" (22) of novels and the "hot-bed of the circulating library" (130) are considered "vehicles of wider mischief" (22), the Bible and Milton are sacred texts for More; yet she is not blind to the inequities of Rousseau's treatment of Sophie. Equally suspicious of worldly praise as of a passive noblewoman sitting "with gratifying docility at the foot of a professor's chair," More perorates: "In those parasites who offered this homage to female genius, the homage was the effect neither of truth, nor of justice, nor of conviction. It arose out of gratitude, or it was a reciprocation of flattery; it was sometimes vanity, it was often distress, which prompted the adulation; it was the want of a patroness; it was the want of a dinner" (228).

More's analogies from the theater, where she first earned acclaim, and from her lifelong passion for gardening preface the final point of comparison: the sensibility and predisposition each brings to the task of writing about women's education. Toward the end of *Strictures*, More draws another comparison from the world of theater to describe the need to combine curiosity with a certain cultivated capacity. In her explanation, "the drawing up the curtain at the theatre, though it serve to introduce us to the entertainments behind it, does not create in us any new faculties to understand or to relish those entertainments: these must have been already acquired; they must have been provided beforehand, and brought with us to the place; for the entertainment can only operate on that taste we carry to it" (368). One of the prevailing mental habits shared by Wollstonecraft and More, both of whom pay tribute to Locke, is their associative thinking. Wollstonecraft tends to be most expansive when describing the restrictions hemming women in. Images of chains, polished but not snapped, lead naturally enough to mentions of Egyptian bondage and to the yoking and harnessing of asses and horses. Such metaphors, though clarifying situations of enslavement, also locate the subject within a wide, natural world. They emphasize the inextricable linkage between social conditions and authority on one hand and the devaluation and voicelessness of women on the other. As predictable and unyielding as the parts of a chain is Wollstonecraft's logical insistence on the consequences of these mind-forged manacles in terms of women's education and station in society. All meliorist forecasting is necessarily based on a liberating social outlook; Wollstonecraft concludes that "it is reasonable to suppose that they will change their character, and correct their vices and follies, when they are allowed to be free in a physical, moral, and civil sense" (319). More's most associative writing, always blunt and unequivocal, relates to careful nurturance and organic growth; it can encourage and excoriate, build up and eradicate. She has the curious knack of being able to use a jeremiad to promote a view of the organicity of change; however, her determination to chop, uproot, and nip vanity in the bud is every bit as pronounced. Evil tempers and troublesome passions—either in children or alluring but empty-headed ladies—are at the top of More's list for extermination: "the subduing hand cannot cut off the ever-sprouting heads so fast as the prolific hydra can reproduce them" (61). In her garden of associative delights More is the chief horticulturalist, deciding which sprouts to tend and which to slice.

Whether snapping chains or tending gardens, these authors live in and represent realms of privilege. A "servant-maid to take off her hands the servile part of the household business" (254) is as necessary to Wollstonecraft's picture of a woman's domestic happiness as, in fact, the French nurse Marguerite was essential to her during the trip to Scandinavia accompanied by her infant daughter by Imlay. More attempts public-spiritedly to meet her audience on their own ground by exhorting them to seize "all the little occasions of doing good, which every day presents to the affluent," through comparing these opportunities to the mere "sacrifice of an opera ticket" (154).

As the vindicator, concerned with avenging, emancipating, defending, and justifying, Wollstonecraft constantly extends the influence of the domestic sphere to a wider social and political setting. She looks from the inside out, aligning manners with morals, affirming the importance for men to "become more chaste and modest" (84), and stressing that "reserve," which "has nothing sexual in it," is "equally necessary for both sexes" (236). As the formulator of strictures, which both tighten and, as in phonetics, allow for the articulation of certain speech sounds, More writes to lift "the reader from sensation to intellect," to abstract "her from the world and its vanities" (136). But, looking from the outside into the home, she also relies on a privileged and uncommon acquaintance with the public world to advance her argument, disparaging the Chinese practice of binding and crippling women's feet and comparing it to the "stinted and cramped" (236) state of women's minds. To correct trifling this observer of faddish modes directs women, with their "delicacy and quickness of perception and . . . nice discernment between the beautiful and the defective," to "see the world, as it were, from a little elevation in [their] own garden" (234). Despite her claim that "co-operation and not competition is indeed the clear principle we wish to see reciprocally adopted by those higher minds in each sex which readily approximate the nearest to each other" (226), the predominant characteristic of More's trope about women's gardens is their distinction from men's. While Wollstonecraft concentrates on mutuality, More emphasizes—more temperately and expansively than in *Essays*—what for her are the inherent, determining, essential differences.

Coelebs in Search of a Wife: *Old Adam and New Eve*

Austen's "universally acknowledged" truth about "a single man in possession of a good fortune" underwent a curious alteration in More's immensely popular novel.[55] Expressing no erotic voltage, she explores the marriage quests central to the works of Fielding, Burney, and Austen in a narrative so determined that the outcome is "a foregone conclusion."[56] With customary dispatch—in this instance linking therapy with combat—the sixty-three-year-old novelist, who had railed against the novel "drug" in *Strictures*, explained her motives: "I wrote it to amuse the languor of disease, . . . to raise the tone of that mart of mischief [the circulating library], and to counteract its corruptions."[57] When Edmund Gosse, generations later, encountered this instrument of edification in his father's "swept and garnished library," from which "novels were excluded," he recalls that "the moralising part of the book made no impression on my infant mind which was fascinated by the pictures of frivolous society and even perilous intrigue," and refuses to "disturb the ancient illusion that 'Coelebs in Search of a Wife' was rather naughty."[58] Most readers see the first-person narrative as the furthest thing from naughtiness, applying such labels as "an extended tract,"[59] "a counterpoint to . . . life,"[60] a "fictionalized conduct book,"[61] "an attempt to rewrite the story of Eve from a 'modern' point of view,"[62] a revelation of "the temper of the early Victorians,"[63] a faithful record of "the practice of her contemporaries in the Clapham Sect,"[64] a celebration of "the ideal woman,"[65] "evangelical doctrine dressed up in the guise of fiction,"[66] a "lay sermon of 'the vanity of human wishes,'"[67] "a plea for the Christian life in its Evangelical dress,"[68] and "a series of essays modeled on those of *The Spectator* and *The Rambler*."[69] The common assumption is that the text is a defence of "the Burkean model of the patriarchal household" and that its creed of "female self-effacement" genuflects to male systems of representation.[70] Is *Coelebs* a novel at all? If it is, does it warrant Lady Belfield's knowing criticism of being "a sad dull novel" with "no difficulties nor adventures to heighten the interest, . . . not so much as a duel or even a challenge, . . . to give variety to the monotonous scene" (193). As the writer of this critique, why would More ostensibly sabotage her own undertaking? Aware that the cards are stacked against her, I want to suggest that the text itself might explain why—aside from the obvious answer of perversity—More decided to construct the discourse of *Coelebs* in the service of such a rigorous and unsentimental thesis about courtship.

Since the issue of the text as a novel was precisely the one occupying the earliest reviewers, Sydney Smith in the *Edinburgh Review* and Zachary Macaulay in the *Christian Observer*,[71] their responses could provide an instructive start. Characterizing it as "uninspired," "strained and unnatural," and angry with its "false or trite representations of life and manners," its "too common philippics against frugivorous children after dinner," and its severity "upon the ordinary amusements of mankind," Smith judged it a "*dramatic sermon*." Although he temporized slightly, in acknowledging More's "very original, and very profound observations," "most brilliant and inviting style," and ability

to amuse "if amusement was her object," Smith reserved his strongest artillery
for the characters themselves. Because Coelebs and Lucilla "never dance, and
never go to the play," they are too staid, while the "excellent Mr Stanley,
thinking no Christian safe who is not dull, is uniformly paltry." The *Christian
Observer*, mouthpiece of "the Established Church" and the official journal of
the Evangelical Anglicans at Clapham, predictably praised where Smith had
damned. Seeing the author of the anonymous publication as a man and *his*
commendable project as instruction (ironically the reviewer was More's
friend), Macaulay initially "cannot allow this work to be called a novel" and
later condescends to use the term, but with qualifications: "A little more
complication of incident, a little more intensity of passion and feeling, would
have completely ruined his project. The work would have been a novel; a mere
novel;—interesting and useless." The narrative "is merely a frame-work for
better things," among them the introduction of Stanley Grove as "a model of
domestic perfection and felicity," the telling of a story that is "perfectly in
nature," and the presentation of leading characters of "pure, vital, practical
piety." Though admitting that "a religious novel" is "open to ridicule," the
reviewer nevertheless lodges specific objections: to the title ("Girls may be
thought fair game; yet they are not quite on a level with red-legged par-
tridges"); to the "drawling gravity" of the hero ("He is in danger of being a
sad proser at fifty"); to the undervaluing of accomplishments and paradoxical
"display of knowledge"; and to Coelebs' vulgarity ("Lucilla will perhaps
improve him"). From the outset judgments about the genre and quality of the
narrative have been tied to judgments about the principal characters. This
finding provides a cue to reconsider how Lucilla and Coelebs, as constructions
of gender and class, function within the "centripetal"[72] household dynamic
and within the "idealized . . . organic community"[73] of More's Eden.

Lucilla Stanley, Coelebs' predestined mate, is only introduced in Chapter 13 of a forty-nine-chapter narrative. We learn about Lucilla through the
comments of others—Coelebs, her father and mother—rather than through
any declaration of her own. While her name may have been suggested by the
unfortunate character in Lyly's *Euphues*, whose poor judgment and incon-
stancy in love undo her, the fate of More's exemplar is vastly different. Talked
about more than actually talking, Lucilla is an embodiment of the ideals of
her mentors, gazers, and her creator herself. Is this untempted Eve simply a
clotheshanger for their ideas? To an extent she *is* the close-to-beatific product
of her parents' nurturance and an illustration of More's doctrines of benefi-
cence, mental rigour, and separate spheres, developed from her earliest pastoral drama and poems through the extended essays.[74] Does it make sense to
expect or search for an individuated, complex self in an account where "love

itself appears . . . not as an ungovernable impulse, but as a sentiment . . . under the dominion of reason and religion" (x)?

Although she is without inconsistencies and aberrations, Lucilla is not, however, merely a Stanley replica, nor is she just the specularized object of male desire. As More introduces at least a dozen privileged families and individuals, whose visits and extended conversations make up the narrative fabric, acquaintances are continually overlapping. In this network of comparisons and confabs Lucilla clearly enjoys More's (and Coelebs') favor. Unlike the "excess of kindness" (56) of the "constitutionally charitable" (58) Lady Belfield, Mrs. Ranby's exclusive, "disproportionate zeal for a very few doctrines" (32), and the vanity of her three daughters, always "dressed to the very extremity of the fashion" (33), no extravagance in costume or practice characterizes the "rather perfectly elegant than perfectly beautiful" Lucilla, whose "beauty consists of the stamp of mind intelligibly printed on the face" (124). Her "gentle frankness and undesigning temper" distance her from Mrs. Fentham's mastery of "all the phraseology of connoisseurship" (6) and the open assaults of Lady Bab Lawless's "artillery of her own wit" (75). With her younger sisters, the workers on the estate, and the local villagers, Lucilla's charity is engaging and real—far removed from "sober" Lady Denham's habit of indulging in "uncharitable gossip and unfounded calumny" (79), Lady Melbury's aestheticizing of poverty while leaving her bills unpaid, and Lady Aston's living "with a little too much of the scrupulosity of an ascetic" and raising her daughters as "mute and timid, cheerless and inactive" recluses (141).

The most powerfully engineered contrasts involve Lucilla and Amelia Rattle and Miss Sparkes; while intended to polish Lucilla's untarnished reputation, these episodes actually point to the problems underlying the whole stage-managed exercise. Three years younger than Lucilla, Amelia is about the age of Phoebe Stanley, but she undergoes more critical scrutiny. Her "lively loquacity" (223) and desire to ape the modish accomplishments of Lady Di Dash make her more than a figure of fun. Her actions tend to outrage the exalted sense of dignity, propriety, and even omniscience of such arbiters of taste as Coelebs and Mr. Stanley. When the departing Amelia springs up, unassisted, to join the coachman, the narrator entones: " 'Here is a mass of accomplishments,' said I, 'without one particle of mind, one ray of common sense, or one shade of delicacy! Surely somewhat less time, and less money, might have sufficed to qualify a companion for the coachman' " (227). More than the disconcerting matter of familiarity between classes tries Stanley's patience. The mocking tone of his retort about "young ladies, whose vast abilities, whose mighty grasp of mind, can take in everything" (227), is very broad. Relentless too, he derides by contrasting "learned men" to "woman, ambitious, aspiring, universal, triumphant, glorious woman, [who] even at the age of a school-boy encounters the whole range of arts, attacks the whole circle of the sciences!" (228). It is left to Sir John Belfield to underline the flaw in the short duration of these pursuits and their absolute halt "as soon as she *comes out*" (229). Stanley's ridicule is especially unsettling because it represents male fear and hence suppression of unbridled female curiosity. Unlike the tormenting fathers so common in the work of the revolutionary women novelists of the 1790s, the danger of More's patriarch lies not in hypocrisy or selfish ambition. Dean William's hypocritical winking at his son's promiscuity in Elizabeth Inchbald's *Nature and Art* is as foreign to Stanley as the blind ambition of Laura Glenmorris's parents and their readiness to sacrifice this younger daughter to "some old man" in Charlotte Smith's *The Young Philosopher*. But Stanley's hold on propriety, although it does not stray into the realm of sex, is every bit as firm, as intolerant of objection or singularity, as the more lascivious control of the other despots.

Age and imperturbability make the quick tongued Miss Sparkes a greater challenge to the text's self-styled judges. The most flummoxing woman in the account, this spinster who, by Stanley's own admission, is "charitable with her purse, but not with her tongue" (343) injects a zesty confrontational edge to the otherwise self-congratulatory chats that occupy most of the time; however, she is definitely not as extreme as Edgeworth's cross-dressing, practical-joking, cruel Harriot Freke in *Belinda*. Perhaps because she senses Lucilla's "dislike of her coarseness," Miss Sparkes slaps Lucilla on the shoulder and recommends an understanding of animal husbandry over "wast[ing] her time in studying confectionary with old Goody Comfit, or in teaching the Catechism to little ragged beggar brats" (341). An ideal illustration of Erasmus Darwin's caution, in *Plan for the Conduct of Female Education* (1798), about "great apparent strength of character . . . [being] liable to alarm both her own and the other sex" (3), Miss Sparkes' independent spirit results in some trenchant comments on marriage and domestic economy. The men try, unsuccessfully, to jolly her out of the tart observation "that a man of talents, dreading a rival, always [takes] care to secure himself by marrying a fool" (390). What really puts them on the defensive against abandonment to the "vagrant faculty" of imagination is her reproof of the wastage of the strictly domestic life: " 'All the plodding employments cramp the genius, degrade the intellect, depress the spirits, debase the taste, and clip the wings of imagination. And this poor, cramped, degraded, stinted, depressed, debased creature is the very being whom men, men of reputed sense, too, commonly prefer to the mind of large dimensions, soaring fancy, and aspiring tastes' " (398).

While the priggish narrator's criticism of Amelia Rattle sounds antifeminist, Miss Sparkes' diatribe and her determined kicking against the pricks are assuredly profeminist. The Rattle and Sparkes episodes are problematic because they disclose the text's ambivalence toward the issues of women's accomplishments and freedom, an ambivalence intensified by the fact that there are no authorial interventions[75] to censure what has been said.

Specific comments about and, more rarely, by Lucilla herself contribute to this sense of contrariety. It is difficult to talk of Lucilla as fully individuated because we seldom have her direct speech and because Coelebs' mediation constructs a formal, scarcely flesh-and-blood image of this young woman. Admired by her suitor for her "intelligent silence [and] well-bred attention" (217), described by her mother as "half a nun [who] likes the rule, but not the vow" (353), and hailed by an envious neighbor, whose children are "fond of the gay world" as "a pattern daughter [who] will make a pattern wife" (534), Lucilla stands in some danger of being seen as a mere plaster saint. Although for her siblings she is a beloved teacher, gardener, and organizer of parties and charitable expeditions, those who apparently know Lucilla also supply some sobering admonitions; Mrs. Stanley insists that her daughter is "no prodigy dropped down from the clouds" (288) and the local clergyman points approvingly to Lucilla's consciousness "of her own imperfections" and "inward conviction of unworthiness which prevents an assuming manner" (307). As with everything in More, goodness—in order to be both credible and didactic—must be controlled. When Lucilla finally speaks, though, she does much more than parrot pieties. Adroit at parrying the narrator's pompous talk, she conveys humility but not self-abasement. Although initially (Chapter 24) her speech is reported indirectly, she makes it clear to Coelebs, as they walk home from church on Sunday, that she does not intend to criticize the sermon since "the custom of pointing out the faults cannot be maintained without the custom of watching for them" (237). She abides by this counsel from her father about "animadversion" and "display" being "symptom[s] of an unhumbled mind" (237). Acute as well as unassuming, her own words (Chapter 33) underline how self-possessed yet unproud Lucilla is. As for being humbled by compliments, she admits honestly to feeling "like an imposter" (347). Without sounding imbecilic or infantilized,[76] she explains: "If I contradict the favourable opinion, I am afraid of being accused of affectation; and if I silently swallow it, I am contributing to the deceit of passing for what I am not" (347). While Coelebs drones on in his generally censorious mode, Lucilla is down-to-earth and thoughtful. Aware of the difference between praise and practice ("Self-deception is so easy . . . commending a right thing is a cheap substitute for doing it" [349]), she is not averse to chiding Coelebs for his simplistic concept of worldliness: "The world, I believe, is not so much a place as a nature. It is possible to be religious in a court, and worldly in a monastery" (350). Even on the topic that most unites them, veneration of Milton and *Paradise Lost*, Lucilla's views are her own—though they happen to chime in nicely with Coelebs' and More's. In her disquisition on Eve in Chapter 41, Lucilla not only echoes the sentiments of Coelebs' opening encomium, by considering Eve "in her state of innocence as the most beautiful model of the delicacy, propriety, grace, and elegance of the female character, which any poet ever exhibited," but she also adds a note of poignant reflection on Eve "after the fall," who exhibits "something wonderfully touching in her remorse, and affecting in her contrition" (470).[77]

More's refashioned Eve has no autobiographical moment at the pool, no dream narrative, and no period of solitary temptation—possibly because she is so busy.[78] As well as maintaining an intimate knowledge of the poetry of Milton and the texts of the Bible, Lucilla reads Latin with her father, supervises the kitchen at Stanley Grove, conducts a school for village children, tends a garden whose flowers embellish family celebrations, and runs her own nursery, which provides presents of fruit trees and shrubs for local brides. Visible and vigilant, she overturns many of the traits that Nancy Armstrong attributes to the domestic woman; Lucilla does not disappear "into the woodwork to watch over the household," shows no "prevalent tendency toward anti-intellectualism," and has a keen interest in "producing goods to be consumed by the household."[79] By incarnating "the new bourgeois notions of self-regulation and surveillance," Lucilla is, in Beth Tobin's characterization, "More's example of the new domestic woman, one whose temperament and tastes are not driven by vanity, greed, or sexual desire, but are rather the product of a liberal education combined with the discipline of 'Christian principle.' "[80] True, in the "rational scene of felicity" (563) that unfolds as Lucilla's marriage to Coelebs approaches, she also actualizes some conduct-book directives, exemplifying Mrs. Chapone's instruction, in *Letters on the Improvement of the Mind* (1773), to "form and govern the temper and manners, according to the laws of benevolence and justice."[81] Although More continually resisted the notion of gender equality, her mediated depiction of Lucilla spotlights an energizing family politics that prizes capable, responsible work, harmonious relations, and modest, monitored courtships. With no form of intimate contact or less-than-stilted conversation related, perhaps the biggest mystery involves Lucilla's willingness to marry the pontificating narrator.

For all his talk, there is little chattiness about Coelebs, who finally resumes the name Charles, but whose surname is never disclosed. With willed naiveté resulting in a discourse of control and obedience, he is More's creation through and through. Ruth Yeazell goes as far as to claim that, speaking though Coelebs, More engages "in a form of literary cross-dressing."[82] As Maria Edgeworth observed, most people who knew or met More's purported model, "young Mr. Harford, of Blaise Castle," declared "that he was a much more agreeable man than Coelebs."[83] The formation of the novel along the life-and-opinions model rather than the life-and-adventures one underlines the governing Morean (*not* Sternean) influence. Coelebs is, truly, all talk and no action—light years removed from such vigorous and predatory sorts as the demonic Montoni in *The Mysteries of Udolpho*, the abusive Venables in *The Wrongs of Woman*, and the villainous Osborne in *The Victim of Prejudice*. But is Coelebs simply a neutered *porte-parole* for the novelist?

As he starts his search "on the tiptoe of expectation" (26), a credible yet vulnerable eagerness distinguishes Coelebs. He is a figure of regulation and restraint, acknowledging his father's directive to consult Mr. Stanley before he marries "as a sort of sedative in the slight intercourse [he] had had with the ladies" (18–19), admitting that "religion, though it had not subdued his imagination, had chastised it," and endeavouring "to keep [his] own feelings in order, till [he] had time to appreciate a character, which appeared as artless as it was correct" (128). Less a pupil than an acolyte of Mr. Stanley, Coelebs readily assents to and transcribes his future father-in-law's dicta about indolence and sensuality being "the prevailing evils of the day" (301) and the need for feelings to be "curbed by restraint and regulated by religion" (441).

Coelebs is the character with the true Miltonic naïveté: so assured, purposive, straightforward, and single-minded, yet also so untried, innocent, and cloistered. If he does not encounter temptation, at the very least his aroused feelings for Lucilla prompt action, audacious and surprising for such a passive observer. In his quest of "a directress for his family, a preceptress for his children, and a companion for himself" (49), Coelebs finds that Lucilla's "numberless attractions" disarm his "guard . . . against such a combination of amiable virtues and gentler graces" (155). To the reader it probably seems a long time for him to summon the courage to ask Stanley for his daughter's hand, a gesture he terms "somewhat premature" but one advanced in the hope that Stanley "will not condemn [his] precipitancy" (478). Despite his like-mindedness with Stanley, Coelebs shocks himself by exclaiming "with more vehemence than politeness" that the three-month postponement of the wedding is "impossible" (529).

This inexperienced young man is remarkably opinionated. Without a hint of sport or mischief, his sobering views on marriage and London society are not the ones readily associated with a financially secure country gentleman-bachelor. Motives for marriage, he insists, are often skewed, when parents allow "family, fortunes, and connections, . . . ambition, avarice, or worldliness" to prevail over judgments of "the moral and especially . . . the religious character of the man who proposed himself" (272). He is equally "disappointed" with the norms of polite society, where "the passion for novelty . . . gives an ephemeral importance to every thing, and a lasting importance to nothing" (372). Unlike conversations in which speakers "skim every topic, but dive into none" (372), this high-principled narrator sets out to remake the novel according to his own exacting standards.

The narrative relates his plunging, with a precisian's relish, into such conversation topics as human corruption, the need of learning in the clergy, and the tug-of-war between faith and works—all Morean standards from the extended essays. But more affecting and memorable than these windy, staged dialogues are his axiomatic observations on the life around him, the life of his class. Prizing, as the novel's epigraph directed, "that which before us lies in daily life" as "the prime wisdom," Coelebs observes fashionable life from the inside. Contrasts between the gloomy prognostics of the breakfast table and the morning papers, where all the talk is of "taxes trebling, dangers multiplying, commerce annihilating, war protracted, invasion threatening, destruction impending," and dinner with the same people, "when you hear the frivolous discourse, witness the luxurious dissipation, contemplate the boundless indulgence, and observe the ruinous gaming," usher in remarks on "the whole comet-like eccentric orbit of the human character" (50–51); they also echo the repeated complaint of More's letters a decade or so earlier about "gay, happy, inconsiderate Bath."[84] He comments insightfully on the subtle erosion or subversion of religious views in "men versed in the world, and abstracted from all religious society," who begin to suspect their own religious opinions may be wrong or rigid, "when they see them so opposite to those of persons to whose judgment they are accustomed to look up in other points" (55). The pharisaical practices of the great and gay bring home the force of a biblical pericope (Matthew 23.24), since they allow Coelebs to see "the gnat-strainer and the camel-swallower so strikingly exemplified" (81).

When the reader recalls the object of this bachelor's quest, his punctilious judgments of women are strangely, if dishearteningly, apposite in a narrative where male standards of acceptability hold sway. With Coelebs' admitted "propensity to promote subjects of taste and elegant speculation" (378), it makes sense (galling though it is) for him to opt for a "learned" over a "scientific" woman, to "prefer a fair companion, who could modestly discriminate between the beauties of Virgil and Milton to one who was always dabbling in chemistry and who came to dinner with dirty hands from the laboratory" (379). Man is the initiator, the arbiter, the font, who is flattered by a female's ability "to relish the beauty we quote, and trace the allusion at which we hint" (435). His discourse constantly points to the need to deflate, correct, and "regulate the pride of talents" (445) in women. When Coelebs' favorite mentor, Stanley, whose learning is presumably governed by these same principles, elevates "two contemporary shining examples, the venerable Elizabeth Carter and the blooming Elizabeth Smith," his praise sounds both consistent and paradoxical. Just as Stanley is compelled to revere their genius "chastised by true Christian humility," he feels no compunction in referring to their "acquirements which would have been distinguished in a University" (445). The subjunctive mood emphasizes the gap separating what might have been and what actually was the situation (exclusion from the university)— even for such a distinguished classicist as Carter and scholar and poet as Smith.

In judging this novel or sermon it is too simple, I think, to conclude that More, the spinster, did not know what she was talking about. Nor is it enough to go along with Charlotte Yonge's uncharacteristic severity about More's being "utterly unable to construct an interesting story."[85] Although desire is opaque at best and passion not on display, More is nonetheless deeply concerned to demonstrate the ways in which a couple become, to use her own distinction from *Strictures*, "matched" as opposed to merely "joined." She considered the difference sufficiently critical to be prepared to sacrifice and even reprobate the conventional pangs, misgivings, and excitements of romance. Did she give up too much or adopt too dyspeptic an approach to courtship?

Comparison with a so-called sequel, *Coelibia Choosing a Husband*, Robert Torrens's "modern novel"[86] that followed close on the heels of More's and attempted to cash in on its popularity, shows how daringly singular her rigorous though pristine narrative was. Shifting the spotlight to the heroine, Torrens's two-volume potboiler provides all the sensational details More had declined to include. This young captain in the Royal Marines was an astute judge of what the market would tolerate; he may also have been familiar with *The Memoirs of Emma Courtney*, since he folds in some of the plot line and character names from Hays's novel. Creating two discrete stories about the virtuous, sought-after, rich, but motherless heroine and the death-bed account of a prostitute, Torrens manages to blend them, somewhat incredibly. Characterization relies on generalized, prosaic utterances from the omniscient narrator. His idealized Coelibia, "free and nimble as the mountain roe, . . . roamed where fancy led, and mused, unrestrained, on the magnificence of nature."[87] In the counterpoint story of Mary, Torrens's ambivalent and condescending moral position gets in the way, as he relates her decline beginning with her addiction to novels and her living "in a perpetual reverie."[88] But if character is determined, action, frenetic and jagged, turns on the sexual character of knowledge. Mary's extramarital liaison leaves her disinherited and defenseless. As ecstatically as she once rushed to her lover, when "his arm encircled [her] waist, [and she] sunk upon his shoulder, and felt his heart beating against her bosom with tumultuous throbs," Mary later finds herself "the victim of odious caresses" who must "accept the wages of [her] shame."[89] In contrast to the headlong passions and Gothic torment of Mary's life are the dilatory caution and fairy-tale order of Coelibia's. Of her three suitors, the first two, a poet who is "unstable and diffusive in all his feelings" and an older aristocrat who practises his own "virtuous despotism,"[90] are manifestly wrong, while the third, the miraculously reappearing and reformed lover from the prostitute's interlude, is just right. A forerunner of Harlequin romances in its abundant formulaic details, Coelibia also does not stint on the mush, as in this description of the captivated heroine and her conquering suitor: "Her eye beamed complacency on Harley. . . . Though the word was unuttered he knew he was beloved. He drew her unresisting to his side—their lips touched—their spirits mingled—no accent was uttered to break the enchantment of delight. Harley retired adoring and adored."[91]

In inverting "the usual courtship schema by featuring a male protagonist,"[92] More avoided such grotesquerie. But in her supercilious suitor she may have created a different kind of extravagant oddity. However, because Coelebs repeats and underlines so many of More's own ideas, promulgated over a thirty-year span, he was not simply a diverting one-of-a-kind. "By equating virtue with self-regulation, More launched an attack on the selfishness and laziness of the pleasure-loving upper classes, linking their neglect of social and moral duties to their inability to control their impulses."[93] That More took the risk of attempting to spin a narrative fabric around her schemes for reform, to animate through fiction her social discourse, shows how keenly committed—in the face of ridicule, condescension, and likely defeat—she remained to the needed amendment and evangelization of the upper class.

❀ 5 ❀
Schools and Tracts:
Consuming Zeal

In his sermon for the Sunday following the funeral of Hannah More, "this woman . . . full of good works and almsdeeds" (Acts 9.36), the Reverend Henry Thompson elevated her as "altogether a practical believer" who was "no dogmatist, no controversialist."[1] In fact, the practices of the schools she established and supervised in her own day and the deliberate fictionalization of popular culture reprobated by readers of her tracts today make More an intensely dogmatic controversialist. As a result of the Sunday and day schools that she and Patty started at the very time of the More sisters' retirement from teaching, thousands of children learned to read and count as well as knit, sew, and spin. But the village schools to which More devoted herself for three decades immersed her in public battles over the licensing, staffing, and responsibilities of these institutions.

Erupting around the allegations and counterallegations about Methodism, oral confessions, and private unlicensed conventicles at the Blagdon school, "this warfare of words," as one of More's champions in the twenty-three tracts about the controversy put it, not only "degenerated into a struggle between the friends and enemies of real, vital Christianity"[2] but also became a mud-slinging match of ferocious cruelty. Her detractors pronounced this self-styled educationalist a "female Fanatic,"[3] "the Imperial Juno of Literature and Methodism,"[4] and "more like our Lady of Loretto, garnished in her most glaring fripperies, than a homely plain English-woman."[5] Her supporters erected their own protective wall around More, presenting her as "the real Patriot . . . [who] guarded with the utmost jealousy against the intrusion of Methodism" in her schools, "established by the consent, open to the inspection and removable at the pleasure of the clergymen throughout the several parishes,"[6] and as a victim who should not "think it, in the smallest degree, necessary to say a single syllable in reply to any assertions."[7]

Missions in the Mendips

Similar variations are evident in the critical comments on the Mendip schools in general. Thompson's early biography fastens on her very femaleness as the explanation of More's success. He argues from the point of view of the noble savage encountering the doughty lady: "the rude barbarian, who would have spurned from his door the most conciliating of the ministers of Christ, had yet enough of manliness in his savage heart to abstain at least from outrage to woman."[8] More's flintiness and intransigence lead M.G. Jones to assess this chapter in her life very severely, showing More "as a masterful, dogmatic woman, a high Tory in politics, a rigid Evangelical in religion, using her undeniable talents for organization to dragoon the wretched, ignorant, ill-nourished population into schools which did not attempt to offer an opportunity to children and adults to improve their material conditions." Jones pinpoints the weakness of the educational scheme, symptomatic of More's whole philanthropic enterprise, in "the identification of Christianity and social order" that implicated More "in the acceptance of social wrongs incompatible with the religion she professed."[9] Although More was in the forefront of the movement to educate the masses, the restrictions of her schools, which allowed reading but not writing for most and offered additional tutelage to the more prosperous, are offensive—to us, not to her contemporaries; so is the primness of her addresses to the Female clubs, which censured and excluded any kind of premarital sexual adventure. But there is another side to this story, too; it was an intervention on behalf of forgotten, genuinely backward people, an attempt to relieve grinding poverty by providing the skills to make an income and feed one's family, an indication of the active compassion of Evangelicalism, and an offer of Christian hope and deferred happiness. I believe it is impossible for a contemporary reader of documents about the schools—More's letters and texts, Patty's journal, and the Blagdon tracts—to be entirely a denouncer or a supporter of More's cause. Within the context of other Sunday school projects, More's undertaking emerges as consistent with a growing movement to educate and specifically catechize the poor, which would lead to the establishment of the Sunday School Union in 1803. Patty's *Mendip Annals* is an engaging narrative of the demonstrable changes in the lives of whole communities and named individuals that the sisters' efforts effected. The charges of More's opponents in the Blagdon affair reveal, among other things, the suspicion, fear, and consequent denunciation of one woman's resolve. They illustrate the fearful alarm her plans sounded among "high church bigots" because "her activities threatened to delegitimate and marginalize the orthodox clergy in their own parishes."[10] Embedded in this "new nervousness evoked by female moral imperialism," as Mitzi Myers observes, "the gravamen of the charge is power."[11]

The twelve preparatory visits Hannah and Patty made to farmers' homes in Cheddar in the fall of 1789 to drum up support for their school and their week-long stay at the George Hotel prior to the official opening on 25 October must have initiated them to the popular suspicions and outright criticism that had always attended the business of teaching religion to children. As early as the 1620s at Little Gidding, Nicholas Ferrar encountered dissatisfied parents who wanted him to do more than teach the psalms. Although the Reverend Joseph Alleine had to be carried about in a litter on account of the weaknesses of disease and imprisonment following his refusal to accept the Act of Uniformity in 1662, he continued to catechise the children of Bath every Sunday in his home until, as his wife reported, "he was forced to desist, and the schoolmaster was threatened to be cited to Wells, before the Bishop, and many others affrighted from it."[12] As John Wesley's preaching in Mevagissey in the 1750s had inspired Frances Lelean to teach children in her home on Sundays, so a sermon by Wesley in Gloucester in 1777 likely prompted Sophia Cooke, daughter of a surgeon, to establish her Sunday school in the squalid Pye Corner part of the city. "It was at Pye Corner that Wesley was set upon by the mob and stoned."[13]

So-called Sunday schools followed a variety of formats: the Reverend Henry Venn's school, opened in Huddersfield in 1770, taught catechizing and reading on Sundays; Hannah Ball's establishment, started in 1769 in High Wycombe, met on Sundays and Mondays; the Reverend David Simpson's institution, opened at Macclesfield in 1778, began as a weekly evening school for reading and spelling, where those who could not come on weeknights were taught on Sundays. The originator of an organized attempt at the popular education of the masses was Robert Raikes, whose employment as a publisher, importer, and distributor of literature in Gloucester positioned him advantageously to supply reading material for the "little experiment" he devised "to check the profanation of the Sabbath."[14] Beginning in 1780, he paid a shilling each to four "decent well disposed women in the neighbourhood who kept schools for teaching to read" to instruct "little heathens . . . in reading and in the Church catechism" on Sunday.[15] Raikes's announcement, three years later in the *Gloucester Journal*, consolidated his character as a sensible man of the world who had helped to establish order and control:

> Farmers, and other inhabitants of the towns and villages, complain that
> they receive more injury to their property on the Sabbath than all the
> week besides: this in a great measure, proceeds from the lawless state of

The school in Cheddar (The Francis Frith Collection, Shaftesbury, Dorset).

the younger class, who are allowed to run wild on that day, free from every restraint. To remedy this evil, persons duly qualified are employed to instruct those that cannot read. . . . By thus keeping their minds engaged, the day passes profitably, and not disagreeably. In those parishes where the plan has been adopted, we are assured that the behaviour of the children is greatly civilized, the barbarous ignorance in which they had before lived being in some degree dispelled.[16]

A similar brand of Christian pragmatism accounted for Sarah Trimmer's establishment of Sunday schools in Old Brentford, in the parish of Ealing, Middlesex, in 1786. Having hired three teachers for the 140 girls and two for the 80 boys, Trimmer issued very clear directives, enjoining the teachers "to hear them read, spell, repeat prayers and catechisms, and to give them the best instructions in their power, respecting their duty to God and men."[17] Her morning and evening admonitions to the children stressed a combination of sobriety and hard work, outlawing "swearing, stealing, drinking" and encouraging them to "read your book, and study your lessons, . . . be industrious, and strive as much as possible to ease your parents from the burden of maintaining you."[18] Through a course of appropriate instruction provided by her own books (*Spelling Book, Scripture Lessons, Moral Instructions to be committed to memory*) Trimmer rested content that she was qualifying children "to fill their respective stations in society" and affirming the received wisdom about a practical education. "It is generally thought injudicious to excite an emulation in *Charity Boys* to write a fine hand," Trimmer observed, "and unless they are intended for teachers in schools, this certainly had better be avoided; neither should any but these be encouraged to make a proficiency in figures beyond what may be wanted for apprentices to common trades."[19]

In addition to "ferretting about . . . among the neglected villages of this hardly Christian country"[20] and attempting to generate local support, More familiarized herself with such primers as the *Salisbury Spelling Book* and *Parochial Exercises* as preparatory models for her own *Questions and Answers for the Mendip and Sunday Schools* and *Historical Questions from the Bible with Answers for the Mendip Schools*. Framed copies of the Church Catechism were hung in the classrooms whose libraries consisted of More's Questions and Answers, Spelling Books, the Psalter, the Book of Common Prayer, the Bible, and Watts's Hymns. Practical psychology guided More's pedagogical strategies. Rote-learned answers, usually unencumbered with verbs and predicates, about first Christian principles relied heavily on monosyllables.

> Who made you and all the world?
> God.
> Who redeemed you?
> Jesus Christ.
> Who is Jesus Christ?
> The Son of God.
> Who sanctified you?
> The Holy Ghost.
> Who is the Holy Ghost?
> The Holy Spirit of God.
> Where did you learn all this?
> In the Holy Scriptures.

With an uncompromising matter-of-factness, her little twelve-page tract introduced "the terms of the Christian religion" as "repentance, faith and renewed obedience." Following its own methodology, the primer reached a pragmatic conclusion about the benefits of Christian allegiance.

> What is promised to the Christian when he dies?
> To go to Heaven and to dwell in happiness with God and Jesus Christ.
> What must the sinner expect?
> To dwell with the Devil and his angels in Hell.
> Are you now convinced of the advantages of Religion?
> Yes.
> What are they?
> It sanctifies our hearts, fits us for Heaven, and makes us acceptable to God, and useful to the world.[21]

Avoiding any "system of terror," More "found that kindness produces a better
end by better means."[22] As well as the acknowledged bribes (a penny for four
Sundays of uninterrupted attendance or for memorizing scriptural texts and
a little gingerbread), More's annual gifts of clothes—hats, shirts, shoes,
aprons, and tippets—and books—with the most deserving getting a Bible,
the next the Prayer Book, and all the rest copies of the Cheap Repository
Tracts—insured that religion continued to be allied with material well-being
and safe reading.

Within scarcely two years, the sisters had nine parish-based schools "in
hand,"[23] at Cheddar, Rowberrow, Shipham, Congresbury, Yatton, Nailsea,
Banwell, Sandford, and Axbridge, and close to one thousand children en-
rolled. Patty's journal is a wonderfully rich archive of the triumphs and
setbacks, the cajolings and ironies attending the labors of the "two noble-
hearted Atlasses," "these mothers in Israel."[24] Although the otherworldly
sisters rejoiced at the growing number of "new recruits" and trainees "for the
mansions of the blessed," although Patty's "recollection of having been all
morning with young men from eighteen to twenty-eight years of age in
reading the 8th of the Romans . . . levelled mountains to molehills," and
Hannah's recording of "our own unworthiness for this work" meant for her
that "*we* are nothing, *have* nothing, can *do* nothing,"[25] they also accomplished
a great deal in this world. Patty included many noteworthy examples of
real-life transformations that may have dictated some story lines in the Cheap
Repository Tracts. Like so many of the inspired choices of the Tracts, especially the job given to the shepherd of Salisbury Plain's wife, the sisters hired
the dairy maids, Patience Seward and Flower Waite, as schoolmistresses at
Rowberrow and Shipham; when, at Yatton, the "pious farmer"—as resigned
as the Salisbury exemplar but less needy—with seven sons "well instructed in
their catechism, . . . lost his wife in child-bed, [he] led a long family proces-
sion in deep mourning up the church"; perseverance transformed Mr. Hyde,
a "profligate, abusive, depraved sinner" at Cheddar, into a great champion of
the school, with the same energetic beliefs as reformed Tom White and John
Brown in the Tracts; the effect of the "good Spirit" of Robert Reeves of
Cheddar brought his two successive masters to the evening reading; a possible
nonfictional precursor of Hester Wilmot's story, the example of Sally
Thatcher on her parents, who "often beat and punished [her] for her attach-
ment to the school," eventually turned them around to "coming some evening
to hear the sermon"; and, like the reforms effected by the teetotal Carpenter,
once a drunkard, the pacified Tom Hod, won over from rioting, and the
Orange Girl Betty Brown, once easily duped but later an industrious sausage-
shop keeper, the conversion by "poor Samuel" of his "profligate wife" and "old

profane mother" meant that "a few sheep, a little orchard, a field, and a house are now cleared of all debt and quite their own."[26]

Lamenting that "we are sending missionaries to our distant colonies, [while] our own villages are perishing for lack of instruction," the sisters concentrated on the home mission front, finding the populous and "almost pagan" Mendip villages "as dark as Africa" and confronting the poverty and voluptuousness at the glass-works at Nailsea as "our little Sierra Leone."[27] Although the savagery of these villages is a constant theme, the idea of communal improvement also becomes a refrain. "Gentlemen" at Yatton are shamed into collecting clothes; at Congresbury "two great, ignorant farmers each Sunday [sit] the whole day with people they oppress and trample on during the week, listening to these poor children"; at Banwell not only can some students recite "forty-six chapters by heart" but "the rich, frigid farmers, . . . once so hostile," have been shamed into clothing the children; "Congresbury can *read* the Bible"; Nailsea has become "a righteous coal-pit" and "one hundred and forty children [are] taught the Scriptures by two young colliers, whom [Hannah] taught their letters"; at Cheddar, the model "great" school, where "not a syllable we tell them [is] ever forgotten," the number of communicants has grown so large "as to prolong the service for nearly two hours."[28] The sisters' favorites, promoted on account of their ardent piety, ranged from the fabled mistress at Cheddar, the loved and feared Mrs. Baber, at whose funeral every one of the two hundred children wore "some little badge of mourning, according as their little pence could be spared," to John Haskins, collier and promising schoolmaster at Nailsea, whose injuries in a cave-in led to his death, "a great affliction and a great blow" for Patty and Hannah.[29]

These Mendip missionaries endured a lot—severe coughs, headaches, fatigue, frequently impassable country roads, uncomfortable circuit travel by cart, horseback, or foot to three or four parishes each Sunday, being out for up to thirteen hours—for the sake of promoting "peace and content" over "riot and disorder."[30] Exercised and indignant at the Shipham girls dancing at a fair, the "daring and dreadful sin" of Sunday shopping, the "sink of sin" of the Cheddar paper mill, and the "drunkenness and indolence" prevailing "in almost every cottage in that village,"[31] Hannah stoutly defended her principles and maintained decades later, "I have not at the end of thirty-six years altered my opinion."[32] With inimitable punctiliousness she had outlined her "extremely simple and limited . . . plan of instruction" to the Bishop of Bath and Wells: "They learn, on week-days, such coarse works as may fit them for servants. I allow of no writing for the poor. My object is not to make fanatics, but to train up the lower classes in habits of industry and piety. I know no way of teaching morals but by teaching principles; nor of inculcating Christian principles without a good knowledge of scripture."[33]

The sisters tolerated, dealt with, and often tried to transform many irritants, such as "our incessant and unwearied enemy," Mr. Jacobs of Nailsea, who ended up sipping tea hospitably; the "old rogue" of a schoolmaster at Congresbury who precipitated their closure of the school; the "sad" and "artful" hypocrisy of one Cheddar schoolmistress, Mrs. Thompson, who "was daring to use extempore prayer" and "introducing much cant and abominable self-righteousness," which resulted in her dismissal; the rich Wedmore farmer's wife who opposed the school, "vehemently declaring it was a very wrong measure: the poor were where they ought to be and where they were placed by Providence"; and the prosperous farmer who intercepted their plans because he did not want "to make his ploughmen wiser than himself: he did not want saints but workmen."[34] But by far the most sustained, venomous, and draining attack centered on the "malicious tales" about the schoolmaster at Blagdon, "cruelly misrepresented as an enthusiast."[35] Lasting more than three years and acquiring notoriety by the twenty-three tracts "written for and against" More, the dispute, as her diary entry for late 1803 indicates, took a very great personal toll. Although she shows a high-minded pride in having "never once *replied* to [her] calumniators," she admits that "they had nearly destroyed [her] life" and that their "false witness . . . has caused [her] works to be much less read and more condemned."[36] As Mitzi Myers's examination of More's correspondence with Thomas Sedgwick Whalley illustrates, More was powerfully and clandestinely active in Blagdon's "cultural politics," with her almost daily bulletins to Whalley constituting "a feminized domestic locale whereby she [could] safely exert pressure on the public space."[37]

Yet More's refusal to intervene publicly proved to be a strategy that backfired. Virtually everyone else was talking about it, and having their opinions molded by shamelessly tendentious essays in the magazines. The *British Critic* favoured More and the cause of injured merit; The *Anti-Jacobin* not only supported her opponent, Thomas Bere, curate at Blagdon, but defended Bere's intemperate style; The *Christian Observer*, entering the fray in 1802, came down solidly on More's side and in the process crystallized some of the underlying reasons for the animus against her. As the *Observer's* editor, her friend Zachary Macaulay argued the schools both embarrassed some clergy, "very few of whom resided at that period in the parishes in question," and upset local plutocrats "who, suspecting her intentions, invented and propagated various calumnies against her." The *Anti-Jacobin's* protest, he noted, was fired "chiefly by its hatred of Methodism." While the Clapham coterie at the *Observer* expressed the "hope that no considerations will induce Mrs. More to engage in this controversy," they continued to enlist her aid in "the cause of rational piety, and good old Church-of-England religion, by devotion without cant and zeal without enthusiasm."[38]

An unfunny comedy of errors, the dispute came to a head with the curate of Blagdon's charge, in a letter of 5 April 1800 to More in London, that her schoolmaster, Henry Young, was encouraging extempore prayer at the Monday evening adult class, thus making the schoolroom an unlicensed conventicle. Martha More wrote to Young, directing him to stop such irregularities immediately. Despite a letter from Mrs. Bere to More reporting that "the school goes on well,"[39] Bere, who was also a Justice of the Peace, collected affadavits on his own behalf attesting to Methodism at the Blagdon school. From London More replied with the suggestion that the charges be investigated by Sir Abraham Elton. Bere's positive refusal to consent shocked her. As she later defended herself, "I could have no partial motives in the reference, for I knew so little of Sir A. Elton, that he had never been in my house, whereas he had been long known to Mr. Bere, and I could not have suggested a more fair and peaceable mode of setting all to rights."[40] In retrospect she also realized that prudent expediency would have called for the instant dismissal of Young; recasting the event, though, More justified her decision:

> I grant that it would have saved me infinite distress. But I not only thought myself bound to protect an innocent man, whom I still consider to have been falsely accused; but I was also convinced, that, as the event has proved, the object in view was not merely to ruin *him*, but to strike at the principle of *all* my schools, and to stigmatize them as seminaries of fanaticism, vice, and sedition.[41]

Although More never relaxed in a close-to-phobic response to Methodism, the actual events at Blagdon did nothing to help her schools. On the advice of the Bishop of Bath and Wells, she dismissed Young and closed the school. However, because of Bere's unseemly jubilance at his victory (ringing bells, shouting from the rectory), the bishop reversed his decision and dismissed Bere on 23 January 1801; the Blagdon school was reestablished and Young, the old schoolmaster, reinstated. Feeding Bere's sense of betrayal and martyrdom was the unsubstantiated claim that More "had lodged private accusations against him"[42] as early as August 1800. The pens of both parties literally flew into action, with one of Bere's champions, Edward Spencer, maintaining that the abused curate had "exposed the Machiavelian machinations of a furious set of red hot zealots, whose aim seems to be subversive of all that is good,"[43] while More's apologist, Sir Abraham Elton, drew attention to the discrepancy in Bere's claims. In a letter to Dr. Crossman, his rector, Bere had stipulated that with the removal of Young he would support the school, whereas in his public letter he had declared that under no circumstances would he support the school. Exasperated, Elton exclaimed, "it is extremely difficult to maintain entire confidence in any man, who, having written privately with so much positiveness in one way, writes publicly, with equal positiveness in another!"[44] Another of More's spokesmen, the Reverend Thomas Drewitt, devoted a whole pamphlet, *The Force of Contrast*, to assessing the veracity of Bere's claims. Point by point Drewitt illustrated how Bere suppressed information and sensationalized his plight, leading this More partisan to conclude that Bere was "far more anxious about pathos than about propriety; and that he has completely lost sight of common sense, and simple matter of fact, in his attempt to prepossess his reader with compassion for himself and indignation against Mrs. H. More."[45] The upshot was another reversal: the reinstatement of the curate and the closing of the school.

The fallout was damaging for More, emotionally and publicly. An unidentified "layman" pointed a finger at More's hurry and reliance on apologists. "If she had not been so hasty and irritable," he observed, "she might have had her favourite teacher reformed of his extravagances; Mr. Bere might have been continued in the curacy; and the peace of the neighbourhood had not been disturbed." The layman's reluctant conclusion, that More should have "defended her own cause" and "that her apologists, with more zeal than judgment, have hurt her,"[46] echoes with a real force in Bere's last salvo. After firing off fifty-four letters and two lengthy pamphlets, Bere finally accused More of being "the criminal cause" and "a secret accuser"; lashing out at her "arrogance" and "ambition," Bere presented More as embodying "the enormities of visionary zealots."[47] Even moderate voices indicted her. The anonymous author of *The Something Wrong Developed* regretted the intemperance of Bere's language, found both parties "culpable," and, most tellingly, located the source of the difficulty in the schools themselves. A supporter of Sunday schools, he nevertheless insisted that they be "in the hands of the Church Governors"; "if they be not systematised, and still permitted to rise in different parts of the Dominion," he warned, "they will be characterised by Caprice and Inconsistency" and "will open the Gates of Sectarism, Fanaticism, and Bigotry."[48]

With the closure of Patty's journal, information about the schools becomes much more scarce. The great schools at Cheddar, Shipham, and Nailsea prospered, and More continued to inspect and examine her institutions. However, just as she did not enter directly into the Blagdon fray, she did not comment on the issue of systematic control by the Church of England. She would have welcomed such control and the responsibilities it would entail, especially since the founding of her schools, in the first instance, exposed the negligence and marginal influence of the clerical Establishment. Another major enterprise, for which More also did not stint her efforts or temper her principles, put her in the spotlight, again, at the close of the century.

Evangelizing Popular Culture

The undertaking of the Cheap Repository for Moral and Religious Tracts, the three-year project most immediately associated with Hannah More's name today, owed much of its acclaim to the problems and notoriety of the village schools. The anxious, unsettled tenor of the times—with the executions of Louis XVI and Marie Antoinette and the "Terror" in Paris in 1793, with the English suspension of habeas corpus and state trials and acquittal of, among others, the dramatist Thomas Holcroft and the radical lecturer John Thelwall in 1794, and with Parliament's passage of two acts outlawing seditious meetings and treasonable practices in 1795—fueled the sense of public alarm, shared by both Revolutionary supporters and opponents. More entered the fray as an anti-Revolutionary warrior. As compelling a reason for launching this enterprise as the runaway success of her anti-Painite dialogue between a blacksmith and a mason, *Village Politics, Addressed to all the Mechanics, Journeymen, and Labourers in Great Britain*, by "Will Chip, a Country Carpenter," was More's equally well-received practice of providing for families in her schoolrooms Sunday evening readings of prayer, a sermon, and a psalm. Following the opening burst of twenty tracts in March 1795, the regular monthly production of three numbers—stories, ballads, and Sunday readings, all under her general editorship—showed the same kind of shrewd, determined, informed preparation in this desire to supply uplifting, sobering, anti-revolutionary reading material for the newly literate as was evident in her scouting of Mendip parishes and boning up on school primers. More collected and studied the immensely popular street literature, the chapbooks and broadsides that Bishop Porteus reprobated as "the vilest penny pamphlets . . . [and] execrable tracts,"[49] to establish the Repository as the counteroffensive to their radical subversion, percolating bottom-up socialism, *carpe diem* morality, and erratic lottery-like economy; by contrast, the tracts promoted a budget-conscious, frugal, investment model, stressing the deferral of happiness, self-restraint, and reliance on paternalistic benefaction. Porteus forecast "this new effort of [More's] active and benevolent mind" would "form the best *sans culotte* library in Europe."[50] Thomas Taylor looked back on the fifty out of 114 tracts More herself contributed to the Repository, tracts that were shipped by the thousands to America, circulated in the West Indies, Sierra Leone, and Asia, and even translated into Russian, as the extraordinary success of "a female, and one, too, in very delicate health, . . . [in] defeating the most daring and open attack on religion that was ever made."[51]

Critical opinion has never been entirely on More's side. The original committee members of the Religious Tract Society, founded immediately after the cessation of the Cheap Repository, judged her tracts "doctrinally inadequate"[52] and insufficient in their Evangelicalism. Even as sympathetic a biographer as Charlotte Yonge tried to preempt Victorian criticism by admitting that More's examples seem "hideous to modern eyes."[53] After his thorough chronological cataloguing of the tracts, which sold three hundred thousand copies in less than two months and two million in the Repository's first year, G.H. Spinney labeled them "sheep in wolves' clothing."[54] Although various explanations and defenses of More's project have been advanced— with her "vigorous action" compensating for "the lack of character drawing,"[55] her ability to "thump home the moral" being comparable to Dickens's,[56] her tracts highlighting "the moral reform priorities of Evangelical womanhood,"[57] and her "vivid and skillful propaganda" modeling "a new, universal Christian culture"[58]—most contemporary readings of the tracts stress the narrowness of their class-based view of the lower ranks. The emphasis is on losses rather than gains in Olivia Smith's view of More's patronizing tactlessness, "cheering on the poor for the suffering that enables the rich to be virtuous," Gary Kelly's charge of More's expropriation of popular culture which results in "a particular distribution of language, selfhood and authority," Donna Landry's analysis of More's "explicitly depoliticizing" lessons for the laboring poor, Elizabeth Kowaleski-Wallace's reading of a text preoccupied "with the containment of explosive appetites," and Moira Ferguson's assessment of an authoritarian narrative prescribing "what is right for the underdog."[59] Another reader contends that More deliberately shifted linguistic registers between the "ballads," the "tales for the common people," and the "stories for the middle ranks," co-opting the poor as hegemonic instruments of the Establishment and speaking blatantly to the middle ranks.[60] In order to accommodate this theory of successive calibration it requires some fiddling of chronology and facts to rearrange the tracts to the generic titles More added for the 1801 edition of her works. More contributed broadsides throughout the lifespan of the Repository—*Dan and Jane* and *The Plum-Cakes* were entered at the Stationers' Hall in October and November 1797, respectively—and one of the longest stories for the middle ranks, the seven-part *Two Wealthy Farmers*, extended over the whole period of More's writing for the Repository.

As an Evangelical cultural warrior, committed to drawing "the profligate multitude . . . off from that pernicious trash" and considering "it lawful to write a few moral stories, the main circumstances of which have occurred within [her] own knowledge, but altered and improved,"[61] More announced her plan "to improve the habits, and raise the principles of the common people, at a time when their dangers and temptations, moral and political, [are] multiplied beyond the example of any former period."[62] Her "humble wish . . . to counteract . . . error, discontent, and false religion"[63] is definitely open to criticism. The fact that most readings today privilege the multitude, whom More dragoons, coerces, belittles, and fictionalizes, lends a retaliatory edge to this revisionism. What often gets lost in the reshuffling of priorities and spokespersons is More's absolute (and, yes, overriding, obsessive, and grossly condescending) confidence that, in alluring "these thoughtless creatures on to higher things,"[64] she was fulfilling a Christian duty. Fortified with her own "superior motives," she was already prepared to face the "proud and arrogant discretion which ridicules, as Utopian and romantic, every generous project of the active and the liberal."[65] Before churning out her colorful, purposive stories, ballads, and meditations, this moral imperialist had also declared that the essence of her philosophy and psychology lay in the scriptures; she found "the whole scheme of the Gospel . . . accommodated to real human nature; laying open its mortal disease, presenting its only remedy; exhibiting rules of conduct, often difficult indeed, but never impossible; and . . . holding out a living pattern, to elucidate the doctrine and to illustrate the precept."[66] When, in one of her lengthy (six-part) tales, *The Two Shoemakers*, More's thrifty, charitable tradesman, the exemplary James Stock, catechizes his apprentice, Will Simpson, he turns his attention to Will's "favourite song": "But let us see to what different purposes the apostle and the poet turn the very same thought. Your song says, because life is so short, let us make it merry: let us divert ourselves so much on the road that we may forget the end. Now what says the apostle? *Because the end of all things is at hand, be ye therefore sober, and watch unto prayer.*"[67] More, too, is on the side of the apostle (St. Peter, in this case), as throughout the tracts she relies on a combination of biblical knowledge, usually italicized pericopes or knowing paraphrases, and her own shrewd skills in narration to guide the training of readers' sights on a heavenly minded sobriety.

Scribbled "one sick day," intended to be "as vulgar as heart can wish, and sent to Rivington instead of her usual publisher Cadell, *Village Politics* clarified More's "utter aversion to liberty according to the present idea of it in France."[68] The distillation of this idea in Thomas Paine's populist, plain, and forthright manifesto is "Will Chip's" particular target. Rivington dispensed

More's best-seller by the thousands; her friends, Porteus, Mrs. Montagu, Walpole, and Mrs. Boscawen, sent packets of the dialogue far and wide; not only was it a hit at Windsor and with the attorney general but a Northumberland parson promptly ordered a thousand copies. As with the tracts themselves, the rave reviews for this prototype came from the members of More's own class or the nobility; beyond the fact that it was distributed to cottages, workshops, coal pits, and public houses, exactly mimicking the circulation of *The Rights of Man*, we know next-to-nothing about the unmediated response of real miners, blacksmiths, masons, and carpenters.

The ways in which More empowers Jack Anvil, patriotic spokesman for the status quo, over restless but fuzzy-thinking and malleable Tom Hod show some of the strategy used thoughout the tracts and the often unintentional ironies that cause this privileging to backfire. Jack is the master of the pithy observation, snorting about the "good sign . . . that you can't find out you're unhappy without looking into a book for it!" and concluding that "envy is at the bottom of your equality works."[69] But for all of his catechetical quickness in rattling off definitions to French *liberty* ("to murder more men in one night than ever their poor king did in his whole life"), a democrat ("one who likes to be governed by a thousand tyrants, and yet can't bear a king"), and *the new Rights of Man* ("battle, murder, and sudden death"),[70] there is a hammering righteousness, a real intransigence about this spokesman. For him the hierarchy of power is entrenched and immutable: "duties are fixed, Tom—laws are settled."[71] His tendency to be hyperbolic, as in claiming that poor patients at the infirmary are "taken as much care of as a lord," goes unchallenged; similarly, the questionable logic of his argumentation, especially about differences in talents ruling out equality and their need of the "very extravagance" of the rich whereby "as poor men we are benefited," meets no rebuttal.[72] Despite the pseudonymn, Morean control and vigilance are everywhere.

From the earliest ballads, the upholding of a paternalistic hierarchy supports an insistence on temperance and self-denying moderation. In the extended, sung conversation between Jack Anvil and Tom Hod, "The Riot; or, Half a Loaf is Better than No Bread," Jack attacks the "whimsey" of filling bellies "by breaking the mill" and "by abusing the butchers"—"What a whimsey to think we shall mend our spare diet / By breeding disturbance, by murder and riot—" and, through commanding most of the talk, links this quietism to basic issues in household economy ("the more ale we drink, boys, the less we shall eat") and national governance.[73] Quelling a riot means the renunciation of power and the acceptance of the benefactor mode. The poor are to be contented drudges, without money or voice, while "the King and Parliament manage the rest" and the "gentlefolks . . . give up their puddings and pies."[74] Consistently the ballads present this kind of distorted argumentation, whether from within the lower ranks or through the voice-over of an omniscient narrator, as compelling and reformative. Such histrionics as the carpenter's wife serving her child as a meal to her drunkard husband prompts immediate confession and redemption, while exposing the ploy of the Market Woman known for fraud and gin leads to isolation from her husband and community as a "good warning" against "lawless weights and measures." Despite the minatory cautions and the prophet-like zeal to transform, a congruent feature of the ballads is that the unregenerate are not redeemed. The Roguish Miller who takes the toll three times ends up in jail; the antagonist of the Newcastle collier, Tim Jenkins, "who drank and who gamed, / Who mock'd at his Bible, and was not ashamed," is killed in a cave-in; libertine Richard sinks more deeply into debauchery and drunkenness, leading to an early death after the drowning of the sweetheart he ruined and their baby.

In a project as overtly didactic as the tracts, it makes sense that judgments be hard-hitting and unequivocal. Echoing the conviction of the weaver who shows his fellow tradesman the "plan" and "pattern" in which "all order and design appear," More explains the world and mitigates its gloom by supplying her own salutary perspective: "This world, which clouds thy soul with doubts, / *Is but a carpet inside out.*"[75] As for "the folly of going out of our element," she wastes no time underlining the moral in the four-part broadside "John the Shopkeeper Turned Sailor"; as well as losing his wife, daughter, mother, and boatman, John serves as an emblem for restless countrymen.

> When Britons, wearied with their lot,
> Grow wild to get they know not what,
> And quit, thro' love of Revolution,
> Our good old English Constitution;
> When Frenchmen lead the mazy dance,
> And Britons ape fantastic France;
> Methinks, like Johnny once so brave,
> They're quitting ancient house and home
> 'Mid the wild winds, and seas to roam.[76]

The yearnings of Tom White, the postboy, for smart clothes prompt the narrator's immediate censure of the "foolish fellow! [who] never considered that though it is true, a waggoner works hard all day, yet he gets a quiet evening at home, and undisturbed rest at night"; however, the underlying malady, neglect of religious practice, warrants a generalizing admonition that "'tis a pity that people don't look at their catechism when they are grown up;

for it is full as good for men and women as it is for children; nay, better; for though the answers contained in it are intended for children to *repeat*, yet the duties enjoined in it are intended for men and women to put in *practice*."[77] The principal character in "The Sunday School," its foundress Mrs. Jones, holds forth at length on the value of her institution, contrasting the probity of its reading material to the "poison for the soul" in the "vile trash" peddled by the fiddler's woman and encouraging the custom of "many of the parents, pleased with the improvement so visible in the young people, [who] got the habit of dropping in, that they might learn how to instruct their own families."[78] Virtue resides in religious observance, especially praiseworthy under adverse conditions. Although the heroine of "The History of Hester Wilmot," the sequel to "The Sunday School," has nonobservant parents, "poor Hester" delights in school and church, "for so great is God's goodness, that he is pleased to make religion a peculiar comfort to those who have no other comfort."[79] A judgmental as well as self-referential exercise, the tracts underscore the effectiveness of lessons inculcated by continuing to advertise intertextually. Just as the saintly Shepherd of Salisbury Plain has pasted the broadside of "Patient Joe or the Newcastle Collier" on his clean white walls, so too Hester Wilmot starts to catechize her derelict parents by buying "of a pious hawker, for three halfpence, the Book of Prayers, printed for the Cheap Repository."

Such strict narrative control also requires simplified detail, which More manages through various means. Abrupt erasure is a favorite. When the reformed Tom White marries, his bride, the "prudent, sober, industrious, and religious upper maid [of] the vicar's lady,"[80] remains anonymous, her modesty and frugality being more important than a name. The Shepherd of Salisbury Plain provides the necessary check to his own loquacity—albeit biblically sound and cheerfully contented—as he begins "to feel that he had made too free, and had talked too long."[81] Despite the frequent encouragement of home baking and brewing, the recipes for mutton stew and onion or leek porridge, and the demonstration of simple cure-alls like a bread and milk poultice, the diet of most characters in the tracts is grossly inadequate; yet invariably—and implausibly—the children are referred to as cherry-cheeked. A similar kind of reality-denying formula separates the virtuous poor from unregenerate sinners. Black Giles, the poacher, lives in a mud cottage that is the essence of dinginess and neglect, "with broken windows stuffed with dirty rags"; although the Shepherd's hovel is no more commodious, it is the epitome of "perfect neatness," with gleaming trenchers "almost as white as their linen" and wooden chairs rubbed "as bright as a looking glass."[82] Giles's wife, the fortune teller Tawney Rachel, is not only as deceiving as her mate

CHEAP REPOSITORY.

THE

COTTAGE COOK,

OR,

Mrs. JONES's Cheap Dishes;

Shewing the Way to do much good with little Money.

Sold by J. MARSHALL,
(Printer to the CHEAP REPOSITORY for Religi-
ous and Moral Tracts) No. 17, Queen-Street,
Cheapside, and No. 4, Aldermary Church-Yard,
and R. WHITE, Piccadilly, LONDON.
By S. HAZARD, at Bath, J. ELDER, at Edin-
burgh, and by all Booksellers, Newsmen, and
Hawkers, in Town and Country. Great Allow-
ance will be made to Shopkeepers and Hawkers.
PRICE ONE PENNY.
Or 4s. 6d. per 100.—2s. 6d. for 50.—1s. 6d. for 25.
A cheaper Edition for Hawkers.
[*Entered at Stationers' Hall.*]

The Cheap Repository's encouragement of home baking and brewing (The Henry E. Huntington Library, San Marino, Calif.).

but is also a "wretched manager"; the Shepherd's patched clothing and multicolored darned socks illustrate his partner's "good housewifery."[83] While Giles, caught in a conspiracy to trick and cheat, dies "in great misery" and Rachel, one of "these hags" preying on the credulous, is tracked down as "vermin" by a vengeful husband of a duped customer and sentenced as "a nuisance"[84] to Botany Bay, good fortune and coincidence benefit the Shepherd. He falls into a better cottage and job (freeing his Sundays to be a schoolmaster), and his wife is rewarded with the position of a schoolmistress at a small weekly school; as their benefactor observes righteously, " 'I am not going to make you rich, but useful.' "[85]

No more subtle or sophisticated, the Stories for the Middle Ranks rely on similar narrative shorthand. The two most developed plots, "The Two Wealthy Farmers; or, the History of Mr. Bragwell" and "The History of Mr. Fantom, the New Fashioned Philosopher and His Man William," turn on many of the same contrasts of character and environment as the Tales for the Common People. Farmers Bragwell and Worthy are as set in their contrastive ways as were the central characters of "The Two Shoemakers," the doted-on, easily tempted Jack Brown and the modest, industrious James Stock. However, while Bragwell smuggles brandy and Worthy advises him to read the Sermon on the Mount, the tract is not preoccupied with warnings against the demon drink or recommendations of home brew. In light of the wider social opportunities that money affords her middle-class characters, More seems to be looking back to the argument of *Thoughts on the Manners of the Great* and *An Estimate of the Religion of the Fashionable World* and previewing some of the observations of *Strictures on the Modern System of Female Education*, by focusing on the education these two farmers provide their daughters.

> As persons in the middle line, for want of that acquaintance with books, and with life and manners, which the great possess, do not always see the connection between remote consequences and their causes, the evils of a corrupt and inappropriate system of education do not strike *them* so forcibly; and provided *they can pay for it*, which is made the grand criterion between the fit and the unfit, they are too little disposed to consider the value, or rather the worthlessness, of the thing which is paid for; but literally go on to *give their money for that which is not bread*.[86]

The affectations of a boarding school and addiction to the circulating library are two strikes against Bragwell's daughters; their mother's vain ambition and father's absorption in "practical arithmetic" ("spend a shilling to gain a pound")[87] make tragedy inevitable. Since More clearly favors Worthy's "spiritual calculations, arithmetic in the long run," she does not restrict the sentimental details of the daughters' ruinous marriages: a strolling player leads one to the workhouse and a bankrupt fortune hunter and suicide leaves the other to die after a stillbirth. Although one daughter and her predictably "rosy face[d]" son are rescued from the workhouse, the reformation in the Bragwell home is incomplete. Despite the fact that Bragwell has his son-in-law's suicide note framed and glazed, his "unfeeling" wife stays as vain as ever. Wholesale when it finally takes effect, reformation is certainly delayed in the two tracts concerning Mr. Fantom. The contrasts between Fantom, a discontented retail merchant turned philosopher, and Trueman, "an honest, plain, simple-hearted tradesman of the good old cut," are the most pronounced and developed of More's whole contribution to the Repository because she demonstrates forcibly how "morality is but an empty name, if it be destitute of the principle and power of Christianity."[88] A thinly disguised parody of Godwin's Caleb Williams, Fantom is the consummate hypocrite, arguing that money is "trash, . . . dirt, and beneath the regard of a wise man" to justify his refusal to relieve the family of a tradesman imprisoned for debt, watching a neighbor's cottage burn while he sits down "to work on a new pamphlet . . . on universal benevolence," and causing his servant to be sentenced to the gallows through teaching "principles" about there being "no hereafter, no judgment, no future reckoning."[89] Whether supplied through the juxtaposition of words and actions or through knowing authorial observations, the irony is very thick. The narrator does not hesitate to ridicule Fantom's patriarchalism, noting how "in his zeal to make the whole world free and happy, [he] was too prudent to include his wife among the objects on whom he wished to confer freedom and happiness."[90] Irony melts into the bathos of remorse in "The Death of Mr. Fantom, the Great Reformist," a sequel that More wrote two decades later to help to quell the 1817 riots occasioned by poor crops and the collapse of trade and fanned by William Cobbett's Twopenny Trash and Weekly Political Register. Along with the thirteen tracts she was prevailed upon to submit to The Anti-Cobbett; or, Weekly Patriotic Register, this extension, like the adaptation of Village Politics into Village Disputants, is a disappointingly pale renunciation of all the former bravado and self-assurance. Instead of Fantom's cockiness there is a fearful whimper and disclosure of infidelity to his "excellent wife" with a "virtuous" woman whom he "seduced from her husband."[91] Like the Ephesian sorcerers (Acts 19), Fantom resolves to burn his books. No hard-fought debate or feisty dialogue with Trueman leads to this decision, for a renunciatory tone casts a pall over the whole tract.

The major projects of the schools and the tracts reveal many different yet complementary sides of More. As an establisher and inspector of schools she gives a local habitation and name to the concept of meliorism. The poor can learn, she attests, and if she shames neglectful clergy and local despots by her interventions, she remains undeterred in the conviction that the forgotten miners, glassblowers, and farmhands, and particularly their children, *must* be taught. The Bible, Prayer Book, and Catechism are ready-made for conveying the rudiments of spelling, grammar, and Christian principles. Pedagogical and social theories interlace: control and firmness go hand in hand with a specially tailored curriculum and rewards for effort. Since she believes in "a newer form of social control based on self-discipline and the internalization of the mechanics of control,"[92] schooling will, in More's view, modify behavior and deter vice more efficaciously than punishment. The related venture of the Cheap Repository confidently addresses a larger audience. As determined as she was in confronting and generally overcoming Mendip objections to the village schools, More marshalls truth and fiction to vindicate divine justice in the unequal distribution of goods. As searingly as she indicts the avarice, irresponsibility, and irreligious cant of the middle ranks, she orders the rhetoric of hierarchy and contentment to counter the *ché sera* attitudes and penchant for insurgence among the lower class. Religious duty and social theory cohere, as they did in the philosophy of the schools. The economy of More's charity means industrious piety for the poor and responsible stewardship for their masters or employers.

Instruments of social control, both enterprises presuppose and promote subalternism. A class-based, hereditary hierarchy is as immutable for More as are duties and laws for her blacksmith-mouthpiece, Jack Anvil. For all the vigour and exertions of her activity, she defends a static social order and aligns it to a notion of Christian discipline. In studying the works of British "charitable ladies," Beth Tobin draws a striking parallel between More's Christian discipline and "what Michel Foucault has called 'disciplinary power,' which operates through 'its invisibility' and . . . 'imposes on those whom it subjects a principle of compulsory visibility.' "[93] In Foucauldian terms More's discipline implicates her in assuming "responsibility for the constraints of power" and, by extension, in making her pupils, readers, and supporters "the principles of [their] own subjection."[94] But the Morean Panopticon was not just a counterinsurgent strategy; it unsettled other so-called disciplinary agents, too. The stories, biographical and purposively fabricated, of the village schools and Cheap Repository disclose the intelligence and wholehearted commmitment of this principal agent. The fact that we can look back through a theoretical lens and measure the extent and limitations of her accomplishment should not blind us to the other important issue: that these very attainments also made her, for contemporaries, an *agent provocateur*.

❀ 6 ❀

"The language of sympathy rather than of dictation":[1] The Unread Hannah More

In her sixties and seventies and on into her eightieth year, More published four major distillations of her religious principles. *Practical Piety; or, The Influence of the Religion of the Heart on the Conduct of the Life* (1811), *Christian Morals* (1812), *An Essay on the Character and Practical Writings of Saint Paul* (1815), and *The Spirit of Prayer* (1825) are invariably dismissed as the pathetic rambling effusions of an old "saint" who, with no firm understanding of theology or philosophy and in her "widowhood of the heart,"[2] had withdrawn into the "fat complacency" of her own "narrow doctrine."[3] Ironically this essential More—practical, confessional, self-aware, strong minded, compelling, adept at blending historical and contemporary references, and totally committed to the animating principle of faith—remains unread. Since the titles are daunting and the texts long and digressive, the simplest solution is to bypass them altogether as the unfortunate consequences of a radical conversion to Evangelicalism. Yet at least three reasons should encourage us to take these documents seriously. They testify to the remarkable homogeneity of her thought over almost half a century. This octogenarian is as steadfastly trained on heavenly sights, on weaning from earth, as she was as a teenaged playwright; she is as ferocious in her opposition to irreligion, two decades later, as she was in warning Christian readers of the "pestilence" that "will insinuate itself imperceptibly with those manners, phrases, and principles which you examine and adopt" in Monsieur Dupont's speech "on the subjects of Religion and Public Education" in the French National Convention.[4] These final volumes also tally with the candor of her letters. Though a devoted and ecumenical reader of sermons, especially those of Ridley, Jewell, Taylor, Hooker, Porteus, Leighton, and Horne, with a sprinkling of Chrysostom and Augustine, and really "fascinated"[5] with the Port Royal authors in the forty-volume set bequeathed by Mrs. Boscawen, More had no illusions about her scholarly preparations. She admitted being "a poor divine" and "a miserable theologian" and went as far as to voice the fear that "under the mask of religion," she could perhaps "indulge [her] own humours and resentments."[6] However, she made it clear that her greatest dread was party narrowness. "I wish there was no such thing as party!"[7] is a characteristic expression of frustration. Finally, these works of avowed piety by a woman who has been both venerated and vilified for daring to comment on the practical applications of a discipline, from which her sex was systematically excluded, should warrant attention as bold examples of a unique and still unrecognized capability. They could provide a test case for ways of according justice to Hannah More. Is she simply a tiresome old woman whose ideas never changed for fifty years, or a discerning and strict observer of humankind who believed passionately in placing her intelligence at the service of an acknowledged higher power?

In this intensely revealing writing, More provides ample evidence that she is not handing down tablets from a mountaintop of complacent smugness. "As a Christian who must die" and "with a deep practical sense of the infirmities against which she has presumed to caution others,"[8] she examines religion and morality to remind and not to inform, to learn and not to teach. She writes for the readership she knows best, "amiable and interesting, . . . virtuous and correct" females with "characters so engaging, so evidently made for better things, so capable of reaching high degrees of excellence, so formed to give the tone to Christian practice, as well as to fashion."[9] A brand of highminded meliorism stamps all of More's works, but in these final volumes explicitly devoted to religion she is especially concerned to engage the attention of readers prone to what she terms "one of the greatest errors of our moral life, . . . miscalculation of the relative value of things."[10] As much, it seems, to direct her own resolve as to prepare the reader for her purposiveness is the canny observation that "things can only influence our practice as they engage our attention."[11] Fully aware that the consequences of this engagement involve a humbling look at her own practice and motives, she is ready for both extremes, yet predictably she casts them in the distancing third-person masculine. Finding "*his* life" falling short of "the strictness of his writings . . . is a disparity almost inseparable from this state of frail mortality," while "being immediately the object of *his* own attention . . . may lead *him* to be too full of *himself*."[12] Of the four volumes the one in which More seems most at ease is the study of Saint Paul. She not only admits to and absolves herself of "deficiencies in ancient learning, Biblical criticism, and deep theological knowledge," but she preempts charges by explaining that "as she never aspired to the dignity of an Expositor, so she never meant to enter into the details of the Biographer."[13] Her personal and idiosyncratic reading matches the revelation of the epistles themselves, since Saint Paul "lets us into the secrets of our own bosoms, . . . discloses to us the motives of our own conduct, and . . . lays bare the moral quality of action."[14]

In her positively charged review, Saint Paul is a model stylist as well as moralist. In keeping with the biblical scholarship of her time More treats as genuine all fourteen epistles attributed to Paul: the authentically Pauline (1 Thessalonians, 1 and 2 Corinthians, Philippians, Galatians, Romans, Philemon), those of debatable authenticity (2 Thessalonians, Colossians, Ephesians), and those of the Pauline school (Hebrews, Titus, 1 and 2 Timothy). Her writerly observations on the language and stratagems of the epistles show a real fascination with the genius of the Apostle to the Gentiles, a fascination that claims the writer as both a universal and a remarkably contemporary figure. Eulogizing Paul, who "is equally the property of each successive race of beings," and speculating that "he would have wished his lot assigned him . . . IN GREAT BRITAIN IN THE BEGINNING OF THE NINETEENTH CENTURY!,"[15] More appreciates the complexity and calculatedness of his ideas. His handling of vast ideas, such as "the extent of the love of God, its height and depth, its length and breadth" accommodates the hugeness of the concept, as "his soul seems to expand with the dimensions he is unfolding [and] his expressions . . . acquire all that force with which he intimates that the soul itself, so acted upon, is invested."[16] When launching his pointed reproofs to the church at Corinth, Paul is an accomplished strategist, "so in no Epistle is there more preparatory soothing, more conciliatory preliminaries, to the counsels or the censures he is about to communicate."[17]

Because More sees Saint Paul "always writing like a man of the actual world" and acutely, compassionately penetrating "the weaknesses of the wise, . . . the failings of the virtuous, and the inconsistencies of even the conscientious,"[18] she is herself inspired to undertake a defense of Paul on two hugely contentious issues: his treatment of women and of authority. Highly opinionated, these exercises, while not entirely whitewashes, remake Paul in More's particular image, dismissing opposing views as uninformed and prejudiced. In contrast to opponents' objections proceeding "from a prejudice lightly taken up on hearsay evidence—a prejudice propagated without serious enquiry, without having themselves closely examined his writings," More catalogues Paul's valuable friendships with women, citing Phoebe, Priscilla, Mary, Julia, Chloe, Tryphena, and Tryphosa, and highlighting Claudia, "our countrywoman," whom she contends Paul met when "in all probability [he] preached the Gospel in Britain."[19] As for Paul's dicta to the Corinthians about marriage, More explains that the "suggested suspension" applied only to a "present distress" and waves off the disgruntled with the bluff rhetorical question, "Is it not absurd to suppose that this zealous Apostle of Christ would suggest, as a permanent practice, a measure which must in a few years, if persisted in, inevitably occasion the entire extinction of Christianity itself?"[20] Her comments on the inflammatory Pauline directives about silence and submission are so placidly unperturbed, expressing surprise that these injunctions "can possibly be the cause of the hostility of any Christian ladies," that I wonder if More assumed blitheness deliberately to foreclose debate. This aspect of her defense of Paul can only provoke howls today, with our understanding of the feminist critical principle of the "hermeneutics of suspicion" and its work in searching out the hidden and the not-so-hidden androcentric bias of culturally honored texts.[21] Despite the sale of the entire first edition of *Saint Paul* in one day, this particular view may not have been swallowed whole in 1815 either!

In her chapter entitled "Saint Paul's Respect for Constituted Authorities," she resorts to similar strategies to shrink and dismiss opposition. More's Paul is no hothead or renegade. With his religion characterized by "a peculiar sedateness,"[22] this Paul appears to have no connection to the Apostle who was snubbed by Jews and Christians alike in Jerusalem, whom the Jews of Lycaonia greeted with violent hostility, on account of whom the silversmiths at Ephesus rioted, and for whom the deep hatred of the Jews of Jerusalem resulted in arrest. More's claim about Paul's desire "to stengthen a natural by a lawful and moral obligation"[23] glosses over many of the inherent tensions of Paul's teaching: most prominent, that Christianity did not impose the obligations of Judaism on Gentiles, that his rabbinical training and Semitic, as opposed to Greek, background led to a preference for extreme, absolute statements rather than tempered or qualified ones, and that the influences of Judaism and Hellenistic urban civilization were constantly jousting in his writing. More's Paul seems to be entirely removed from what current biblical scholars refer to as "the apocalyptic atmosphere of his era," showing no development or modification from 1 Thessalonians to Romans, no progress "from an apocalyptic-transcendent orientation . . . to a more immanent, anthropocentric, and humanist orientation."[24] Yet curiously, although More is content to neuter Paul and blunt at least one edge of his sword, she relies on the characterization of him as "a firm supporter of established authorities" to move her own argument's praise of this proselytizer *par excellence* into a denunciation of those subversive contemporary authors (especially Voltaire and Godwin) who rail, mistake, and discolor.

Who now reads the "Leviathan?" Who has *not* read Candide? . . . Little wits came to sharpen their weapons at the forge of this Philistine, or to steal small arms from his arsenal. . . . "Political Justice," a more recent work, subversive of all religious and social order, was too ponderous to be popular, and too dry to answer the end of general corruption. But when the substance, by that chemical process well known to the preparers of poison, was *rubbed down* into an amusing novel, then it began to operate.[25]

Although her voice strives for sympathetic understanding, More's lenses for viewing the world around her are always specially adjusted. Her admiration of Paul reduces merely secular figures as secondary. Conviction makes him superior to Copernicus, who "recanted what he knew to be truth and was set free"; for More "the philosopher was irresolute; the Apostle persevered."[26] As a martyred moralist he towers above Seneca, since "Paul lived a Christian, and Seneca died a Heathen."[27] Her strong advocacy places Paul's writings above those of "the learned speculatists of the German school," which she considers "airy," "mystic," and "shadowy."[28] It is probable that More had heard of and even consumed some English abridgment or review of Friedrich Schleiermacher's *On Religion; Speeches to Its Cultured Despisers*, which had appeared in 1799. A veritable manifesto of the young Romantic school, *On Religion* defined its subject as deep emotion, intuition, and feeling in which "religion never appears quite pure" but "its outward form is ever determined by something else."[29] Although More may have agreed with many aspects of Schleiermacher's engaging attempt to interpret Christian faith in relation to the intellectual life of modern times, she remained too loyal to fixed doctrines and principles to accept his resort to the shifting sands of human reflection and creation. No doubt More would have registered real opposition to this kind of apologetic argument:

> Whence do those dogmas and doctrines come that many consider the essence of religion? Where do they properly belong? And how do they stand related to what is essential in religion? They are all the result of that contemplation of feeling, of that reflection and comparison, of which we have already spoken. The conceptions that underlie these propositions are, like your conceptions from experience, nothing but general expressions for definite feelings. They are not necessary for religion itself, scarcely even for communicating religion, but reflection requires and creates them.[30]

By contrast, Paul's "devout," "earnest", and "humble" faith, which More tries to emulate, is a stable entity, embedded in a tradition: "His religion is definite and substantial, . . . a homage to Christianity."[31] Such substantiality, she maintains, would have given Lord Chesterfield's advice "a right direction; . . .

he would have found the *suaviter in modo* accompany the *fortiter in re* more uniformly in our Apostle than in any other writer."[32]

Her knowledge of the customary, worldly judgments of her society is not a liability for More. She knows how unpopular her reminders can be and, undeterred, presses on. I do not believe this is the result of perversity; admittedly she felt she had nothing to lose, but at no stage in her conservative Christian career did she ever temporize or deliver to her readership what they wanted or expected to hear. She never relaxes in her view of man as a fallen, not an imperfect, creature; hence, "a thorough renovation of heart"—in the face of ridicule that such enthusiasm is "criminal," "mischievous," and "destructive"—[33] is the sure remedy she adduces. She is also capable of some rhetorical pyrotechnics, especially asyndeton and parataxis, to meet these objections. The authorities she cites are impressive, not just as an arsenal of allies, but as an illustration of the ways in which widening the supportive circle ultimately silences objection.

> But if these charges be really well founded, then were the brightest luminaries of the Christian Church—then were Horne, and Porteus, and Beveridge; then were Hooker, and Taylor, and Herbert; Hopkins, Leighton, and Usher; Howe, Doddridge, and Baxter; Ridley, Jewell, and Hooper;—then were Chrysostome, and Augustine, the Reformers and the Fathers; then were the goodly fellowship of the Prophets, then were the noble army of Martyrs, then were the glorious company of the Apostles, then was the Disciple whom Jesus loved, then was Jesus himself—I shudder at the implication—dry speculatists, frantic enthusiasts, enemies to virtue, and subverters of the public weal.[34]

Equally adept at refashioning the past to suit her own purposes, More can excite her readers to a patriotic pitch; by contrasting the Saint Bartholomew Massacre and the Inquisition to "three noble and . . . lasting monuments as ever national virtue erected to true piety, . . . The Society for Promoting Christian Knowledge, the British and Foreign Bible Society, and the Abolition of the African Slave-trade," she emphasizes only the positively charitable interventions of "this happy land of civil and religious liberty."[35]

The conciseness with which More pinpoints the ironies of so-called Christian practice means that readers are not lulled into complacency, but constantly—albeit gently—urged to evaluate themselves. More's acquaintances often furnish instructive examples. The "lady of rank who, though her benevolence was suspected to bear no proportion to the splendour of her establishment, was yet rather too apt to make her bounties a subject of conversation" is self-deluded; More minces no words in commenting on the lady's conversational fillip, " 'notwithstanding my large family I give all this to charity *besides paying the poor rates*,' " as "converting a compulsory act, to which all are equally subject, into a voluntary bounty."[36] Though willing to see prejudice as "not so much the fault of the individual, as of our common nature," she stresses how difficult it is to eradicate with the pithy observation, "by disguising itself under the respectable name of firmness, it is of infinitely slower extirpation than actual vice."[37] She does not gloss over faults with omniscient detachment but with a feeling grasp of both human motives and spiritual losses. In contemplating why good nominal Christians are not better, she draws her simile from the beloved subject of gardening. "They live, it is true, but it is as the vegetable world lives in the winter's frost, which does not indeed kill it, but benumbs its powers, and suspends its vitality."[38] More's most persuasive summations usually rely on very simple devices; contrasting monosyllabic adverbs, for example, drive home the point about Christian inconsistency when she notes, "To suppose that we shall possess hereafter what we do not desire here, that we shall complete then, what we do not think of beginning now, is among the inconsistencies of many who pass muster under the generic title of Christians."[39]

Even in her last major work, the fourteen chapters on prayer sent "from a sick, and, in all probability a dying bed," which the subtitle identifies as "compiled by the author, from various portions exclusively on that subject, in her other works,"[40] she produces more than a cut-and-paste job. Her urge to define and categorize is as strong as that to exhort and reform. Convinced as she is of human corruption and of the "imaginary dignity [of] self-sufficiency," it is logical for More to proceed to a definition of prayer as "the urgency of poverty, the prostration of humility, the fervency of penitence, the confidence of trust."[41] Urgency, prostration, fervency, and confidence are, by this point in More's writing, quintessential signature terms. Her awareness of the arguments of those who neglect or reject prayer, as evidenced in two separate catalogues, does not diminish her conviction to stand apart from and, if need be, alone against these received ideas. However, in her eightieth year, she still is more concerned with faith-directed community and action. The distinction drawn between the Creed and the Lord's Prayer hinges on the opening pronouns. "We cannot exercise faith for another, and, therefore, can only say *I* believe. But when we offer up our petitions, we address them to *our* Father, implying that he is the Author, Governor, and Supporter, not of ourselves only, but of his whole rational creation. It conveys also a beautiful idea of that boundless charity which links mankind in one comprehensive brotherhood."[42] The contrasts between strength and weakness now poignantly combine physiology and spirituality. "Let us not impair that faith on which we rested when our mind was strong, by suspecting its validity now it is weak. That which had our full assent in perfect health, which was then firmly rooted in our spirit, and grounded in our understanding, must not be unfixed by the doubts of an enfeebled reason, and the scruples of an impaired judgment."[43] The controlling yet ultimately unquestioned assumption of these volumes is the shared, wide interest in the subject of religion. More poses the question, "where will topics be found more universal in their application to all times, persons, places, and circumstances as well as more important than those which relate to the eternal welfare of mankind?"[44] as entirely rhetorical. The preoccupation with final things sanctions and actually requires strict control of imaginative energies, of the sort that Paul exemplified in being "too devout to be ingenious, too earnest to be fanciful, too humble to be inventive."[45] As calmly as the lion of imagination was tamed in *Strictures* (Chapter 12), the ingenious, the fanciful, and the inventive are thereby excluded from any thoroughgoing Christian enterprise. Her extended praise of Wilberforce, called "Candidus" in *Christian Morals*, epitomizes the engaged, active, diligent, kind member of the Establishment, whose "invariable conformity with Scripture" sharpens his awareness of "what abuses have been and are still practised, and what deceits carried on, under pretence of being *the work of the Spirit*."[46] As a "genuine son of the Reformation," Candidus, "catholic, but not latitudinarian; tolerant, not from indifference, but principle," censures only one group, "the sect of the *Non-doers*."[47] Just as the portrait of Wilberforce reflects the temperament and aspirations of the author herself, so too, Wilberforce's own *Practical View of the Prevailing Religious System of Professed Christians*, first published in 1797, provided a reciprocal summary of many of More's cherished principles. He succinctly forecast such developed Morean themes as "our own natural depravity," "the essential practical characteristics of true Christians" consisting in their having "cordially and unreservedly devoted themselves to God," and "the tendency of Religion in general to promote the temporal welfare of political communities"; *Practical View* also paid attention to the "more favourable disposition to Religion in the female sex" in a way More surely endorsed.[48] In fact, his image of women as "the medium of our intercourse with the heavenly world, the faithful repositories of religious principle for the benefit both of the present and of the rising generation"[49] encapsulates the very features on which More founded her writing career.

The congruence of More and Wilberforce is unsurprising, but what about connections between More and us? Is there any hope at all for mutuality linking these texts to readers almost two centuries removed? Can we simply content ourselves with charting the differences between More's enthusiastic spiritualizing of the social affections, without hesitancy, equivocation, or problematizing nuance, and our own suspicion of regnant models, certitude, and domination, our sense that there is no longer any grand story, only local stories? In addressing the topic of "the Bible and postmodern imagination," Walter Brueggemann suggests that the "responsibility" of a religious community or leader today "is not a grand scheme or a coherent system, but the voicing of a lot of little pieces out of which people can put life together in fresh configurations."[50] Concessions about the shift from hegemony, the weakening of a centrist synthesis, and the welcoming of interpretation that is contextual, local, and pluralistic would all be foreign to More. But there is strangeness on both sides. Informed by protective strategies that preclude dissent, her sense of the infinite and of religious experience, more descriptive and evocative than analytical and explanatory, is confidently mediated through linguistic representation. Since belief in a transcendent Creator and associated metaphysical doctrines have been rejected by many, More's passionate certitude and lifelong commitment may seem equally remote to us.

Despite the cultural and ideological distances, a couple of considerations might make More less of a sister from another planet. Reflections on and inquiries into Christian faith and practice affect, actually saturate, all aspects of her life. Her apologetic exercise often goes far beyond the religious perspective; or, seen from another angle, it promotes the universality of religious experience and belief in organizations outside of the church, in politics, economics, and the arts. Such a universalizing assumption, although it rests on a huge commonality of belief and appropriateness, illustrates remarkably a contemporary position that "the authority of religious doctrine or of the religious form of life cannot be disconnected from other concepts and beliefs."[51] Of course one position homologizes, and the other differentiates. Whereas More assumes that the infiltration of religion into every activity should be tolerated willingly, contemporary theorists of religion maintain that "concepts and beliefs that are not distinctively religious" cannot be subsumed indiscriminately within the doctrine of "a tacit explanatory commitment."[52] In a curious way, and without a hint of bad faith, More writes from the inside, assuming, however, that her beliefs transcend and transform boundaries, and thus exteriorize her insidedness. This sense of public possibility and urgency in More's writing indicates an understanding of covenantal fidelity which, though removed from the sinking doubt of many well-intentioned believers, is closely allied to Brueggemann's explanation of "the counterworld of evangelical imagination" in its "readiness to receive life . . . from God." Brueggemann contrasts modern greed, acquisitiveness, and idolatry with trust in a covenant that decisively reshapes and redefines.

At the heart of the matter, the contrast of *commodity* and *covenant* hinges upon the reliability of the other. And that reliability is known through a rich memory marked by generous origins, and a vivid hope marked by a full, joyous completion. Commoditization knows no reliable other, having scuttled a generous memory and a buoyant hope, and is left with a thin, administrable present. Thus everything depends upon an enduring, palpable fidelity that lives with us and for us through time.[53]

In her faithfulness to the rich memory and vivid hope that she found in the Christian tradition, More shifted no gears at the end of her life. She saw no reason to retract or revise the doctrines that had provided, from her earliest efforts, the ligature binding private and civic concerns, personal and institutional ethics. It is so easy to carp at More's critical pronouncements and at her intent, though blinkered, desire to strengthen the meaning of a common good. But such dismissal may be the result of our own commoditization. Though it is more difficult and often exasperating, listening to her individualistic voice on matters of practical religion seems to me a more generous response, allowing for difference and, perhaps, evoking a certain awe.

❀ EPILOGUE ❀
The Georgian Britomart

On the face of it, no one could be worse suited to the errancy of Arthurian romance than Hannah More. Her writing suggests that she never raised her visor or endorsed serendipity. Securely oriented in moral space, her work stayed focused on national, local, and domestic issues. Although she presented herself as operating on the side of the apostles, one of their agents, such affiliations did not shield her from charges of stiffness and intransigence; in fact, they may have contributed to her amazing (for detractors, completely predictable) naïveté. Despite the phalanx of her supporters, More shunned direct confrontation, preferring to disclose the financial accounting about the Yearsley Trust to Mrs. Montagu rather than to Ann Yearsley herself, and deputizing Sir Abraham Elton to speak to the aggrieved Mr. Bere rather than doing so herself. As a meliorist it is curious that, once stung, she would recoil. A sense of control—of her philanthropy as well as literary style—was of paramount importance to More. Hence, she often wrote her own ticket, declaring that imaginative, fanciful forays were not appropriate to the true Christian yet to some extent indulging in them, renouncing the stage yet permitting her dramas to be republished, reprobating the chapmen's wares yet discerningly mimicking their popular tone in her ballads and stories, and denigrating the novels of the circulating library yet providing her own form of competition. By thus reshaping the world to accord with her ideology, does More exemplify that false state of society George Eliot found so distasteful?

For More, whose letters are filled with candid self-appraisals, the circles in which she moved along with her fervent attempts to be a doer, not merely a hearer, of the word, and keep herself "unspotted from the world" (James 1.27) were all evidence of good faith and unflinching commitment. Though not widely traveled, this goal-oriented Britomart who, in her advocacy of living to some purpose, roamed over almost every literary genre (with the exception of comedy) inspired both admiration and dread in her day. When Anna Seward visited More's "silvan cottage," Cowslip Green, she was impressed by the peace of the spot and the dwellers, praising More and her sisters as "bright examples of an heedless age, . . . true disciples of the sacred page" and extending the call of Urania's followers in her desire "to live like you—to be what we admire."[1] In the face of the venomous attacks of her contemporary critics, who were most indignant at her widely publicized projects of reforming the upper ranks and establishing schools for the poor, More experienced no dislocated sense of the present moment, always combining the practical and the cerebral in her aesthetic. She was equally at home arguing over Shakespeare with Dr. Johnson and discussing gardening with Capability Brown, catechizing miners and compiling ironic observations on the domestic habits of lords and ladies. The ebullience of her temperament was remarkable, whether corresponding as Rhyney the rhinoceros with Ele the elephant and Dromy the dromedary, alias Dr. and Mrs. Kennicott, or rhapsodizing over a pair of stockings of her own knitting and a soon-to-be-roasted pig. But she felt deep and lasting wounds too. Although in the "long-protracted trial" of the Blagdon controversy she prayed for her "enemies," trying "to indulge neither resentment nor misanthropy," she admitted to an unnerving erosion of confidence: "Battered, hacked, scalped, and tomahawked as I have been for three years, and continue to be, brought out of every mouth as an object of scorn, and abhorrence, I seem to have nothing to do in the world."[2]

When she was not assailed or vilified, More could be thoroughly at ease writing to her friends and talking about worldly things. While scribbling to Mrs. Garrick, in one instance, about her love and honor for Johnson "with all his faults" and about Patty's rest cure in Dorsetshire, she announced "a plate of rasberries is just overset on my letter—will you forgive?"[3] and promptly carried on with her chatty news. She never, however, catered for popular tastes, even within presumably loyal religious circles. When, as she admitted to Wilberforce in 1824, she begged some books and tracts for her 620 schoolchildren from the British and Foreign Bible Society, the society not only complied but "desired leave to print a good many of [her] tracts on condition that they might leave out whatever they did *not* like, and put in whatever they *did*." Almost three decades after the Repository's heyday More's reply blended curt common sense with a tacit understanding of a different political and economic climate: "I did not accept the terms as I will be answerable for nobody's faults but my own."[4]

Biblically inspired principles, royalist sympathies, and a keen observation of social mores directed all More's work. Her writing, in my estimate, does not illustrate the conversion thesis, that in the eighties, following her withdrawal from the theater, and the nineties, with her friendships among the Clapham sect, she became one of the saints and eschewed fashionable society. Her whole career was devoted to moral reform and the difficulties of adopting and pursuing an otherworldly perspective. Public and private documents consistently rehearse these longings. With their firm, legible, cursive hand and practical use of the whole page, both sides and at times from different angles, her manuscript letters provide at least one glimpse of the private More. Yet the disclosures are not at odds with the public persona. Like the palindrome of her name, Hannah remains the same, read forward or backward, in public or private settings.

Figures associated with religious principles and reform, whether canonized or with irony labeled saints, have been notoriously difficult subjects for biographers and critics. The problems are greater than ever today. How can the biographer adopt *le ton juste* when huge gaps in culture and disposition separate writer and subject? What ethical decisions can be made about the useful disclosures of a letter headed "Burn this"? And how muffled, cautious, or discreet should analysis be when the biographer shares many of the convictions of the subject? Conversely, how vituperative should it get when views clash? These questions were pressing on me, as I was trying to settle my thoughts about Hannah at the same time as I was reading a new biography of Ignatius of Loyola. When sifting through the nearly seven thousand letters that Ignatius of Loyola wrote to "fellow Jesuits, . . . kings and queens, princes and princesses, and nobility of all ranks, to popes, bishops, cardinals, priests, and nuns, and to large numbers of lay people including the poor and humble," his most recent biographer, W. W. Meissner, a Jesuit psychiatrist, concludes that these "exclusively public documents . . . , with rare exceptions, present a public persona—always tactful, devout, courtly in manner, and gracious in tone."[5] Meissner sees aspects of Inigo the courtier, diplomat, and hidalgo throughout the life of this idealizing mystic and saint. His psychoanalytic portrait argues "the remarkable transvaluation of Inigo de Loyola . . . as an effect of grace that found expression through powerful and dynamic psychological processes."[6] Comparisons with More are really quite striking. Although Meissner extracts many psychoanalytic insights, about phallic narcissism, masochistic perversion, and obsessionality, for instance, from these largely public documents, the interchangeable public and private portraits of More show a determined, resilient, strong willed, and independent woman. Aside from highly opinionated comments on religion and public morality, there is a certain opacity about sex. Without sounding infantilized or regressive, she inquires after friends' children, makes gifts for them, longs to romp with them on the lawns, and clearly enjoys their company. After the disappointment of Mr. Turner, there are no liaisons or affairs, not even any hinted at or revealed fantasies. Her closeness to her sisters and friendships with many older women notwithstanding, there is also no discernible evidence of homosexuality. I find the suggestion of a colleague, who works in another area, that

More's interest in Yearsley could be construed as lesbian, very doubtful. For all their shared dedication as reformers and letter writers, it seems to me, ultimately, that more contrasts than congruencies exist between the Georgian cultural warrior and one of the foremost saints of the Counter-Reformation.

Meissner's revealing study prompted me to reconsider the curious silences in Hannah More. Are these sexual lacunae so strange, or inexplicable, or pathetic after all? Because her long, strictly devout and presumably celibate life, with its migrainous bouts, digestive disorders, and pulmonary weakness lacks the saucy gossip of Catharine Macaulay and her toy-boy husband, the lurid anguish of Frances Burney's unanaesthetized mastectomy, and the early tragedy of Mary Wollstonecraft's death from postpartum septicemia, is it therefore less compelling? For me Hannah More remains a complex human phenomenon. Her incorrectness, in terms of the uncritical acceptance of hierarchy, the equation of rank with mental capacity, and the endorsement of the two spheres, means that I continue to grapple and wrestle with her sense of surety. "Unrecognized and unmodulated countertransference," warns Meissner, "distorts objectivity and impairs judgment throughout the process."[7] There is little chance, I believe, that any reader today will idealize Hannah More, whose outlook on philanthropy, women's importance, and religious integrity was defined and limited by her age. Yet More is not simply a cold, strange figure of the past. She devoted her long career to one overriding cause: galvanizing women of the middle and upper ranks to act, not as domestic ornaments, but as thinking, engaged, and responsible social beings.

Notes

1. More is Less

1. In their planning of Barley Wood the sisters may have been influenced by two books of design by architect John Plaw: *Ferme Ornée; or, Rural Improvements; A Series of Domestic and Ornamental Designs* (1795) and *Sketches for Country Houses, Villas, and Rural Dwellings Calculated for Persons of Moderate Income and for Comfortable Retirement* (1800). From 1824–26, although she was confined to her second-floor apartment, More had spent nearly £1,000 in repairs and had exceeded her income in doing so. She wished to sell the reversion of Barley Wood with the buyer becoming its owner and occupant only on her death. But the prodigality of her servants, unknown to the largely bedridden More, forced her to sell Barley Wood. William Henry Harford, a younger brother of John Scandrett Harford (the touted model for "Coelebs" in More's novel *Coelebs in Search of a Wife*), bought the estate in a private sale. The Harfords occupied Barley Wood—with few major changes—for most of the nineteenth century. Henry Herbert Wills, of the tobacco empire, bought the house in 1897. He and his wife Monica (later Dame Monica) made several changes, replacing the home's Georgian symmetry with pseudo-Jacobean wings, a new dining room, and a billiard room, and laying out the formal garden. Barley Wood stayed in the Wills family for seventy years. In 1974 a consortium of building companies, the H.A.T. Group Limited, bought and occupied Barley Wood as their administrative headquarters. In 1978 the Locke and Porteus urns were re-erected on the porch outside the group chairman's office. See Alice Harford, ed., *Annals of the Harford Family* (London: Westminster Press, 1909); John Rutter, *Delineations of the North Western Divisions of the County of Somerset and Its Antediluvian Bone Caverns* (London: Longman, Rees, 1829); Mrs. L.H. Sigourney, *Pleasant Memories of Pleasant Lands* (Boston: James Munroe, 1842); *The History of Barley Wood* (booklet prepared by the H.A.T. Group, Wrington, 1980).

2. Frank K. Prochaska, *Women and Philanthropy in Nineteenth-Century England* (Oxford: Clarendon, 1980), 6–7.

3. Deborah M. Valenze, *Prophetic Sons and Daughters: Female Preaching and Popular Religion in Industrial England* (Princeton: Princeton University Press, 1985), 9–10. In tracing the steps from "cottage solidarity" to "conservative domesticity" in popular evangelicalism, Valenze isolates Hannah More, Susannah Wesley, and Mary Bosanquet, who "determine our notions of eighteenth-century female piety" (50).

4. E.P. Thompson, "The Moral Economy of the English Crowd in the Eighteenth Century," *Past and Present* 50 (1971): 136. Thompson does not mince words about More's "sententious" caroling in "The Riot": "the nature of gentlefolks being what it is, a

133

thundering good riot in the next parish was more likely to oil the wheels of charity than the sight of Jack Anvil on his knees in church" (126).

5. Mitzi Myers, " 'A Peculiar Protection': Hannah More and the Cultural Politics of the Blagdon Controversy," in *History, Gender & Eighteenth-Century Literature*, ed. Beth Fowkes Tobin (Athens: University of Georgia Press, 1994), 239.

6. Marlene LeGates, "The Cult of Womanhood in Eighteenth-Century Thought," *Eighteenth-Century Studies* 10 (1976–77): 38.

7. M.G. Jones, *Hannah More* (Cambridge: Cambridge University Press, 1952), 12.

8. William Roberts, *Memoirs of the Life and Correspondence of Mrs. Hannah More* (London: R.B. Seeley and W. Burnside, 1834), 2:414.

9. She was not impressed by the publication of some of Dr. Johnson's letters in 1788. As she remarked to her sisters, "they are such letters as ought to have been *written*, but ought never to have been *printed*" (W. Roberts, *Memoirs*, 2:100). Later when she was solicited as a contributor to the projected Walpole correspondence, she was "extremely careful" and would consent only to those "quite disencumbered of private history, private characters, &c" (W. Roberts, *Memoirs*, 3:22–23).

10. Annette M. B. Meakin, *Hannah More: A Biographical Study* (London: John Murray, 1911), 8.

11. Letters from H. More to her sisters, dated 1783 and 1781; Roberts, 1:270–71, 202, 206, 211.

12. Elizabeth Kowaleski-Wallace, *Their Fathers' Daughters: Hannah More, Maria Edgeworth, and Patriarchal Complicity* (New York: Oxford University Press, 1991), 12, 11, 23. She also accuses Roberts of "repression of the biological mother" by barely disguising "his discomfort over Mrs. More's déclassé origins" (24).

13. Letter from Miss More, London 1774; W. Roberts, *Memoirs*, 1:49.

14. Sylvia Harcstark Myers characterizes More as a bit of a parvenue, one "of the younger generation who came to prominence as bluestockings," but "probably the most regressive in her attitudes towards the advancement of women." Myers' treatment of the earlier part of More's career and of her poem "The Bas-Bleu; or, Conversation" as "a rather superficial estimate of the significance of the bluestockings without going deeper into the motives of the older women" is itself cursory; see *The Bluestocking Circle: Women, Friendship, and the Life of the Mind in Eighteenth-Century England* (Oxford: Clarendon, 1990), 260–62.

15. Letter from H. More to one of her sisters, Jan. 1779; W. Roberts, *Memoirs*, 1:147.

16. Letter from H. More to her Sister, Oxford, 19 Aug. 1783; W. Roberts, *Memoirs*, 1:288.

17. Letter from Mr. Newton to Miss H. More, 30 Dec. 1790; W. Roberts, *Memoirs*, 2:243.

18. Letter from Sir James Stonehouse to Miss Sarah More, 17 Oct. 1791; W. Roberts, *Memoirs*, 2:283.

19. Letter from H. More to her sister, 17 Feb. 1786; W. Roberts, *Memoirs*, 2:13.

20. Letter from H. More to her sister, Adelphi 1781; W. Roberts, *Memoirs*, 1:197.

21. Letter from Miss More, London 1776; W. Roberts, *Memoirs*, 1:66.

22. John Latimer, *The Annals of Bristol in the Eighteenth Century* (London: Butler and Tanner, 1893), 331.

23. John Locke, *Some Thoughts Concerning Education*, ed. John W. and Jean S. Yolton (Oxford: Clarendon Press, 1989), section 196, p. 252.

24. Jonathan Swift, "The Furniture of a Woman's Mind," in *Poetical Works*, ed. Herbert Davis (Oxford: Clarendon, 1967), 328.

25. As quoted from the *Spectator* in Marion Phillips and W.S. Tomkinson, *English Women in Life and Letters* (Oxford: Clarendon, 1926), 114.

26. Reginald Blount, ed., *Mrs. Montagu, Queen of the Blues* (London: Constable, 1923), 2:218.

27. As quoted in A.M.B. Meakin, *Hannah More*, 15.

28. Patrick McGrath, *The Merchant Venturers of Bristol* (Bristol: Society of Merchant Venturers, 1975), 90, 100, 101.

29. Gary Kelly, *English Fiction of the Romantic Period, 1789–1830* (London: Longman, 1989), 33, 71.

30. Letter from H. More, London 1775; W. Roberts, *Memoirs*, 1:58.

31. Letter from J. Langhorne to H. More, Blagdon House, 12 February 1775; W. Roberts, *Memoirs*, 1:21.

32. William Blackstone, *Commentaries on the Laws of England*, 3d ed. (Oxford: Clarendon, 1765–69), 1:441.

33. Arthur Roberts, ed. *Mendip Annals; or, A Narrative of the Charitable Labours of Hannah and Martha More in their Neighbourhood* (London: James Nisbet, 1859), 222, 227.

34. Letter from H. More to Mrs. Kennicott, Cowslip Green, 1789: "I hate Bath"; W. Roberts, *Memoirs*, 2:212. Letter from H. More to Mr. Wilberforce, Cowslip Green, 1794; W. Roberts, *Memoirs*, 2:404.

35. Letter from H. More to Mrs. T——, Barley Wood, 1802; W. Roberts, *Memoirs*, 3:172.

36. W. Roberts, *Memoirs*, 3:327. Letter from Mrs. H. More to Lady Olivia Sparrow, 1815: "It is rather ridiculous that I have not a single copy of St. Paul for my sisters to read, the first edition having been sold the first day"; W. Roberts, *Memoirs*, 3:438.

37. Letter from Mrs. H. More to Mr. Knox, June 1816; W. Roberts, *Memoirs*, 3:449.

38. Although the letter is undated, a proposed date is 1816. British Library Egerton MS 1965, 56.

39. Letter from Mrs. H. More to Sir W. Pepys, 17 June 1825, where she "reckoned up thirty physicians who had attended [her]"; W. Roberts, *Memoirs*, 4:235. Letter from Mrs. H. More to the Rev. T. Gisborne, 28 Feb. 1827, where the reckoning has changed to fifteen; W. Roberts, *Memoirs*, 4:274.

40. Letter from Mrs. H. More to Mr. Wilberforce, undated; W. Roberts, *Memoirs*, 4:271.

41. More uses the description in a letter (1 Sept. 1825) to her last attending physician, Dr. Carrick, explaining "the newly opened passage" to the adjoining chamber of her bedroom: "This opening so enlarges my Bastile as to extend my walk from 24 to 48 feet." Bodleian MS Eng. Lett. d.2, 261.

42. W. Roberts, *Memoirs*, 4:86; Letter from Mrs. H. More to Mary and Margaret Roberts, undated, W. Roberts, *Memoirs*, 4:118.

43. Letter from Mrs. H. More to the Rev. Daniel Wilson, 16 Oct. 1819; W. Roberts, *Memoirs*, 4:63.

44. Letter from Mrs. H. More to Mr. Wilberforce, 26 Dec. 1823; W. Roberts, *Memoirs*, 4:192.

45. Letter from Mrs. H. More to Sir W. W. Pepys, 1 July 1823; W. Roberts, *Memoirs*, 4:182.

46. W. Roberts, *Memoirs*, 4:253.

47. Letter from Mrs. H. More to Zachary Macaulay, 19 Feb. 1796; W. Roberts, *Memoirs*, 2:460.

48. Letter from Miss H. More to the Rev. John Newton, Cowslip Green, 1787; W. Roberts, *Memoirs*, 2:88.

49. Letter from Miss H. More to a Friend, 1 Jan. 1792; W. Roberts, *Memoirs*, 2:311.

50. Letter from Mrs. H. More to Mr. Knox, June 1816; W. Roberts, *Memoirs*, 3:449.

51. Letter from Mrs. H. More to W. Wilberforce, 31 July 1824; Bodleian MS Wilberforce c. 48, 35.

52. Letter to Mrs. H. More from Millicent Sparrow, 11 Nov. 1819; British Library, Egerton MS 1965, 80. Letter from Mrs. H. More to Lady Olivia Sparrow (October 1815?); British Library, Egerton MS 1965, 40.

53. A.L. (incomplete) from H. More to Marianne [Thornton], [1828], MY 719; Huntington Library.

54. Letter from Mrs. H. More to Mrs. King, 10 Sept. 1813; Roberts, 3:401.

55. Leonore Davidoff and Catherine Hall, *Family Fortunes: Men and Women of the English Middle Class, 1780–1850* (London: Hutchinson, 1987), 83. Davidoff and Hall offer one of the most nuanced and instructive views of "the contradictory nature of More's philosophy . . . and the space it allowed for alternative interpretations" (171–72).

56. Letter from Mrs. H. More to Sir W. Pepys, October 1825; W. Roberts, *Memoirs*, 4:249. *Articles of Agreement to be observed by a Society of Women Held in the Parishes of Shipham and Rowberrow in Somersetshire, Commenced in September 1792*. This broadsheet is housed in the small library in the vestry of All Saints Church, Wrington.

57. Letter from Mrs. H. More to Misses Mary and Margaret Roberts, 1818; W. Roberts, *Memoirs*, 4:35.

58. Letter from Mrs. H. More to Sir W.W. Pepys, 24 Jan. 1817; W. Roberts, *Memoirs*, 3:471–72. Letter from Mrs. H. More to John Scandrett Harford, 4 Jan. 1827, *Annals of the Harford Family*, ed. Alice Harford (London: Westminster Press, 1909), 105.

59. Letter from Mrs. H. More to Sir W. Pepys, 19 Aug. 1822; W. Roberts, *Memoirs*, 4:161.

60. Ian C. Bradley, *The Call to Seriousness: The Evangelical Impact on the Victorians* (London: Macmillan, 1976), 44.

61. Letter from Miss H. More to Mrs. Carter, 1 Oct. 1789; W. Roberts, *Memoirs*, 2:200.

62. Letter from Miss H. More to Mr. Wilberforce, 1791; W. Roberts; *Memoirs*, 2:303.

63. Letter from Miss H. More to Mrs. Kennicott, 2 Aug. 1791; W. Roberts, *Memoirs*, 2:309–10.

64. Letter from Mrs. H. More to Rev. J. Newton, 15 Sept. 1796; W. Roberts, *Memoirs*, 2:465.

65. W. Roberts, *Memoirs*, 2:465.

66. W. Roberts, *Memoirs*, 2:465–66.

67. Letter from Mrs. H. More to Mr. Wilberforce, 1801; W. Roberts, *Memoirs*, 3:148–49.

68. Donna Landry, *The Muses of Resistance: Laboring-Class Women's Poetry in Britain, 1739–1796* (Cambridge: Cambridge University Press, 1990), 286, n. 28.

69. Letter from Mrs. H. More to Sir W.W. Pepys, 15 Oct. 1821; W. Roberts, *Memoirs*, 4:139.

70. Landry, *Muses of Resistance*, 123. Her argument echoes E.P. Thompson's remarks on the Burkean message given to the laboring poor: " 'Patience, labour, sobriety, frugality, and religion should be recommended to them; all the rest is downright fraud' "; see *The Making of the English Working Class* (London: V. Gollanz, 1963), 61.

71. Charles Dickens, "Covering a Multitude of Sins" (Chapter 8), *Bleak House* (New York: Bantam Books, 1983), 95.

72. Letter from Miss H. More, 17 Jan. 1782 [no addressee]; W. Roberts, *Memoirs*, 1:222.

73. Letter from Miss H. More to Mrs. Boscawen, Sept. 1788; W. Roberts, *Memoirs*, 2:137.

74. Letter from Miss H. More to Rev. J. Newton, May 1791; W. Roberts, *Memoirs*, 2:257.

75. Wilkie Collins, "Second Period. The Discovery of the Truth, First Narrative Contributed by Miss Clack; niece of the late Sir John Verinder, Chapter One," in *The Moonstone: A Romance*, ed. J.I.M. Stewart (Harmondsworth, Middlesex: Penguin Books, 1966), 238.

76. Letter from Miss H. More to Mr. Wilberforce, 1794; W. Roberts, *Memoirs*, 2:409.

77. Judith Hawley, ed., introduction, *Jane Collier: The Art of Ingeniously Tormenting* (Bristol: Thoemmes Press, 1994), xxxvi.

78. Letter from Jane Collier to Mr. Richardson, 4 Oct. 1748, *The Correspondence of Samuel Richardson* (London: Richard Phillips, 1804), 2:62–63.

79. *A Description of Millenium Hall, and the Country Adjacent . . . By a Gentleman on his Travels* (London: J. Newbery, 1762), 7.

80. Walter Marion Crittenden, *The Life and Writings of Mrs. Sarah Scott, Novelist (1723-1795)* (Philadelphia, 1932), 38.

81. *Millenium Hall*, 9, 24, 262.

82. Ibid., 16.

83. Gary Kelly, ed., introduction, *Millenium Hall* (Peterborough: Broadview, 1995), 34.

84. Frances Burney, *Camilla; or, A Picture of Youth*, ed. Edward A. and Lillian D. Bloom (Oxford: Oxford University Press, 1972), 51.

85. Ibid., 36.

86. In assessing his great-aunt, Forster observed, "In form, and sometimes in sentiments, she was indebted to Hannah More, but she had a lighter touch, and sketched rather than underlined her religious and moral conclusions"; see *Marianne Thornton: A Domestic Biography 1797–1887* (New York: Harcourt, Brace, 1956), 265.

87. The Reynolds painting hangs in the Georgian House, Great George Street, Bristol. The Opie, Bird, Clint, and Slater portraits are in the archives of the Bristol Museum and Art Gallery. Slater's drawing is also in the Hannah More Papers at the British Library (MS. Add. 42511. f. 20); another engraving of the Clint portrait is in the Pierpont Morgan

Library, New York. One of the two Pickersgill paintings is in storage at the National Portrait Gallery, London. A Minton statuette (c. 1835) in unglazed biscuit porcelain "after the portrait by H.W. Pickersgill" is displayed in the Bristol Museum and Art Gallery (NX 881). In a letter to Sir W.W. Pepys, 15 Oct. 1821, More complained of being "condemned, sorely against [my] will, and on the verge of eternity, to see 'the lack-lustre eye,' and corrugated visage, snatched a little while from oblivion"; W. Roberts, *Memoirs*, 4:136. My colleague, Robert James Merrett, has examined "how literary men belittled portraiture"; see "Pictorialism in Eighteenth-Century Fiction: Visual Thinking and Narrative Diversity," in *Time, Literature and the Arts: Essays in Honor of Samuel L. Macey*, ed. Thomas R. Cleary (University of Victoria: English Literary Studies, monograph no. 61, 1994), 168. Consider, too, the contrasts between John Bogle's miniature and Edward Francesco Burney's portrait of Frances Burney and the insights Margaret Anne Doody extracts from them; see Margaret Anne Doody, *Frances Burney: The Life in the Works* (New Brunswick, N.J.: Rutgers University Press, 1988), 153–54.

88. Letter from Miss H. More to Mrs. Boscawen, 1786; W. Roberts, *Memoirs*, 2:37.

89. Letter from Mrs. H. More to Lady Olivia Sparrow, 27 Dec. 1813; W. Roberts, *Memoirs*, 3:406.

90. Letters from Mrs. H. More to Hart Davis, 16 Oct. 1821, and to Misses Mary and Margaret Roberts, Nov. 1821; W. Roberts, *Memoirs*, 4:126, 128.

91. In a letter to her sisters in 1782, More reported Johnson's words: " 'it is dangerous to say a word of poetry before her; it is talking of the art of war before Hannibal' "; W. Roberts, *Memoirs*, 1:251–52. In a letter to Hannah and Patty, 2 Oct. 1789, Wilberforce declares, "Your labours can only be equalled by Spenser's lady-knights"; see *Mendip Annals*, p. 21. With Hannah as Britomart, Patty as Belphoebe, and Wilberforce as "the Red Cross Knight" (W. Roberts, *Memiors*, 2:193), the Spenserian connections were well established. Charlotte Yonge refers to "the undaunted Britomart and Belphoebe" and to "the Britomart of Mendip" couching her lance against Sansfoy (Monsieur Dupont); see *Hannah More* (Boston: Roberts Brothers, 1890), 115, 124. "Your Scipio in petticoats . . . mocks gravity into hysterics," charged Thomas Bere, *An Appeal to the Public, on the Controversy Between Hannah More, the Curate of Blagdon, and the Rev. Sir A. Elton* (Bath: R. Cruttwell, 1801), 6. The Reverend Sir Abraham Elton countered Bere's "attempt to asperse the name of that admirable Lady, to diminish her influence, and reduce to nothing her institutions" by reminding him that "(like Scipio) her dignity is best consulted by silence" and then jousting with his opponent over his (Bere's) misuse of classical quotations; see *A Letter to the Rev. Thomas Bere, Rector of Butcombe, Occasioned by his late unwarrantable attack on Mrs. Hannah More* (London: Cadell and Davies, 1801), 1–2.

92. Edmund Spenser, *The Faerie Queene* III.ii.9, *The Works of Edmund Spenser: A Variorum Edition*, ed. E. Greenlaw, C.G. Osgood, F. M. Padelford, *et al.* (Baltimore: Johns Hopkins University Press, 1932–49), 3:22.

93. Pamela Joseph Benson, *The Invention of the Renaissance Woman; The Challenge of Female Independence in the Literature and Thought of Italy and England* (University Park, Pa.: Penn State University Press, 1992), 261.

94. *Faerie Queene*, III.i.61; ii.26; xii.33.

95. "Letters and memoirs are silent on so intimate a theme," observes M.G. Jones; however, Jones does attribute a period similar to "the modern nervous breakdown . . . to

William Turner's defection." See *Hannah More*, 17–18. An early biographer, Henry Thompson, had indicated that More "was recovering from an attack of ague"; see *The Life of Hannah More with Notices of Her Sisters* (London: T. Cadell, 1838), 22.

96. Letter from Horace Walpole to Miss H. More, 21 Aug. 1792; W. Roberts, *Memoirs*, 2:352.

97. Letter from H. More to her sister, 1778; W. Roberts, *Memoirs*, 1:132; W. Roberts, *Memoirs*, 2:56.

98. Letter from Mr. C. Burney to Mrs. H. More, April 1799; W. Roberts, *Memoirs*, 3:69.

99. W. Roberts, *Memoirs*, 4:208.

100. Letter from Reverend J. Bean to Mrs. H. More, May 1799; W. Roberts, *Memoirs*, 3:92.

101. Letter from Reverend Dr. Magee to Mrs. H. More, 7 Sept. 1811; W. Roberts, *Memoirs*, 3:344.

102. Sappho Search, *A Poetical Review of Miss Hannah More's Strictures on Female Education. In a series of Anapestic Epistles* (London: T. Hurst, 1800), 8–9.

103. Ibid., 74.

104. *Nil Admirari, or, A Smile at a Bishop, The Works of Peter Pindar* (London: J. Walker, 1794–1801), 5:180–82.

105. "Expostulation to Miss Hannah More," *Nil Admirari*, 5:201.

106. Rev. Sir Archibald MacSarcasm [William Shaw], *The Life of Hannah More with A Critical Review of Her Writings* (London: T. Hurst, 1802), 202.

107. Thomas B. Macaulay, Letter to Napier, 15 June 1837, *The Life and Letters of Lord Macaulay*, ed. George Otto Trevelyan (New York: Harper, 1876), 1:405–6.

108. Thomas DeQuincey, "Recollections of Hannah More," *The Collected Writings of Thomas De Quincey*, ed. David Masson (London: A. & C. Black, 1897), 14:115, 130, 105.

109. W. Roberts, *Memoirs*, 4:399, 375–76.

110. Henry Thompson, *Life of Hannah More*, 78.

111. Thomas Taylor, *Memoir of Mrs. Hannah More: With Notices of Her works, and Sketches of Her Contemporaries* (London: Joseph Rickerby, 1838), a3.

112. Ibid., 163.

113. Ibid., 241.

114. Ibid., 400.

115. Mrs. E. K. Elwood, "Mrs. Hannah More," *Memoirs of the Literary Ladies of England* (London: Henry Colburn, 1843), 1:260.

116. Mrs. Helen C. Knight, *A New Memoir of Hannah More; or, Life in Hall and Cottage* (New York: M.W. Dodd, 1851), vii, 23.

117. Mrs. Clara Lucas Balfour, *A Sketch of Mrs. Hannah More and Her Sisters* (London: W. & F.G. Cash, 1854), 48. Catherine J. Hamilton, "Hannah More," *Women Writers: Their Works and Ways* (1892; Freeport, N.Y.: Books for Libraries Press, 1971), 94. Two generations earlier Thomas Taylor had scotched possible comparisons with "Harriet Martineau's ingenious but ineffective compositions; the former comes home to the hearts of the poor, the latter scarcely reaches them at all." See Taylor, *Memoir*, 418.

118. Valerie Sanders, *Reason over Passion: Harriet Martineau and the Victorian Novel* (Sussex: Harvester Press, 1986), 142, 160.

119. George Eliot, Letter to John Sibree, *George Eliot's Life as Related in Her Letters and Journal*, ed. J. W. Cross (New York: T. Y. Crowell, 1884), 170.

120. Yonge, *Hannah More*, 12, 227.

121. L.B. Walford, *Four Biographies from 'Blackwoods'* (Edinburgh: W. Blackwood, 1888). Marion Harland [M.V. Terhune], *Hannah More* (New York: G.P. Putnam's Sons, 1900). Norman Pearson, "The Lighter Side of Hannah More," *The Nineteenth Century* 59 (1906): 842–58. Annette Meakin, *Hannah More: A Biographical Study* (London: John Murray, 1911). Margaret Tabor, *Pioneer Women*, second series (London: Sheldon Press, 1927). Betsy Aikin-Sneath, "Hannah More," *London Mercury* 28 (1933): 528–35. Philip Child, "Portrait of a Woman of Affairs—Old Style," *University of Toronto Quarterly* 3 (1933): 87–102. S. Addleshaw, "Hannah More, Blue-Stocking and Reformer," *Church Quarterly Review* 118 (1934): 57–79. Rev. James Silvester, *Hannah More Christian Philanthropist: A Centenary Biography* (London: Thynne, 1934). Margaret Cropper, *Sparks among the Stubble* (London: Longmans, Green, 1955). Paddy Lewis, "The Little Girl Who Wanted to See Bookshops and Bishops," *Illustrated Bristol News*, September 1963, 26–7.

122. Augustine Birrell, "Hannah More," *Men, Women, & Books* (London: Duckworth, 1894), 40.

123. Augustine Birrell, "Hannah More Once More," *In the Name of the Bodleian and Other Essays* (New York: Charles Scribner's Sons, 1905), 174. The only reply to Birrell is Annette Meakin's conservationist note: "surely he would have done better to present them to the London Library in St. James's Square which only possesses a miserably incomplete edition"; see Meakin, *Hannah More*, xi.

124. E. M. Forster, *Marianne Thornton*, 4, 69.

125. Mary Alden Hopkins, *Hannah More and Her Circle* (New York: Longmans, Green, 1947). Marlene Hess, *The Didactic Art of Hannah More* (Ann Arbor: University Microfilms International, 1983). Jeremy and Margaret Collingwood, *Hannah More* (Oxford: Lion, 1990).

126. M.G. Jones, *Hannah More*, 114, 228.

127. Luther Weeks Courtney, *Hannah More's Interest in Education and Government* (Waco, Texas: Baylor University Press, 1929), 64.

128. Eleanor Ty, *Unsex'd Revolutionaries: Five Women Novelists of the 1790s* (Toronto: University of Toronto Press, 1993), 17, 42, 71, 76, 119.

129. Claudia L. Johnson, *Jane Austen: Women Politics and the Novel* (Chicago: University of Chicago Press, 1988), 18.

130. Felicity Nussbaum, *The Autobiographical Subject: Gender and Ideology in Eighteenth-Century England* (Baltimore: Johns Hopkins University Press, 1989), 145. Her view is shared by others; see Moira Ferguson, "Resistance and Power in the Life and Writings of Ann Yearsley," *Eighteenth Century* 27 (1986): 247–68, and Donna Landry, *The Muses of Resistance*, 17–19, 21, 150. Contending that More's response to Yearsley "demonstrates the close relation between aesthetic and social judgements of the peasant poets," Morag Shiach concludes that More wanted Yearsley "to remain dependent, marginal, and constrained by her domestic relations"; see *Discourse on Popular Culture; Class, Gender and History in Cultural Analysis, 1730 to the Present* (Cambridge: Polity Press, 1989), 46, 56.

131. Moira Ferguson, *Subject to Others: British Women Writers and Colonial Slavery, 1670–1834* (London: Routledge, 1992), 220.

132. Mitzi Myers, "Reform or Ruin: 'A Revolution in Female Manners,'" *Studies in Eighteenth-Century Culture* 2 (1982): 211–12.

133. Mitzi Myers, "'A Peculiar Protection,'" in *History, Gender & Eighteenth-Century Literature*, 245–46.

134. Mary Poovey, *The Proper Lady and the Woman Writer: Ideology as Style in the Works of Mary Wollstonecraft, Mary Shelley, and Jane Austen* (Chicago: University of Chicago Press, 1984), 40.

135. Leonore Davidoff and Catherine Hall, *Family Fortunes*, 171.

136. Angela Carter, *The Sadeian Woman: An Exercise in Cultural History* (London: Virago, 1979), 55.

137. Letter from Mrs. H. More to Dr. Beadon, Bishop of Bath and Wells, 1801; W. Roberts, *Memoirs*, 3:130.

138. Barbara Newman, "On the Ethics of Feminist Historiography," *Exemplaria* 2 (1990): 702–3, 705.

139. "Directions for Uniting Amusement with Instruction, in the use of Mrs. Hannah More's Much-Admired Cards," *Hannah More's Cards of Wisdom, Intended as Conversation for Two or More Persons to which is added A Game as a further Amusement for a Party* (Birmingham: J.T. Maund, n.d.).

140. Answer Card no. 15, Ibid.

141. Roberts describes her "pensive parting look upon her bowers," 4:280. More refers to her previous servants in a letter to Mr. Wilberforce, Windsor Terrace, 27 Oct. 1828; Roberts, 4:294. As an example of a "forceful" irony Elizabeth Kowaleski-Wallace maintains that the servants' cheating "reveals both their lack of respect and their perception of her true powerlessness" and concludes that More's "alliance with the superior power of the church establishment failed to empower her"; *Their Fathers' Daughters*, 25.

142. Letter from Mrs. H. More to John Harford, Barley Wood, 5 Mar. 1828; *Annals of the Harford Family*, ed. Alice Harford, 106.

143. Roberts, 4:288.

2. The "Complicated Temptation" of the Theater

1. See the Letter from H. More to her sister, London 1787; W. Roberts, *Memoirs*, 2:51–52.

2. W. Roberts, *Memoirs*, 1:163.

3. Letter from H. More to her sister, Hampton 1782; W. Roberts, *Memoirs*, 1:244.

4. Preface to the Tragedies (1801), *The Works of Hannah More*, a New Edition, 11 vols (London: T. Cadell, 1830), 2:139.

5. General Preface to the Collected Works, *The Works of Hannah More*, I:xv.

6. Peter Pindar, "To the Reviewers," *The Works of Peter Pindar*, 3:7.

7. Ellen Donkin, "The Paper War of Hannah Cowley and Hannah More," in *Curtain Calls: British and American Women and the Theater, 1660–1820*, ed. Mary Anne Schofield and Cecilia Macheski (Athens: Ohio University Press, 1991), 158.

8. Allan Cunningham, "Biographical and Critical History of the Literature of the Last Fifty Years," *The Athenaeum*, 16 Nov. 1833, 777.

9. Henry Thompson, *Life of Hannah More*, 32–33.

10. Thomas Davies, *Memoirs of the Life of David Garrick* (London: Longman, Hurst, Rees, and Orme, 1808), 2:353.

11. Robert Chambers, *Cyclopaedia of English Literature* (London: W. & R. Chambers, 1858), 1:237; 2d ed. (London: W. & R. Chambers, 1870), 1:577.

12. Augustine Birrell, *Men, Women, & Books*, 42.

13. M.G. Jones, *Hannah More*, 35. Allardyce Nicoll's *Late Eighteenth Century Drama* (Cambridge: Cambridge University Press, 1955) holds her up as an example of "a withered pseudo-classicism and a false type of romance" (91). Robertson Davies' contribution to *The Revels History of Drama in English*, vol. 4, *1750-1880* (London: Methuen, 1975) insists that her work exhibits "grotesqueries" yet still "claims attention" (169–70).

14. Ciji Ware, *Wicked Company: A Novel of the Eighteenth Century* (New York: Bantam Books, 1992), 641, 581, 659, 664.

15. Letter from H. More to Mr. W. Pepys, September 1788; W. Roberts, *Memoirs*, 2:131.

16. S. Addleshaw, "Hannah More, Blue Stocking and Reformer," 69.

17. These editions have been consulted: *A Search after Happiness: A Pastoral in Three Dialogues* By a Young Lady (Bristol: T. Farley, [1773]); *The Search after Happiness: A Pastoral Drama* Second Edition (Bristol: S. Farley, 1773); *The Search after Happiness: A Pastoral Drama* Third Edition (Bristol: S. Farley, 1774); *The Search after Happiness: A Pastoral Drama* Seventh Edition (London: T. Cadell, 1778); *The Search after Happiness: A Pastoral Drama* Eighth Edition (London: T. Cadell, 1785); *The Search after Happiness: A Pastoral Drama* Ninth Edition, with additions (London: T. Cadell, 1787); *The Search after Happiness: A Pastoral Drama* Eleventh Edition, with additions (London: T. Cadell, 1796); *The Search after Happiness: A Pastoral Drama for Young Ladies, The Works of Hannah More in Prose and Verse* (London: T. Cadell, 1801), vol. 1; *The Search after Happiness: A Pastoral Drama for Young Ladies, The Works of Hannah More*, A New Edition (London: T. Cadell, 1830), vol. 1. Unless otherwise indicated, all quotations are from the eighth edition.

18. Mary Russell Mitford, "The English Teacher," *Our Village: Sketches of Rural Character and Scenery*, 2d ed. (London: George B. Whittaker, 1827), 158, 165.

19. Elizabeth Carter's complete translation of Epictetus appeared in 1758. Anna Laetitia Aikin's poems were first published in 1773. Elizabeth Montagu's *Essay on the Writings and Genius of Shakespear* appeared in 1769. Two of Frances Brooke's many-deckered novels were on the market: *The History of Lady Julia Manderville* in 1763 and *The History of Emily Montague* in 1769. Catharine Macaulay's *The History of England, from the Accession of James I to that of the House of Hanover* was an eight-volume study appearing between 1763 and 1783; by the time of the first publication of *Search*, five volumes had appeared, with volumes six and seven following in 1781 and volume eight in 1783.

20. John Locke, *Some Thoughts Concerning Education*, section 70, p. 132.

21. Ibid., section 94, p. 152.

22. Ibid., section 94, p. 152; section 167, p. 223.

23. Samuel Richardson, *Pamela; or, Virtue Rewarded* (London: J.M. Dent, 1914), 2:276, 278.

24. James Thomson, "Spring," *The Seasons*, ed. O. Zippel (Berlin: Mayer & Muller, 1908), lines 1061–68.

25. Patricia Meyer Spacks, "'Always at Variance': Politics of Eighteenth-Century Adolescence," *A Distant Prospect: Eighteenth-Century Views of Childhood* (Los Angeles: W.A. Clark Memorial Library, University of California, 1982), 3.

26. Elizabeth Joceline, "To my truly loving, and most dearly loved Husband, Tourell Iocelin," *The Mothers Legacie, to Her Unborne Childe*, Seventh Impression (London: Robert Allot, 1635), n.p. Dorothy Leigh, *The Mothers Blessing; or, the Godly Counsule of a Gentle-woman, not long since deceased, left behind her for her children* (London: John Budge, 1618), 47.

27. Margaret Newcastle, "A True Relation of My Birth, Breeding and Life," *Nature's Pictures* (London: J. Martin and J. Allestrye, 1655), 369–70. Sara Heller Mendelson points out that although "as an adult Margaret bemoaned her 'negligent' education, . . . [she] seems to have enjoyed a happy childhood because her permissive education allowed her leisure to do exactly as she pleased" (a slightly more indulgent attitude than Urania's); see *The Mental World of Stuart Women* (Brighton: Harvester, 1987), 15.

28. Georges Lamoine, *La Vie Littéraire de Bath et de Bristol, 1750–1800* (Paris: Honoré Champion, 1978), 1:447.

29. Katherine D. Duncan-Jones, "Sidney's Urania," *RES* ns 17 (1966): 126.

30. Hannah More, "Thoughts on the Cultivation of the Heart and Temper in the Education of Daughters," *Essays on various subjects, principally designed for young ladies* (London: T. Cadell, 1777), 133, 145.

31. W. Buller, "On Seeing Miss H. More in the title page of the 2d Edition of the Search after Happiness: A Ballad," *Commonplace Book* ca. 1795–1805 M.a. 179: Folger Shakespeare Library.

32. "Self-conquest is the lesson books should preach, / Self-conquest is the theme the Stage should teach." See prologue, *The Fatal Falsehood, The Works of Hannah More* (1830), 2:236.

33. Norman Pearson, "The Lighter Side of Hannah More," *Nineteenth Century* 59 (1906): 856.

34. All page references to these plays will be based on *The Works of Hannah More*, 11 vols. (London: T. Cadell, 1830), in which the tragedies and preface are in vol. 2.

35. M.A. Doody, *Frances Burney: The Life in the Works*, 75.

36. Ibid., 77.

37. Charles Burney, *Memoirs of the Life and Writings of the Abate Metastasio, including translations of his principal letters* (London: C.G. & J. Robinson, 1796), 1:316.

38. Comparing *The Inflexible Captive* to a more pedestrian but precise English translation, the three-act *Regulus*, by John Hoole, drives home the differences. While Hoole's Regulus postures that "a soul resign'd / In freedom leaves my mind," More's hero amplifies his state into a characteristic philosophical observation:

> I am the same; in laurels or in chains,
> 'Tis the same principle; the same fix'd soul,
> Unmov'd itself, though circumstances change.
> The native vigour of the free-born mind
> Still struggles with, still conquers adverse fortune;
> Soars above chains, invincible though vanquish'd. (332)

The speech of Hoole's Regulus, in such instances as " 'Tis virtue with our blood to serve our country" and "I come to save her from a fatal risk," is bland and commonplace. Stressing the moral imperative of action, More's hero speaks of absolutes like virtue, which is "the price of liberty" (335), and his mission "to save [Rome's] *honour*, to preserve her / From tarnishing her glory" (339). Although Hoole's Regulus notes prosaically that "life is servitude," More's hero explains, "The body is the chain that binds the soul; / A yoke that every mortal must endure" (347).

39. John Hoole, trans., *Regulus. Dramas by Metastasio* (London, 1800), 3:238–310.

40. E.V. Knox thinks Elwina resembles "Iphigenia at least"; see " 'Percy' (The Tale of a Dramatic Success)," *London Mercury* 13 (1925–26): 514. Georges Lamoine compares Elwina to Racine's Bérénice; see *La Vie Littéraire de Bath et de Bristol*, 2:459.

41. "Review of *Percy*," *Monthly Review* 3 (1778): 23; Katharine Rogers, *Feminism in Eighteenth-Century England* (Urbana: University of Illinois Press, 1982), 24.

42. "Epilogue to the Tragedy of Percy." W. b. 464: Folger Shakespeare Library.

43. Having "been judged worthy to be preserved, as the Writers are both well known to the Literati," the letters of More and Cowley to the *Chronicle* (August 1779) were reproduced in the *Gentleman's Magazine* (September 1779).

44. Mrs. Cowley, *Albina, Countess Raimond: A Tragedy* (London: T. Spilsbury, 1779), 78.

45. Ibid., preface, vi.

46. Ibid., 57–61.

47. Ellen Donkin, "The Paper War of Hannah Cowley and Hannah More," 158, 153, 144.

48. Ibid., 150.

49. All quotations from *Sacred Dramas: Chiefly Intended for Young Persons* are taken from *The Works of Hannah More* (London: T. Cadell, 1830), vol. 1.

50. Letter from H. More to her sister, London 1782; Roberts, 1:235.

51. Extract of a letter from Mrs. H. More to Lady Olivia Sparrow, undated; Roberts, 3:415.

52. Philip Child, "Portrait of a Woman of Affairs—Old Style," 96.

53. Letter from H. More to her sister, London 1780; Roberts, 1:172.

54. L.B. Walford, *Four Biographies from 'Blackwood'*, 163.

55. Letter to Hannah More, 21 May [1774?]. Y. c. 204 [1]: Folger Shakespeare Library.

56. "A Medallion Portrait of David Garrick." The lines on the portrait are in the autograph of Hannah More. Y. d. 120 [60]: Folger Shakespeare Library.

57. Letter from H. More to her sister, London 1782; W. Roberts, *Memoirs*, 1:252.

58. Letter from H. More to Mrs. Gwatkin, 5 Mar. 1778; W. Roberts, *Memoirs*, 1:141.

59. A.L.S. to Eva Marie Violetti Garrick, 22 Nov. [1804]: Berg Collection, New York Public Library.

3. Poetics of Beneficence

1. Paul Fussell, *The Rhetorical World of Augustan Humanism* (Oxford: Clarendon, 1965), 46.

2. Ibid., 51, 53.

3. Margaret Anne Doody, *The Daring Muse: Augustan Poetry Reconsidered* (Cambridge: Cambridge University Press, 1985), 237.

4. Kelvin Everest, *English Romantic Poetry* (Milton Keynes: Open University Press, 1990), 10.

5. "Sensibility: An Epistle to the Honourable Mrs. Boscawen," *The Works of Hannah More* (London: T. Cadell, 1830), 1:170. Most of More's poetry appears in Volume 1; the three exceptions are "Inscription in a Beautiful Retreat called Fairy Bower," "Slavery" (under the title "The Black Slave Trade") and "The Feast of Freedom," which appear in Volume 2. Parenthetical references will cite page numbers in these volumes.

6. "The Bas Bleu; or, Conversation," *Works*, 1:303.

7. Ibid., 1:301.

8. J.R. de J. Jackson, *Romantic Poetry by Women: A Bibliography, 1770–1835* (Oxford: Clarendon Press, 1993), 69, 71, 75, 80.

9. Letter from H. More to Mr. W. Pepys, Bristol, 17 July 1784; W. Roberts, *Memoirs*, 1:339.

10. Anne K. Mellor, *Romanticism and Gender* (New York: Routledge, 1993), 60.

11. "Inscription in Beautiful Retreat called Fairy Bower," *Works*, 2:47.

12. Letter from H. More to her sisters, London 1776; W. Roberts, *Memoirs*, 1:58.

13. Letters from H. More to her sisters, London 1776, 1777; W. Roberts, *Memoirs*, 1:71, 125.

14. "Florio: A Tale for Fine Gentlemen and Fine Ladies," *Works*, 1:339.

15. Letters from H. More to her sisters, London 1776; Oxford, 13 June 1782; London 1782; W. Roberts, *Memoirs*, 1:64, 262, 251–52.

16. Letter from H. More to Mrs. Boscawen, Bristol 1780; W. Roberts, *Memoirs*, 1:188.

17. In her study of poetry of the preceding age, Margaret Anne Doody claims that "it was in this record of change and rapid alteration that Ovid was most useful to the Augustan poets"; see *The Daring Muse*, 89.

18. M.G. Jones, *Hannah More*, 17.

19. When reading Scott's *Rokeby* almost four decades later, More discovered, as she related in a letter (12 Feb. 1813) to Lady Olivia Sparrow, that "the circumstance of Mortham's stabbing his wife in her brother's arms is precisely the same as the catastrophe in a Legendary Tale, called Sir Eldred of the Bower, written by an unworthy friend of yours"; W. Roberts, *Memoirs*, 3:393.

20. A lightheartedness is evident in More's letters about the poem, especially in the letter entitled "The Bas Blanc," describing the pair of stockings she knitted for one of Mrs. Pepys's children. Writing under the pseudonymn borrowed from Berquin of "L'Amie des Enfans," she comments on the knitting project in literary terms. "The subject is simple, but it has a beginning, middle, and end." She has taken "care to shun too pointed a conclusion" and "to unite the two great essentials of composition, ease and strength." As for the broken thread, she trusts that "none but the eye of a professor, which looks into the interior, will detect it." Pleased with the clockwork as a "bold attempt to unite poetry with mechanics," she deposits this gift "in the Pepys collection, humbly hoping . . . it may be found as useful as many a black-lettered manuscript of more recondite learning." See W. Roberts, *Memoirs*, 1:313–15.

21. *The Bluestocking Circle*, 262. As Walpole assessed the poem (6 Mar. 1784), "though there is a quantity of learning, it has all the air of negligence, instead of that of pedantry"; W. Roberts, *Memoirs*, 1:335–36.

22. More was anxious enough about the poem in its manuscript stages (1783–86) to send separate sections and elaborate instructions for opening them to Mr. Pepys and Miss Hamilton. Although she chattily described a gathering at Mrs. Ord's, where she defended Pope against Dryden, as "delectable in the blue way," and found herself almost "ashamed" to relate Johnson's flattery, she maintained a "strict . . . embargo" on the copying of her text. Since Pepys persisted in encouraging her to print the poem, she relented by admitting in a letter (7 Jan. 1785), "I have been brushing the dust off these blue stockings a little, and have added a few stitches to them." See W. Roberts, *Memoirs*, 1:296, 317, 319–20, 322, 382.

23. *Thoughts on the Importance of the Manners of the Great to General Society*, *Works*, 11:49–50.

24. T. Taylor, *Memoir*, 72.

25. Charlotte Yonge excerpts Barbauld's poem; *Hannah More*, 47. The sixteen-year-old son of the Scottish divine James Beattie took a different notice of the poem by translating it into Latin as a school exercise; see W. Roberts, *Memoirs*, 2:341–42.

26. Letter from H. More to Horace Walpole, Cowslip Green, 27 July 1789; W. Roberts, *Memoirs*, 2:164.

27. Letter from H. More to her sisters, London, 11 Jan. 1788; W. Roberts, *Memoirs*, 2:99.

28. Letter from H. More to her sisters, London 1788; W. Roberts, *Memoirs*, 2:97.

29. Robert Isaac and Samuel Wilberforce, Letter of 28 Oct. 1787, *The Life of William Wilberforce* (London: Murray, 1838), 4:39.

30. More bequeathed £500 to the Anti-Slavery Society and £50 to the Bristol and Clifton Female Anti-Slavery Society. Thomas Taylor includes the particulars of her will and its "princely sums"; see *Memoir*, 421–22.

31. Moira Ferguson, *Subject to Others*, 150.

32. Mrs. Trimmer, "Anecdotes of Negroes," *The Family Magazine; or, A Repository of Religious Instruction, and Rational Amusement* (London: John Marshall, 1788), February 1788, 127.

33. *Family Magazine*, May 1788, 345.

34. "The epilogue to an opera called the padlock," *Family Magazine*, May 1788, 346–47. First published in 1768, "as it is performed by His Majesty's Servants at the Theatre-Royal in Drury-Lane," the libretto of this "comic" opera in two acts by Isaac Bickerstaff included several untitled songs; it was based on *El celoso extrameno* (The jealous husband), one of Cervantes' *Novelas ejemplares*.

35. *Critical Review*, February 1789, 237; as quoted by Ferguson, *Subject to Others*, 163.

36. *Subject to Others*, 163.

37. Ibid., 161, 163, 152.

38. Letter from Mrs. H. More to Miss Buchanan, 11 Feb. 1819; City of Bristol Record Office, 12252.

39. Letter from Mrs. H. More to the Rev. Charles Ogilvie, 2 Dec. 1827; Bodleian Ms. Eng. Lett. d. 124, 138.

40. Preface to the Second Edition, *Bible Rhymes on the Names of all the Books of the Old and New Testament: With Allusions to Some of the Principal Incidents and Characters*, *Works*, 1:184.

41. To Sir Thomas Dyke Acland, Bart. With a Pair of Garters of Mrs. H. More's Knitting; Roberts, 4:159. To Mrs. Carrick with a Pair of Card Racks, 24 Sept. 1828; Bodleian, MS Eng. Lett. d. 2, 269.

42. From my Sty, 29 Apr. 1826; Bodleian, MS Eng. Lett, d. 2, 265–66.

43. This section of the chapter is a revision of my " 'For mine's a stubborn and a savage will': 'Lactilla' (Ann Yearsley) and 'Stella' (Hannah More) Reconsidered," *Huntington Library Quarterly* 56.2 (Spring 1993): 135–150.

44. Robert Southey, *The Lives and Works of the Uneducated Poets*, ed. J.S. Childers (London: Humphrey Milford, 1925), 128–29, 133.

45. Moira Ferguson, ed., *First Feminists: British Women Writers, 1578–1799* (Bloomington: University of Indiana Press, 1985), 381, 25. Moira Ferguson, "Resistance and Power in the Life and Writings of Ann Yearsley," *Eighteenth Century* 27 (1986): 247, 250, 253, 249, 255; and "Unpublished Poems of Ann Yearsley," *Tulsa Studies in Women's Literature* 12, no. 1 (1993): 16.

46. Elizabeth Kowaleski-Wallace, *Their Fathers' Daughters*, 3–5.

47. Donna Landry, *Muses of Resistance*, 17–19.

48. Ibid., 21, 152.

49. Mary Waldron, "Ann Yearsley and the Clifton Records," *The Age of Johnson*, ed. P.J. Korshin (New York: AMS Press, 1990), 318, 310, 314.

50. By contrast, Waldron contends that "Yearsley was in fact rather more practical and far-sighted than More"; ibid., 314.

51. D. Landry, *Muses of Resistance*, 21.

52. M.G. Jones, *Hannah More*, 73.

53. D. Landry, *Muses of Resistance*, 150.

54. Draft of A.L. to Hannah More, 29 Aug. 1796; New York Public Library, Berg Collection. Reproduced in *Horace Walpole's Correspondence with Hannah More . . .*, ed. W.S. Lewis, R.A. Smith, C.H. Bennett (New Haven: Yale University Press, 1961), 31:401–3. The handwriting vividly conveys Walpole's illness and lends an undeniable credence to his tribute.

55. William Shaw, *Life of Hannah More*, 48.

56. The books proved to be a problematic gift; Yearsley complained they were kept from her when, in fact, More was trying to find appropriate shelves on which to display them in Yearsley's home.

57. Letter from H. More to Mrs. Montagu, 27 Aug. 1784, MO 3986; Huntington Library. The letter is also reproduced in *The Female Spectator: English Women Writers before 1800*, ed. M.R. Mahl and H. Koon (Bloomington: University of Indiana Press, 1977), 277–78. The transcription of letters from More to Mrs. Montagu by Mahl and Koon closes with More's letter of 16 Sept. 1785; however, the dispute was not officially resolved until late December 1785.

58. Letter from H. More to Mrs. Montagu, 22 Oct. 1784, MO 3988; Huntington Library. The letter is also reproduced in *Female Spectator*, 279–81.

59. An original broadsheet is in the New York Public Library, Berg Collection.

60. James Silvester, *Hannah More, Christian Philanthropist* (London: Thynne, 1934), 52–53. Silvester reproduces several previously unpublished letters from More to Hamilton.

61. Letter from H. More to Mrs. Montagu, 27 Sept. 1784, MO 3987; Huntington Library. The letter is also reproduced in *Female Spectator*, 279. M. Ferguson, "Resistance and Power," 249.

62. A.L.S. to Hannah More from Horace Walpole, 13 Nov. 1784; New York Public Library, Berg Collection. The letter is also reproduced in *Horace Walpole's Correspondence with Hannah More*, 31:219.

63. Letter from H. More to T. Cadell, 12 June [1785], HM 1837; Huntington Library. I am grateful to the anonymous reviewer of the University Press of Kentucky for this suggestion of an additional defense of More, in safeguarding the money she had collected by endebting herself to influential friends.

64. Letter from H. More to Mrs. Montagu, [June 1785], MO 3990; Huntington Library. The letter is also reproduced in *Female Spectator*, 282.

65. Letter from H. More to Mrs. Montagu, 27 Aug. 1784, MO 3986; Huntington Library. The letter is also reproduced in *Female Spectator*, 277–78.

66. *Poems on Several Occasions by Ann Yearsley A Milkwoman of Bristol* (London: T. Cadell, 1785). In a year and a half, this volume went through four editions.

67. "Deed of Trust," *Poems on Various Subjects by a Milkwoman of Clifton near Bristol, Being Her Second Work* (London: G.G.J. & J. Robinson, 1786), xxviii.

68. M. Ferguson, "Unpublished Poems of Ann Yearsley," 24, 25.

69. Ann Yearsley, *Earl Goodwin, An Historical Play* (London: G.G.J. & J. Robinson, 1791), "Exordium," 38.

70. The epilogue is credited to "Mr. Meyler," though its strong advocacy argument suggests that Yearsley may have had a hand in it.

71. Letter from Mrs. Boscawen to H. More; W. Roberts, *Memoirs*, 1:370.

72. Letter from Mrs. Montagu to H. More, 1784; W. Roberts, *Memoirs*, 1:374.

73. Letter from H. More to Mrs. Montagu, 21 July 1785, MO 3991; Huntington Library. The letter is also reproduced in *Female Spectator*, 283–84.

74. A.L.S. to Eva Marie Violetti Garrick, 12 Aug. 1785; Folger Shakespeare Library.

75. Letter from H. More to Mrs. Montagu, 21 July 1785, MO 3991; Huntington Library.

76. Letter from H. More to Mrs. Montagu, 16 Sept. 1785, MO 3992; Huntington Library. The letter is also reproduced in *Female Spectator*, 284–86.

77. Letter from H. More to Mrs. Montagu, 20 Oct. 1785, MO 3993; Huntington Library.

78. A.L.S. to Eva Marie Violetti Garrick, 30 Nov. [1785]; Folger Shakespeare Library.

79. Letter from H. More to Mrs. Montagu, 21 Dec. 1785, MO 3994; Huntington Library.

80. Letter from H. More to Mrs. Montagu, 27 July 1787, MO 3995; Huntington Library. In the letter More refers to Yearsley's slandering of her (Yearsley's) "servants." Yearsley vilifies More throughout the "Autobiographical Narrative" prefaced to *Poems on Various Subjects*.

81. Letter from H. More to Mrs. Montagu, 16 Sept. 1785, MO 3992; Huntington Library.

82. Letter from H. More to Mrs. E. Carter, Bristol 1785; W. Roberts, *Memoirs*, 1:391.

83. Joseph Cottle, *Early Recollections, Chiefly Relating to the Late Samuel Taylor Coleridge* (London: Longman, Rees, 1837), 1:74. "Mrs. Yearsley's Proposals, in Behalf of her Children, presented to Mrs. H. More, and rejected," *Poems on Various Subjects*, xxx.

84. W. Roberts, *Memoirs*, 1:369.

85. H. Thompson, *Life of Hannah More*, 58.

86. T. Taylor, *Memoir*, 53.

87. C. Yonge, *Hannah More*, 80.

88. Richard D. Altick, *The English Common Reader* (Chicago: University of Chicago Press, 1957), 240.

89. Martha Vicinus, *The Industrial Muse: A Study of Nineteenth Century British Working-Class Literature* (New York: Barnes & Noble, 1974), 177.

90. J.M.S. Tompkins, "The Bristol Milkwoman," *The Polite Marriage* (Cambridge: Cambridge University Press, 1938), 77.

91. Rayner Unwin, *The Rural Muse: Studies in the Peasant Poetry of England* (London: George Allen and Unwin, 1954), 78–80.

92. M. Ferguson, "The Unpublished Poems of Ann Yearsley," 25.

93. "A Prefatory Letter to Mrs. Montagu By A Friend," *Poems on Several Occasions*, vii, x.

94. "Night. To Stella," *Poems on Several Occasions*, lines 209–10.

4. 'That which before us lies in daily life'

1. Part of the passage from *Paradise Lost*, 8:191–94, which More chose as the epigraph to *Coelebs in Search of a Wife*.

2. "Introduction," *Essays on various subjects*, 2; hereafter referred to as *Essays*.

3. "Introduction," *Strictures on the Modern System of Female Education, The Works of Hannah More* (London: T. Cadell, 1830), 5:xi; hereafter referred to as *Strictures*.

4. *Thoughts on the Importance of the Manners of the Great to General Society, The Works of Hannah More* 11:56–57; hereafter referred to as *Thoughts*.

5. *Strictures*, 3.

6. Letter from H. More to her sister, Adelphi, February 1786; W. Roberts, *Memoirs*, 2:10. Cowper's religious temperament was the prime attraction. In her diary entry for 5 May 1803, she records, "Cowper's letters are interesting, as they present to view the genuine, affectionate, benevolent heart of the incomparable author. I was disappointed to find so few of his religious letters printed. The biographer seems to forget or not to know that religion was the grand feature, the turning point in the character of Cowper." See W. Roberts, *Memoirs*, 3:195.

7. William Cowper, *The Task*, Book 4, 88–89, *The Poetical Works of William Cowper*, 4th ed., ed. H.S. Milford (London: Oxford University Press, 1934), 184.

8. *Strictures*, xi.

9. Ibid., 4–5, 138, 248.

10. Ibid., 229.

11. *Thoughts*, 18.

12. *An Estimate of the Religion of the Fashionable World, The Works of Hannah More* 11:18–19; hereafter referred to as *Estimate*.

13. *Thoughts*, 54.

14. Ibid., 42.

15. *Estimate*, 135.

16. *Thoughts*, 18.

17. *Estimate*, 175.

18. *Strictures*, 255.

19. *Estimate*, 172.

20. Ibid., 172.

21. *Strictures*, 390.

22. *Hints Towards Forming the Character of a Young Princess*, *The Works of Hannah More*, 6:143; hereafter referred to as *Hints*.

23. S. H. Myers, *Bluestocking Circle*, 260.

24. *Essays*, 3.

25. Ibid., 6.

26. Ibid., 9.

27. Ibid., 14. More extends this assertion in *Strictures*, where she accepts, paradoxically, both women's excellence and their secondariness: "Is it not desirable to be the lawful possessors of a more limited domestic territory, rather than the turbulent usurpers of a wider foreign empire? to be good originals instead of bad imitators? to be the best thing of one's own kind, rather than an inferior thing, even if it were of a higher kind? to be excellent women rather than indifferent men?" (232).

28. *Essays*, 9–10.

29. Letter from Mrs. H. More to Cadell and Davies, 2 July 1810; Bodleian MS. Facs. c. 44, ff. 83–84.

30. Catharine Macaulay, *Letters on Education with Observations on Religious and Metaphysical Subjects*, ed. G. Luria (New York: Garland, 1974), 47, 202.

31. Ibid., 206.

32. Ibid., 208.

33. John Bennett, *Strictures on Female Education; Chiefly As It Relates to the Culture of the Heart* (London: T. Cadell, 1787), 76. I am grateful to Tania Smith for the loan of her copy of Bennett. In her examination of Mary, Lady Chudleigh, Hester Chapone, and Hannah More, Smith contends that Bennett's text, though satirical and misogynist, was an influence on More's *Strictures*; see "Beyond Conduct: Three Eighteenth-Century Women Moralists" (M.A. thesis, Department of English, University of Alberta, 1995).

34. Smith, "Beyond Conduct," 123.

35. More, *Strictures*, 217; Bennett, *Strictures*, 112.

36. *Strictures*, 15.

37. Ibid., 111.

38. Ibid., 112.

39. Ibid., 76.

40. Ibid., 225–26. Mr. Badcock's letter in *Gentleman's Magazine* (September 1789) about Catharine Macaulay's *History*, commending "Mrs. Macaulay Graham's work [as] really wonderful considering her sex," underlines the pertinence of More's *quid pro quo* ridicule.

41. *Strictures*, 226.

42. Mary Wollstonecraft, *Vindication of the Rights of Woman: With Strictures on Political and Moral Subjects*, ed. Miriam Brody (London: Penguin Classics, 1983). Hannah More, *Strictures on the Modern System of Female Education; With a View of the Principles and Conduct Prevalent Among Women of Rank and Fortune*, *The Works of Hannah More*, vol. 5. Subsequent parenthetical citations will refer to pages in these editions.

43. Theobald J. Boucher, "Art. X. Review of Hannah More's *Strictures on the Modern System of Female Education,*" *Anti-Jacobin Review and Magazine* 4 (1799): 190, 192, 198–99.

44. Sappho Search, *A Poetical Review of Miss Hannah More's Strictures on Female Education*, 23.

45. The Rev. Charles Daubeny, *A Letter to Mrs. Hannah More on Some Part of Her Late Publication entitled "Strictures on Female Education<F255D170 (London: J. Hatchard and F. & C. Rivington, 1799), 43, 52.*

46. Ibid., 46.

47. More's French correspondence is in the City of Bristol Record Office (26168). In a letter from Bristol dated le 10 juillet 1783, she thanks the members of the Académie for electing her "une membre de votre savante et tres célèbre Académie," calling the announcement "la circonstance la plus honorable et la plus flatteuse de ma vie." Another copy of this letter is at the Huntington (HM 31107).

48. Sappho Search, *Poetical Review*, 11.

49. Nancy Cott, "Passionlessness: An Interpretation of Victorian Sexual Ideology, 1790–1850," *Signs* 4, no.2 (1978): 226.

50. Dr. Gregory, *A Father's Legacy to His Daughters* (London: W. Strahan and T. Cadell, 1781), 92.

51. Bishop Porteus assumed More had devoured Gisborne's book when it first appeared with her "usual voracity"; letter to Mrs. H. More, 16 Jan. 1797; Roberts, 3:4. Gisborne and his "amiable family" (he was the father of nine) stayed at Barley Wood for a few days, in 1811, and More returned by visiting Yoxall Lodge later that year; see Roberts, 3:341.

52. Thomas Gisborne, *An Enquiry into the Duties of the Female Sex* (London: T. Cadell, 1797), 80.

53. Mitzi Myers, "Reform or Ruin: 'A Revolution in Female Manners,' " 209.

54. While her English contemporaries John Cartwright and Jeremy Bentham were enumerating objections to female suffrage and, by contrast, the Marquis de Condorcet was writing openly of improved education and citizenship for women, Wollstonecraft made no comment on these differing constitutional agendas.

55. *Coelebs in Search of a Wife: Comprehending Observations on Domestic Habits and Manners, Religion and Morals, The Works of Hannah More,* vol. 7; all quotations will be based on this edition. Appearing anonymously in two octavo volumes in December 1808, *Coelebs* sold out in less than a fortnight. Within nine months eleven editions had been printed. During More's lifetime thirty editions of one thousand copies each were printed in America. Subtitled *"le choix d'une Epouse, Roman Moral," Coelebs* was also translated into French and enjoyed by Madame de Stael. More herself expressed some reservations about how "this plain Westmoreland Squire can ever suit the meridian of Paris"; see letter to Sir W. Pepys, 24 Jan. 1817; W. Roberts, *Memoirs,* 3:473. By contrast she was "pleased to learn" that *Coelebs* was "much read in Sweden"; see letter to Lady Tryphena Bathurst, 7 Apr. 1818; Roberts, 3:501. Through citing such nineteenth-century periodicals as the *New Monthly Magazine* and Chambers' *Cyclopedia of English Literature,* Ann H. Jones charts Austen's growing reputation as well as More's initially greater fame; see *Ideas and Innovations: Best Sellers of Jane Austen's Age* (New York: AMS Press, 1986), 257, 260. Although Austen herself disliked the Evangelicals, she admitted in a letter (1809) to her

sister about *Coelebs*: "Of course I shall be delighted, when I read it, like other people"; see *Jane Austen's Letters to her Sister Cassandra and Others*, ed. R.W. Chapman (Oxford: Clarendon, 1952), 256.

56. Ruth Bernard Yeazell, *Fictions of Modesty; Women and Courtship in the English Novel* (Chicago: University of Chicago Press, 1991), 33.

57. Letter from H. More to Sir W. Pepys, Barley Wood, 13 Dec. 1809; Roberts, 3:313.

58. Edmund Gosse, "Review of The Letters of Hannah More, selected by R. Brimley Johnson," *Sunday Times*, 15 November 1925, 15. Despite his willingness to defend More as "a voice in the wilderness" and "a link with the past," Gosse quickly added, "I shall never read it again."

59. Sam Pickering, Jr., "Hannah More's *Coelebs in Search of a Wife* and the Respectability of the Novel in the Nineteenth Century," *Neuphilologische Mitteilungen* 78 (1977): 80.

60. J.M.S. Tompkins, *Polite Marriage*, 129.

61. Mitzi Myers, "Reform or Ruin: 'A Revolution in Female Manners,'" 201.

62. E. Kowaleski-Wallace, *Their Fathers' Daughters*, 44.

63. Maurice J. Quinlan, *Victorian Prelude: A History of English Manners, 1700–1830* (New York: Columbia University Press, 1941), 149.

64. Elisabeth Jay, *The Religion of the Heart: Anglican Evangelicalism and the Nineteenth-Century Novel* (Oxford: Clarendon, 1979), 135.

65. Lawrence Stone, *The Family, Sex and Marriage in England, 1500–1800* (New York: Harper & Row, 1977), 668.

66. F.K. Prochaska, *Women and Philanthropy in Nineteenth-Century England*, 118.

67. James Silvester, *Hannah More, Christian Philanthropist*, 94.

68. M.G. Jones, *Hannah More*, 194.

69. Mary Alden Hopkins, *Hannah More and Her Circle*, 229.

70. Eleanor Ty, *Unsex'd Revolutionaries: Five Women Novelists of the 1790s*, 17.

71. Sidney Smith, "Art. XI *Coelebs in Search of a Wife*," *Edinburgh Review* 14 (April 1809): 145–51. "Review of *Coelebs in Search of a Wife*," *The Christian Observer* 8 (1809): 109–21. Unlike M.G. Jones I do not believe that "the disparaging comments of the organ of Evangelicalism" delivered "the coup de grâce" to Hannah's ambitions as a novelist; see *Hannah More*, 198. First, the review is primarily laudatory. Second, Hannah herself admitted that the exercise was a diversion, though—as always—purposive and sober; there is no hint that at sixty-three she was planning to launch a career as a religious novelist. In his article cited above, Sam Pickering, Jr., contends that the endorsement of the *Observer*, "a journal formerly hostile to the novel, was remarkable," and that More's work fulfilled the hopes lying "between the lines" of such periodicals as the *Methodist Magazine* and the *Evangelical Magazine* "that the 'right sort' of novel would be published"; see S. Pickering, 84.

72. Nancy Armstrong, "The Rise of the Domestic Woman," in *The Ideology of Conduct*, ed. N. Armstrong and L. Tennenhouse (New York: Methuen, 1987), 136.

73. Leonore Davidoff and Catherine Hall, *Family Fortunes: Men and Women of the English Middle Class, 1780–1850*, 168. In their insightful examination of "the contradictory messages which More develops," Davidoff and Hall contend that "her Garden of Eden had no politics and no sexuality" (168). True, passions are muted and sexual attractions, implied rather than acted out. But politics and sex do play a part—albeit covertly and subliminally—in *Coelebs*. Mrs. Carlton's longsuffering marriage and her

eventual reform of her husband show, as Mrs. Stanley maintains, "the power of religion in subduing the passions, that of love among the rest" (165). As for Coelebs' highmindedness, Sir John Belfield is shrewd enough to bring it down to earth. "You pretend to be captivated only with *mind*. I observe, however, that previous to your raptures, you always take care to get this mind lodged in a fair and youthful form. This mental beauty is always prudently enshrined in some elegant corporeal frame, before it is worshipped" (195).

74. In *Search* Florella epitomizes the emphasis on mental cultivation ("to live to some purpose we constantly try"), while the widow Urania locates this purposiveness at a domestic site ("Women born to dignify retreat"). The female figures of the longer poems—from the rejected Ianthe ("The Bleeding Heart") and the doubted Birtha ("Sir Eldred") to the rescuing Celia ("Florio")—all effect reformation or penitence in their suitors. Her criticism of the so-called age of benevolence takes direct aim in *Thoughts*: "if it appear that, though more objects are relieved by our money, yet incomparably more are debauched by our licentiousness—the balance, perhaps, will not turn out so decidedly in favour of the times as we are willing to imagine." The criterion of usefulness was always uppermost for More and especially rigorous as it applied to women's activities; *Strictures* clearly reprobates display and self-indulgence. When she concentrates on the rare examples of women performing offices in public life, as in *Hints*, the subject's "mental and moral cultivation" is her "supreme concern," particularly since "the well-being of . . . millions . . . may be at this moment suspended on lessons and habits received by one providentially distinguished female."

75. Although the hinges of the novel's action creak audibly, the only passage that could qualify as an authorial observation involves the introduction of the Belfields to Stanley Grove (Chapter 17). More is at pains to insert the Belfields into the narrative and cites Aristotle's observation about "the introduction of a new person [being] of the next importance to a new incident" (156). She had become influenced by—some argue, addicted to—the Aristotelian unities during her playwrighting tutelage under Garrick.

76. Elizabeth Kowaleski-Wallace charges that the price Lucilla pays "for such protection is an ongoing infantilism that inhibits her ability to act on her own authority"; see *Their Fathers' Daughters*, 52.

77. Because Lucilla so feelingly addresses "the fall," I do not find justification in Eleanor Ty's claim that "More's suppression of the self-willed, disobedient, and unsettling side of Eve indicates the inadequacy and the one-sidedness of her ideal"; see *Unsex'd Revolutionaries*, 18.

78. This industry, however obsessive it seems, is truly the hallmark of More's women. Elanor Ty's judgment that the " 'insipid' " and " 'indolent' " Virginia (in Edgeworth's *Belinda*) possesses the qualities Hannah More believed would be "sufficient for a useful . . . life" does not tally with the evidence of More's writing or life; see *Unsex'd Revolutionaries*, 21.

79. Nancy Armstrong, "The Rise of the Domestic Woman," *Ideology of Conduct*, 119, 106, 105.

80. Beth Fowkes Tobin, *Superintending the Poor: Charitable Ladies and Paternal Landlords in British Fiction, 1770–1860* (New Haven: Yale University Press, 1993), 89, 80.

81. Mrs. Chapone, *Letters on the Improvement of the Mind* (London: J. Walter, 1774), 8 n.d., 66.

82. R. Yeazell, *Fictions of Modesty*, 8.

83. Letter from M. Edgeworth to Mrs. Ruxton, Edgeworthstown, January 1810; *The Life and Letters of Maria Edgeworth*, ed. Augustus J.C. Hare (London: Edward Arnold, 1894), 170. Alice Harford notes that the association of Coelebs with her relative was "a family tradition"; she also suggests that John Scandrett Harford's eventual wife, Louisa Davis, the elder daughter of the MP for Bristol, Richard Hart Davis, may have been the model for Lucilla. See *Annals of the Harford Family*, 66.

84. As More observed in a letter from Bath (1 Jan. 1792) to a friend, "we run about all morning lamenting the calamities of the times, anticipating our ruin, reprobating the taxes, and regretting the general dissipation; and every night we are running into every excess, to a degree unknown in calmer times"; see W. Roberts, *Memoirs*, 2:312. She repeated these sentiments almost verbatim in a letter to Mrs. Boscawen, 27 Dec. 1797; W. Roberts, *Memoirs*, 3:27.

85. C. Yonge, *Hannah More*, 177.

86. Robert Torrens, *Coelibia Choosing a Husband: A Modern Novel* (London: J.F. Hughes, 1809).

87. Ibid., 1:14.

88. Ibid., 1:56.

89. Ibid., 1:77, 130.

90. Ibid., 2:6, 75.

91. Ibid., 2:161.

92. Katherine Sobba Green, *The Courtship Novel, 1740–1820: A Feminized Genre* (Lexington: University Press of Kentucky, 1990), 113.

93. B.F. Tobin, *Superintending the Poor*, 89.

5. Schools and Tracts

1. The Reverend Henry Thompson, *The Christian An Example. A Sermon Preached in the Parish Church of Wrington, Somerset, on the Sunday after the Funeral of Mrs. H. More, which took place there September 13, 1833.* (London: J.G. and F. Rivington, 1833), 8.

2. The Reverend Thomas Drewitt, *Illustrations of Falsehood, in A reply to Some Assertions Contained in Mr. Spencer's late Publication.* (Bath: S. Hazard, 1802), 15–16.

3. Edward Spencer, *Truths, respecting Mrs. Hannah More's Meeting-Houses, and the Conduct of her Followers; Addressed to the Curate of Blagdon.* (Bath: W. Meyler, 1802), 65.

4. "The Blagdon Controversy," *Anti-Jacobin Review and Magazine*, 11 (1802): 425.

5. The Reverend Thomas Bere, *An Appeal to the Public, on the Controversy Between Hannah More, the Curate of Blagdon, and the Rev. Sir A. Elton* (Bath: R. Cruttwell, 1801), 31.

6. The Reverend Sir Abraham Elton, *A Letter to the Rev. Thomas Bere, Rector of Butcombe, Occasioned by his late unwarrantable attack on Mrs. Hannah More* (London: Cadell and Davies, 1801), 30–31.

7. [The Reverend Thomas Drewitt], *The Force of Contrast; or, Quotations, Accompanied with Remarks, Submitted to the consideration of all who have interested themselves in what has been called the Blagdon Controversy* (Bath: S. Hazard, 1801), 25.

8. H. Thompson, *Life of Hannah More*, 107.

9. M.G. Jones, *Hannah More*, 152, 159.

10. B.F. Tobin, *Superintending the Poor*, 111.

11. M. Myers, "'A Peculiar Protection,'" 246.

12. J. Stratford, *Robert Raikes and Others: The Founders of Sunday Schools* (London: Sunday School Union, 1880), 40.

13. Philip B. Cliff, *The Rise and Development of the Sunday School Movement in England, 1780–1980* (Nutfield, Redhill, Surrey: National Christian Education Council, 1986), 24.

14. Letter from Robert Raikes to Richard Townley, 25 Nov. 1783; quoted in P.B. Cliff, *Rise and Development of the Sunday School Movement*, 3.

15. Ibid., 3.

16. Ibid., 27.

17. Sarah Trimmer, "Appendix. An Account of Sunday Schools established in Old Brentford, in the parish of Ealing, Middlesex, June 1786," *The Oeconomy of Charity; or, An Address to Ladies Concerning Sunday Schools; the Establishing of Schools of Industry under Female Inspection; and the Distribution of Voluntary Benefaction* (London: T. Bansley, 1787), 167.

18. Ibid., 172–73.

19. Sarah Trimmer, *Reflections Upon the Education of Charity Schools; with the Outlines of a Plan of Appropriate Instruction for the Children of the Poor* (London: T. Longman, 1792), 4, 20–21.

20. Letter from H. More to Mrs. Kennicott, Cowslip Green 1789; W. Roberts, *Memoirs*, 2:210.

21. [H. More], *Questions and Answers for the Mendip and Sunday Schools*, 16th ed. (Bath: J. Binns, 1795), 3, 10–11.

22. Letter from Mrs. H. More to W. Wilberforce, 1801; W. Roberts, *Memoirs*, 3:151.

23. Letter from Mrs. H. More to Mrs. Kennicott, 2 Aug. 1791; W. Roberts, *Memoirs*, 2:308.

24. Arthur Roberts, "Introduction," *Mendip Annals*, 2, 3.

25. *Mendip Annals*, 91, 99, 129–30, 131.

26. Ibid., 39, 43, 78, 92, 104–5, 137.

27. Ibid., 31, 26, 43.

28. Ibid., 68, 70, 81, 95, 99, 98, 205, 106, 239.

29. Ibid., 121, 196.

30. Ibid., 113.

31. Ibid., 114, 142, 158.

32. Letter from Mrs. H. More to W. Wilberforce, 1823; W. Roberts, *Memoirs*, 4:173.

33. Letter from Mrs. H. More to Dr. Richard Beadon, 1801; W. Roberts, *Memoirs*, 3:133–34.

34. *Mendip Annals*, 176, 197, 201, 203, 208, 210.

35. Ibid., 221.

36. Diary entry for 27 Nov. 1803; Roberts, 3:203.

37. M. Myers, "'A Peculiar Protection,'" 242.

38. "Mrs. H. More's Schools; or, The Blagdon Controversy," *Christian Observer* 1 (1802): 180, 183, 184.

39. As quoted in a letter from Mrs. H. More to the Bishop of Bath and Wells, 1801; W. Roberts, *Memoirs*, 3:132.

40. Ibid., 126.

41. Ibid., 126.

42. "The Blagdon Controversy," *Anti-Jacobin Review* 9 (1801): 278.

43. Edward Spencer, *Truths, respecting Mrs. Hannah More's Meeting-Houses, and the Conduct of her Followers; Addressed to the Curate of Blagdon* (Bath: W. Meyler, 1802), 10.

44. The Rev. Sir Abraham Elton, *A Letter to the Rev. Thomas Bere, Rector of Butcombe, Occasioned by his late unwarrantable attack on Mrs. Hannah More* (London: Cadell & Davies, 1801), 42.

45. [Thomas Drewitt], *Force of Contrast*, 7.

46. *The Blagdon Controversy; or, Short Criticisms on the Late Dispute between The Curate of Blagdon, and Mrs. Hannah More, Relative to Sunday Schools, and Monday private Schools, by a Layman* (Bath: W. Meyler, 1801), 13, 34.

47. Thomas Bere, *An Address to Mrs. Hannah More, on the Conclusion of the Blagdon Controversy, With Observations on an Anonymous Tract Entitled 'A Statement of Facts'* (Bath: T. Cruttwell, 1801), 2, 3, 6, 5, 67.

48. *The Something Wrong Developed; or, Free Remarks on Mrs. H. More's Conventicles* (Bristol: Harris and Bryan, 1801), 19, 10–11.

49. Letter from Bishop Porteus to Mrs. H. More, 1794; W. Roberts, *Memoirs*, 2:427.

50. Ibid., 429.

51. Taylor, *Memoir of Mrs. Hannah More*, 153.

52. Jones, *Hannah More*, 150.

53. Yonge, *Hannah More*, 130.

54. G. H. Spinney, "Cheap Repository Tracts: Hazard and Marshall Edition," *The Library* 20 (1939–40): 295.

55. Jones, *Hannah More*, 148.

56. Paul Sangster, *Pity My Simplicity: The Evangelical Revival and the Religious Education of Children, 1738–1800* (London: Epworth, 1963), 66.

57. Mitzi Myers, "Hannah More's Tracts for the Times: Social Fiction and Female Ideology," in *Fetter'd or Free? British Women Novelists, 1670–1815*, ed. Mary Ann Schofield and Cecilia Marcheski (Athens: Ohio University Press, 1986), 269.

58. Susan Pedersen, "Hannah More Meets Simple Simon: Tracts, Chapbooks, and Popular Culture in Late Eighteenth-Century England," *Journal of British Studies* 25 (1986): 97, 106.

59. Olivia Smith, *The Politics of Language, 1791–1819* (Oxford: Oxford University Press, 1984), 93; Gary Kelly, "Revolution, Reaction, and the Expropriation of Popular Culture: Hannah More's *Cheap Repository*," *Man and Nature* 6 (1987): 153; D. Landry, *Muses of Resistance*, 123; E. Kowaleski-Wallace, *Their Fathers' Daughters*, 75; M. Ferguson, *Subject to Others*, 215.

60. Bonnie Herron, "Cheap Shots or Trenchant Tactics? Hannah More's *Cheap Repository Tracts* as Cultural Warfare" (M.A. thesis, Department of English, University of Alberta, 1994); I am endebted to Bonnie Herron for illuminating More's stylistic mastery in writing for different audiences.

61. Letter from Mrs. H. More to the Rev. J. Newton, Bath 1794; W. Roberts, *Memoirs*, 2:429.

62. Advertisement to Tales for the Common People (1801), *The Complete Works of Hannah More* (New York: Derby & Jackson, 1857), 1:190.

63. Ibid., 190.

64. Letter from Mrs. H. More to the Rev. J. Newton; Roberts, 2:429.

65. *Thoughts on the Importance of the Manners of the Great, Works,* 11:41.

66. *An Estimate of the Religion of the Fashionable World, Works,* 11:124.

67. *The Two Shoemakers, Tales for the Common People, Works,* 3:631.

68. Letter of H. More to her sister, 20 Mar. 1790; W. Roberts, *Memoirs*, 2:225.

69. *Village Politics: Addressed to All the Mechanics, Journeymen, and Labourers in Great Britain, Works,* 3:365, 378.

70. Ibid., 3:379–80.

71. Ibid., 3:373.

72. Ibid., 3:377, 376.

73. "The Riot; or, Half a Loaf is better than no Bread: in a Dialogue between Jack Anvil and Tom Hod: written in 1795, a Year of Scarcity and Alarm," *Works,* 2:87.

74. Ibid., 2:88–89.

75. "Turn the Carpet; or, The Two Weavers: in a Dialogue between Dick and John," *Works,* 2:17.

76. *John the Shopkeeper Turned Sailor; or, The Folly of Going Out of Our Element, In Four Parts* (London: J. Hatchard, J. Evans & Sons, n.d.), part 1, 4.

77. *The History of Tom White the Postboy: in Two Parts, Works,* 4:9.

78. *The Sunday School, Works,* 3:309.

79. *The History of Hester Wilmot: in Two Parts; being the Sequel to the Sunday School, Works,* 4:53.

80. *The History of Tom White, Works,* 4:14.

81. *The Shepherd of Salisbury Plain: in Two Parts, Works,* 3:402.

82. *Black Giles the Poacher: in Two Parts. Containing some Account of a Family who had rather live by their Wits than their Work, Works,* 4:115; *The Shepherd of Salisbury Plain, Works,* 3:419.

83. *Black Giles, Works,* 4:124; *The Shepherd of Salisbury Plain, Works,* 3:399.

84. *Black Giles, Works,* 4:146; *Tawney Rachel; or, the Fortune-teller: with some Account of Dreams, Omens, and Conjurers, Works,* 4:156, 161–62.

85. *The Shepherd of Salisbury Plain, Works,* 3:437.

86. *The Two Wealthy Farmers; or, The History of Mr. Bragwell, Works,* 3:123.

87. Ibid., 196.

88. *Mr. Fantom; or, The History of the New-fashioned Philosopher, and his Man William, Works,* 3:5, 41.

89. Ibid., 14, 21, 38.

90. Ibid., 16.

91. *Tracts written during the Riots in the Year 1817: The Death of Mr. Fantom, the Great Reformist, Works,* 3:54–5.

92. B.F. Tobin, *Superintending the Poor*, 115.

93. Ibid., 115. Tobin quotes Foucault's *Discipline and Punish*, p. 187.

94. Michel Foucault, *Discipline and Punish: The Birth of the Prison*, trans. A. Sheridan (New York: Random House, 1979), 202–3.

6. "The language of sympathy rather than of dictation"

1. *Practical Piety; or, The Influence of the Religion of the Heart on the Conduct of Life*, *Works*, 8:ix.

2. Charlotte Yonge, *Hannah More*, 201.

3. M.G. Jones, *Hannah More*, 235.

4. *Remarks on the Speech of M. Dupont, made in the National Convention of France in 1793*, *Works*, 11:234.

5. Letter from Mrs. H. More to Mr. Wilberforce, Barley Wood, 16 Oct. 1805; Roberts, 3:324.

6. Letter from Mrs. H. More to the Bishop of Bath and Wells, 1801; Roberts, 3:129. Letter from Mrs. H. More to the Rev. D. Wilson, Barley Wood, 2 Sept. 1825; Roberts, 4:246. Diary entry for 25 Mar. 1798; W. Roberts, *Memoirs*, 3:57.

7. Letter from Mrs. H. More to Sir W.W. Pepys, 1819; Roberts, 4:48.

8. *Practical Piety*, *Works*, 8:ix.

9. Ibid., 8:103.

10. Ibid., 8:104.

11. Ibid., 8:103.

12. *Christian Morals*, *Works*, 9:10, 16.

13. *An Essay on the Character and Practical Writings of Saint Paul*, *Works*, 10:vii, xi.

14. Ibid., 10:407.

15. Ibid., 10:378.

16. Ibid., 10:218–19.

17. Ibid., 10:195.

18. Ibid., 10:357, 230.

19. Ibid., 10:242–44. Although More buttresses this claim by referring "the enquirer to 'Henry's Ecclesiastical History of Great Britain,' Vol. i, p. 189," the evidence that Paul, during his two years of easy house arrest in Rome, actually undertook a final journey to the west (which could have included Spain and Britain) is very speculative and unconvincing. A journey to Spain, however, is still a probability. In his careful reconstruction of Paul's three missionary journeys and final journey to Rome, Emil Kraeling allows that during a period of exile or relegation, which banished Paul for a time from Judaea or Rome, "it is very probable that he would have chosen to go to Spain"; see *Rand McNally Bible Atlas* (New York: Rand McNally, 1966), 463.

20. *Saint Paul*, *Works*, 10:244.

21. Elisabeth Schüssler Fiorenza explains the "hermeneutics of suspicion" in two essays: "The Will to Choose or to Reject: Continuing Our Critical Work," in *Feminist Interpretation of the Bible*, ed. Letty Russell (Philadelphia: Westminster Press, 1985), 125–36 and "Remembering the Past in Creating the Future: Historical Critical Scholarship and Feminist Biblical Interpretation," in *Feminist Perspectives on Biblical Scholarship*, ed. A. Y.

Collins (Chico, Calif.: Scolars Press, 1985), 43–64. Mieke Bal takes specific aim at Pauline injunctions in "Sexuality, Sin, and Sorrow: The Emergence of Female Character (A Reading of Genesis 1–3)," *The Female Body in Western Culture, Contemporary Perspectives*, ed. S.R. Suleiman (Cambridge: Harvard University Press, 1986), 317–38. See also Phyllis Trible, "Five Loaves and Two Fishes: Feminist Hermeneutics and Biblical Theology," *Theological Studies* 50 (1989): 279–95.

22. *Saint Paul, Works*, 10:225.

23. Ibid., 10:284.

24. Peter F. Ellis, *Seven Pauline Letters* (Collegeville, Minn.: Liturgical Press, 1982), 37.

25. *Saint Paul, Works*, 10:298–99.

26. Ibid., 10:175.

27. Ibid., 10:264.

28. Ibid., 10:179.

29. Friedrich Schleiermacher, *On Religion: Speeches to Its Cultured Despisers*, trans. John Oman, with an introduction by Rudolf Otto (New York: Harper & Row, 1958), 33.

30. Ibid., 87.

31. *Saint Paul, Works*, 10:179.

32. Ibid., 10:239.

33. *Practical Piety, Works*, 8:6, 9.

34. Ibid., 8:9–10.

35. Ibid., 8:296.

36. *Christian Morals, Works*, 9:149.

37. Ibid., 155.

38. Ibid., 259.

39. Ibid., 332–33.

40. Preface, *The Spirit of Prayer, Selected and Compiled by the Author, from Various Portions Exclusively on That Subject, in Her Other Works, Works*, 11:239.

41. Ibid., 11:249, 255.

42. Ibid., 11:327.

43. Ibid., 11:421.

44. *Practical Piety, Works*, 8:258–59.

45. *Saint Paul, Works*, 10:179.

46. *Christian Morals, Works*, 9:421.

47. Ibid., 9:414, 431.

48. William Wilberforce, *A Practical View of the Prevailing Religious System of Professed Christians, in the Higher and Middles Classes in this Country, contrasted with Real Christianity*, 13th ed. (London: T. Cadell and W. Davies, 1818), 35, 127, 307, 366.

49. Ibid., 367.

50. Walter Brueggemann, *Texts under Negotiation: The Bible and Postmodern Imagination* (Minneapolis: Fortress Press, 1993), 20.

51. Wayne Proudfoot, *Religious Experience* (Berkeley: University of California Press, 1985), 236.

52. Ibid., 236.

53. Brueggemann, *Texts under Negotiation*, 54.

Epilogue

1. Anna Seward, "On visiting the Silvan Cottage, Inhabited by Miss Hannah More and her sisters 1791," *The Juvenile Forget Me Not*, ed. Mrs. S. C. Hall (London: Frederick Westley & A. H. Davis, 1831), 159.

2. Quoted by T. Taylor, *Memoirs of Mrs. Hannah More*, 206–7.

3. A.L.S. from Hannah More to E.M.V. Garrick, dated Bristol 27 July 1783. (Folger Shakespeare Library).

4. Letter to W. Wilberforce, 31 July 1824, Bodleian MS. Wilberforce, c. 43, f. 37.

5. W.W. Meissner, S. J., M. D., *Ignatius of Loyola: The Psychology of a Saint* (New Haven: Yale University Press, 1992), xxiii.

6. Ibid., 398.

7. Ibid., xvii–xviii.

Works Cited and Consulted

More's Published Work

The Accomplished Lady; or, Strictures on the Modern System of Female Education. Boston: J. Loring, 1838.

The Apprentice's Monitor; or, Indentures in Verse, Shewing What They are Bound to Do. London: J. Marshall, at the Cheap Repositories, n.d.

Articles of Agreement to be observed by a Society of Women Held in the Parishes of Shipham and Rowberrow in Somersetshire, Commenced in September 1792. Broadsheet in the library of All Saints Church, Wrington.

On Carrying Religion into the Common Business of Life; A Dialogue between James Stock and Will Simpson, the Shoemakers, as they sat at Work. Cheap Repository Sunday Reading. London: J. Marshall, n.d.

Coelebs in Search of a Wife: Comprehending Observations on Domestic Habits and Manners, Religion and Morals. 2 vols. 12th ed. London: T. Cadell, 1809.

The Complete Works of Hannah More. 2 vols. New York: Derby & Jackson, 1857.

The Cottage Cook; or, Mrs. Jones's Cheap Dishes; Shewing the Way to do much good with little Money. London: J. Marshall, n.d.

The Day of Judgment; or, The Grand Reckoning. London: J. Marshall, n.d.

An Essay on the Character and Practical Writings of Saint Paul. 3d ed. London: T. Cadell & W. Davies, 1815.

Essays on various subjects, principally designed for young ladies. London: J. Wilkie, T. Cadell, 1777.

The Good Militia Man; or, The Man that is Worth a Host, Being a new song. By Honest Dan the Plough-boy turned Soldier. London: J. Marshall, n.d.

The Inflexible Captive: A Tragedy. Bristol: S. Farley, 1774.

John the Shopkeeper Turned Sailor; or, The Folly of Going Out of Our Element, in Four Parts. London: J. Hatchard, n.d.

The Lancashire Collier Girl; A True Story. London: J.G. & F. Rivington, 1833.

The Market Woman; or, Honesty is the Best Policy. Dublin: W. Watson, n.d.

Miss More's Essays. In *The Lady's Pocket Library.* 3d American ed. Philadelphia: Dover and Harper, 1797.

Ode to Dragon, Mr. Garrick's house-dog, at Hampton. London: T. Cadell, 1777.

Percy: A Tragedy in Five Acts. Bristol: J.W. Arrowsmith, 1911.

Questions and Answers for the Mendip and Sunday Schools. Bath: John Binns, [1795?].

The Roguish Miller; or, Nothing Got By Cheating. Bath: S. Hazard, Printer to the Cheap Repository for Religious and Moral Tracts, n.d.

Sacred Dramas. Philadelphia: T. Dobson, 1787.

A Search after Happiness: A Pastoral in Three Dialogues. Bristol: S. Farley, [1773].

The Search after Happiness: A Pastoral Drama. 2d ed. Bristol: S. Farley, 1773.

The Search after Happiness: A Pastoral Drama. 3d ed. Bristol: S. Farley, 1774.

The Search after Happiness: A Pastoral Drama. 7th ed. London: T. Cadell, 1778.

The Search after Happiness: A Pastoral Drama. 8th ed. London: T. Cadell, 1785.

The Search after Happiness: A Pastoral Drama. 9th ed. with additions. London: T. Cadell, 1787.

The Search after Happiness: A Pastoral Drama. 11th ed. with additions. London: T. Cadell, 1796.

The Search after Happiness: A Pastoral Drama for Young Ladies. The Works of Hannah More in Prose and Verse. 8 vols. London: T. Cadell, 1801.

Slavery; A Poem. London: T. Cadell, 1788.

The Sorrows of Yamba; or, The Negro Woman's Lamentation. Newcastle: RTS, 1823.

The Twelfth of August; or, The Feast of Freedom. London: J. and T. Clarke, 1819.

The Works of Hannah More in Prose and Verse. 8 vols. London: T. Cadell, 1801.

The Works of Hannah More. New ed. 18 vols. London: T. Cadell & W. Davies, 1818.

The Works of Hannah More. New ed. 11 vols. London: T. Cadell, 1830.

Roberts, William, Esq. *Memoirs of the Life and Correspondence of Mrs. Hannah More.* 4 vols. London: R.B. Seeley and W. Burnside, 1834.

Manuscript Letters

At the Bodleian: Ms. Wilberforce d. 17, ff. 6–7 (letter of 24 Sept. 1789 about Cheddar School); c.3, ff. 31–32, 45–46, 89, 242–47 (letters to Wilberforce 1797–1807); d. 15, ff. 70–71 (letter of 24 Sept. 1804); c. 48, ff. 2–55 (letters to and from Wilberforce 1819–25); d. 4, ff. 8, 48–49 (letters of 1828).

Letters to or from other correspondents: Ms. facs. c. 44, ff. 26–29 (letter to Hannah More from Elizabeth Carter, 29 Oct. 1789); Ms. Wilberforce c. 3, ff. 270–72 (letter to Mrs. Clark, 20 Jan. 1792); Ms. Wilberforce c. 49, ff. 127–128 (letter to Hannah More from John Newton, 4 June 1793); MS. Eng. lett. c. 461, ff. 14–15 (letter to Hannah More from Charles Burney, 26 Sept. 1793); MS. Eng. lett. c. 19, ff. 83–84 (letter to Cadell & Davies,2 July 1810); MS. Eng. lett. c. 651, ff. 274–275 (letterto Mr. Manning, Esq., M.P., 13 Feb. 1811); Ms. Eng. lett. d. 124, ff. 97–139 (letters to Charles Ogilvie 1812–27); MS. Eng. lett, d. 310, ff. 172–73 (letter to Mrs. Dawson, 17 Apr. 1816); MS. Eng. lett. d. 2, ff. 236–304 (letters to Dr. Carrick 1816–32); MS. Autogr. d. 36, ff. 374–77 (letter to unknown recipient, 1 Mar. 1829).

At the City of Bristol Record Office: 26168 ff. (letters in English and French, 1779–1833); 12252 (letter to Miss Buchanan, 11 Feb. 1819); 39015 (letter to unknown recipient, 26 May 1821); 35521 (poem to Master John MacGregor, 23 May 1825); 8033, f. 14 (letter from Edward Protheroe to John Hare, about a visit to Hannah More); 28672 (engraving of E. Bird, 1809).

At the British Library: BM MS. Add. 42511, ff. 1–50 (Hannah More Papers: ff. 2–4, letter to Mrs. Boscawen, 14 Nov. 1788; ff. 5–7, letter to W. Bankes, 20 Sept. 1798; ff. 9–10, letter to Mrs. Garrick, 1 Jan. 1806; ff. 11–12, letter to Mrs. Barker, 25 May 1818; f. 15, card to Miss Maria Whitney, 1827; f. 16, "The Bazaar"; f. 17, paper work cutout of Roman arch at Barley Wood; f. 20, drawing by Mr. Slater; f. 27, engraving of Barley Wood).

   BM MS. 46362, ff. 62–63 (letter to Countess Haddington, 6 July 1794); BM MS. 18204, f. 139 (letter to Mrs. King from Bath, n.d.); BM MS. 39312, ff. 220–21 (letter to Mrs. Kennicott, 11 Mar. 1810); BM MS. 32491, ff. 5–6 (letter to Mrs. Nash, 23 Jan. 1811); BM Egerton MS., ff. 1–103 (letters to Lady Olivia Sparrow, 1812–27); BM MS. 47458, f. 25 (letter to Miss Weir, 15 Nov. 1822); BM MS. 42711, ff. 50–55 (letters to Lord Bexley, 1823–27).

At the Folger Shakespeare Library: Volume 3 of Garrick Correspondence (letters from Hannah More to Mrs. Garrick, 1783–1818); Y.c. 204 (1) (letter to Hannah More from Mrs. Boscawen, 21 May 1774); Y.c. 2600 (183, 215, 222) (letters to Hannah More from David Garrick); W.b. 492 (letter to Hannah More from David Garrick, 19 Dec. 1777); W.b. 487 (60) (*Hannae Morae, Virgini piae, eruditae, eleganti*, poem by Robert Lowth, Bishop of London); Y.d. 199 (poem for Hannah More by Mrs. Garrick); W.b. 464 (Epilogue to the Tragedy of Percy); Y.d. 156 (42) (Prologue to Percy, 1777); M.a. 179 (Commonplace Book, *ca.* 1795–1805, poem about More's authorship of *Search*); Y.d. 120 (60) (Medallion Portrait of David Garrick); W.b. 489 (letter from Marianne Thornton to Mrs. Garrick about Hannah More's sickness, 22 Apr. 1799); Y.d. 195 (letter from Hannah More to Mr. Wylde on the death of his child, 3 Jan. 1811).

At the Henry E. Huntington Library: MO 3983–4003 (Letters to Mrs. Elizabeth Montagu: 3983, 6 Jan. 1776; 3984, 28 Sept. 1777; 3985, 23 Feb. [1780?]; 3986, 27 Aug. 1784; 3987, 27 Sept. 1784; 3988, 22 Oct. 1784; 3989, 7 Dec. 1784; 3990, June [1785]; 3991, 21 July 1785; 3992, 16 Sept. 1785; 3993, 20 Oct. 1785; 3994, 21 Dec. 1785; 3995, 27 July 1787; 3996, 20 July 1788; 3997, 7 July [1789]; 3998, 2 Sept. 1789; 3999, 10 Oct. 1789; 4000, 8 Jan. 1790; 4001, 20 Dec. [1790]; 4002, 14 Aug. 1791; 4003, 12 Sept. 1791).

   MY 665–73, 675–92 (letters to Zachary Macaulay 1799–1828); MY 674, 693–710 (letters to Mrs. Selina [Mills] Macaulay 1816–24; MY 713–20 (Letters to Marianne Thornton, 1814–28); MY 723 (letter to Tom Macaulay, *ca.* 1820).

   JE 596–97 (Letters to Edward Jerningham, 1789).

   HM 1837 (letter to Cadell, 12 June 1785); HM 20641 (letter to Cadell, 22 Mar. 1809); HM 30580–30623 (letters to the Reverend Charles Hoare, 1808–

22); HM 30636 (letter to Cadell & Davies, 5 Apr. 1811); HM 30639–30648 (letters to Dr. Lovell, 1820–22); HM 31107 (draft letter to Académie Royale de Rouen, 10 July 1783); HM 31108 (letter to Mrs. Holroyd, 29 Oct. 1807); HM 31109 (incomplete letter to "my dear friends," *ca.* 1807).

At the New York Public Library, Berg Collection: Letters to Eva Marie Violetti Garrick (12 Aug. 1785; 17 Jan. 1802; 22 Nov. 1804; 2 Aug. 1806; 7 Aug. 1813; 3 Dec. 1814). Note and letter to Frances Burney d'Arblay [1786?]. Subscription notice for Ann Yearsley's poems (1785). Note from Beilby Porteus (28 Jan., n.d.). Draft letter from Horace Walpole (29 Aug. 1796).

     Two letters to G. I. Beltz (31 Oct. 1822; 23 Apr. 1823). An undated letter to the British and Foreign Bible Society.

At the Pierpont Morgan Library: Letter to Mrs. Horne (10 Jan. 1793). Letters to Mrs. Garrick (22 May 1801; 31 Jan. 1803). Letter to Messrs. Cadell & Davies (6 Oct. 1818). Letter to an unknown recipient (3 Nov. 1818). Letter to Dr. Carrick (24 Jan. 1823). Letter to Mrs. Pigott (3 July 1824). Letter to Hannah More from Horace Walpole (13 Nov. 1784). Letter to Hannah More from Legh Richmond (17 Jan. 1804). Letter from Sir Thomas Acland to Right Reverend Bishop McIlvaine of Ohio, regarding More's will (30 Apr. 1835).

Other Published Works

Addleshaw, S. "Hannah More, Blue-Stocking and Reformer." *Church Quarterly Review* 118 (1934): 57–79.

Aikin-Sneath, Betsy. "Hannah More." *London Mercury* 12 (1933): 528–35.

Altick, Richard D. *The English Common Reader.* Chicago: University of Chicago Press, 1957.

Armstrong, Nancy. "The Rise of the Domestic Woman." In *The Ideology of Conduct and the History of Sexuality,* edited by N. Armstrong and Leonard Tennenhouse, 96–141. New York and London: Methuen, 1987.

Awdry, Miss F. *Hannah More.* (1896) Bodleian MS. Eng. misc. e. 1125, 284–91.

Balfour, Mrs. Clara Lucas. *A Sketch of Mrs. Hannah More and Her Sisters.* London: W. & F. G. Cash, 1854.

Barbauld, Anna Laetitia, ed. *The Correspondence of Samuel Richardson.* 6 vols. London: Richard Phillips, 1804.

Bennett, John. *Strictures on Female Education; Chiefly As It Relates to the Culture of the Heart.* London: T. Cadell, J.J.G. and J. Robinson, Rivington, J. Murray, 1787.

Benson, Pamela Joseph. *The Invention of the Renaissance Woman; The Challenge of Female Independence in the Literature and Thought of Italy and England.* University Park, Pa.: Penn State University Press, 1992.

Bere, Rev. Thomas. *An Address to Mrs. Hannah More, on the Conclusion of the Blagdon Controversy, with Observations on an Anonymous Tract Entitled 'A Statement of Facts'.* R. Cruttwell, 1801.

————. *An Appeal to the Public, on the Controversy Between Hannah More, the Curate of Blagdon, and the Rev. Sir A. Elton*. Bath: R. Cruttwell, 1801.

————. *The Controversy between Mrs. Hannah More and the Curate of Blagdon; relative to the Conduct of her Teacher of the Sunday School in that Parish, With the Original Letters and Explanatory Notes*. London: J. S. Jordan, 1801.

Birrell, Augustine. "Hannah More." In *Men, Women, & Books* (1894), *Papers and Essays*. London: Duckworth, 1912, 40–45.

————. "Hannah More Once More." *In the Name of the Bodleian and Other Essays*. New York: Charles Scribner's Sons, 1905, 172–82.

Blackstone, William. *Commentaries on the Laws of England*. 3d ed. 4 vols. Oxford: Clarendon, 1765–69.

"The Blagdon Controversy." *Anti-Jacobin Review* 9 (July–August 1801): 277–96.

The Blagdon Controversy; or, Short Criticisms on the Late Dispute between the Curate of Blagdon, and Mrs. Hannah More, Relative to Sunday Schools, and Monday private Schools. By a Layman. Bath: W. Meyler, 1801.

Blunt, Reginald, ed. *Mrs. Montagu "Queen of the Blues"; Her Letters and Friendships from 1762 to 1800*. 2 vols. London: Constable, 1923.

Boucher, Theobald J. "Review of Hannah More's *Strictures on the Modern System of Female Education*." *Anti-Jacobin Review and Magazine* 4 (1799): 190–200.

Bradley, Ian C. *The Call to Seriousness; The Evangelical Impact on the Victorians*. London: Macmillan, 1976.

Brueggeman, Walter. *The Bible and Postmodern Imagination*. Minneapolis: Fortress Press, 1993.

Buller, W. "On Seeing Miss H. More in the title page of the 2d Edition of the Search after Happiness: A Ballad." *Commonplace Book* ca. 1795–1805. M.a. 179. Folger Shakespeare Library, Washington.

Burke, Peter. *Popular Culture in Early Modern Europe*. London: Temple Smith, 1978.

Burney, Charles. *Memoirs of the Life and Work of the Abate Metastasio, including translation of his principal letters*. 3 vols. London: C.G.J. Robinson, 1796.

Burney, Frances. *Camilla; or, A Picture of Youth*. Edited by Edward A. and Lillian D. Bloom. Oxford: Oxford University Press, 1972.

Candid Observations on Mrs. Hannah More's Schools: in which is considered their Supposed Connection with Methodism. Bath: S. Hazard, 1802.

Carter Angela. *The Sadeian Woman: An Exercise in Cultural History*. London: Virago, 1979.

Carter, Elizabeth. *Letters from Mrs. Elizabeth Carter to Mrs. Montagu, Between the years 1755 and 1800*. 3 vols. London: F.C. & J. Rivington, 1817.

Chambers, Robert, editor. *Cyclopaedia of English Literature; A History, Critical and Biographical, of British Authors From the Earliest to the Present Times*. 2 vols. London: W. & R. Chambers, 1858.

Chapman, R. W., ed. *Jane Austen's Letters to Her Sister Cassandra and Others*. Oxford: Clarendon, 1952.

Chapone, Mrs. Hester. *Letters on the Improvement of the mind*. London: J. Walter, 1774.

Child, Philip. "Portrait of a Woman of Affairs—Old Style." *University of Toronto Quarterly* 3 (1933–34): 87–102.

Cliff, Philip B. *The Rise and Development of the Sunday School Movement in England, 1780–1980.* Nutfield, Redhill, Surrey: National Christian Education Council, 1986.

Collier, Jane. *The Art of Ingeniously Tormenting.* Introduced by Judith Hawley. Bristol: Thoemmes Press, 1994.

Collingwood, Jeremy and Margaret. *Hannah More.* Oxford: Lion, 1990.

Collins, Wilkie. *The Moonstone, A Romance* [1868]. Edited by J.I.M. Stewart. Harmondsworth: Penguin Books, 1966.

Cott, Nancy. "Passionlessness: An Interpretation of Victorian Sexual Ideology." *Signs* 4, no. 2 (1978): 219–36.

Cottle, Joseph. *Early Recollections, chiefly relating to the late Samuel Taylor Coleridge.* 2 vols. London: Longman, 1837.

Courtney, Luther Weeks. *Hannah More's Interest in Education and Government.* Waco, Texas: Baylor University Press, 1929.

Cowley, Mrs. *Albina, Countess Raimond: A Tragedy.* London: T. Spilsbury, 1779.

Cowper, William. *The Poetical Works of William Cowper.* Edited by H.S. Milford. London: Oxford University Press, 1934.

Crittenden, Walter Marion. The *Life and Writings of Mrs. Sarah Scott, Novelist (1723–1795).* Philadelphia: A thesis presented to the faculty of the Graduate School, 1932.

Cropper, Margaret. *Sparks among the Stubble.* London: Longman, Green, 1955.

Cross, J.W., ed. *George Eliot's Life as Related in Her Letters and Journal.* New York: T.Y. Crowell, 1884.

Cunningham, Allan. "Biographical and Critical History of the Literature of the Last Fifty Years." *The Athenaeum,* 16 Nov. 1833, 769–77.

Darton, F.J. Harvey. *Children's Books in England: Five Centuries of Social Life.* 3d ed. Revised by Brian Alderson. Cambridge: Cambridge University Press, 1982.

Daubeny, Charles. *A Letter to Mrs. Hannah More, on Some Part of Her Late Publication Entitled "Strictures on Female Education."* London: J. Hatchard and F. & C. Rivington, 1799.

Davidoff, Leonore, and Catherine Hall. *Family Fortunes: Men and Women of the English Middle Class, 1780–1850.* London: Hutchinson, 1987.

Davies, Robertson. *The Revels History of Drama in English 1750–1880.* London: Methuen, 1975.

Davies, Thomas. *Memoirs of the Life of David Garrick.* 2 vols. London: Longman, Hurst, Rees, and Orme, 1808.

Demers, Patricia. "'For mine's a stubborn and a savage will': 'Lactilla' (Ann Yearsley) and 'Stella' (Hannah More) Reconsidered." *Huntington Library Quarterly* 56, no. 2 (1993): 135–50.

DeQuincey, Thomas. *The Collected Writings of Thomas DeQuincey.* Edited by D. Masson. 14 vols. London: A. & C. Black, 1897.

Dickens, Charles. *Bleak House* [1853]. New York: Bantam Books, 1983.

Donkin, Ellen. "The Paper War of Hannah Cowley and Hannah More." In *Curtain Calls: British and American Women and the Theater, 1660–1820*, edited by Mary Anne Schofield and Cecilia Macheski, 143–62. Athens: Ohio University Press, 1991.

Doody, Margaret Anne. *The Daring Muse: Augustan Poetry Reconsidered.* Cambridge: Cambridge University Press, 1985.

——. *Frances Burney: The Life in the Works.* New Brunswick, N.J.: Rutgers University Press, 1988.

[Drewitt, Rev. Thomas.] *The Force of Contrast; or, Quotations, Accompanied with Remarks, Submitted to the consideration of all who have interested themselves in what has been called the Blagdon Controversy.* Bath: S. Hazard, 1801.

——. *Illustrations of Falsehood, in A reply to Some Assertions Contained in Mr. Spenser's late Publication.* Bath: S. Hazard, 1802.

Duncan-Jones, Katherine. "Sidney's Urania." *RES* ns 17 (1966): 123–33.

Ellis, Peter F. *Seven Pauline Letters.* Collegeville, Minn.: Liturgical Press, 1982.

Elton, Rev. Sir Abraham. *A Letter to the Rev. Thomas Bere, Rector of Butcombe, Occasioned by his late unwarrantable attack on Mrs. Hannah More.* London: Cadell & Davies, 1801.

Elwood, Mrs. E.K. *Memoirs of the Literary Ladies of England.* 2 vols. London: Henry Colburn, 1843.

Everest, Kelvin. *English Romantic Poetry.* Milton Keynes: Open University Press, 1990.

Ewert, Leonore Helen. *Elizabeth Montagu to Elizabeth Carter; Literary Gossip and Critical Opinions from the Pen of the Queen of the Blues.* Ph.D. dissertation, Claremont Graduate School, 1967.

Ferguson, Moira. "Resistance and Power in the Life and Writings of Ann Yearsley." *Eighteenth Century* 27 (1986): 247–68.

——. *Subject to Others: British Women Writers and Colonial Slavery, 1670–1834.* London: Routledge, 1992.

——. "The Unpublished Poems of Ann Yearsley." *Tulsa Studies in Women's Literature* 12, no. 1 (1993): 13–46.

Ferguson, Moira, ed. *First Feminists: British Women Writers, 1578–1799.* Bloomington: University of Indiana Press, 1985.

Fielding, Sarah. *The Governess; or, Little Female Academy.* Introduced by Jill E. Grey. London: Oxford University Press, 1968.

Figes, Eva. *Sex and Subterfuge; Women Novelists to 1850.* London: Macmillan, 1982.

Foner, Philip S., ed. *The Complete Writings of Thomas Paine.* New York: Citadel Press, 1945.

Forster, E.M. *Marianne Thornton: A Domestic Biography, 1797–1887.* New York: Harcourt, Brace, 1956.

Foucault, Michel. *Discipline and Punish: The Birth of the Prison.* Translated by A. Sheridan. New York: Random House, 1979.

Freeman, Michael. *Edmund Burke and the Critique of Political Radicalism*. Oxford: Basil Blackwell, 1980.

Fucilla, Joseph G., trans. *Three Melodramas by Pietro Metastasio*. Lexington: University of Kentucky Press, 1981.

Fussell, Paul. *The Rhetorical World of Augustan Humanism: Ethics and Imagery from Swift to Burke*. Oxford: Clarendon, 1965.

Gaull, Marilyn. *English Romanticism: The Human Context*. New York: Norton, 1988.

Gisborne, Thomas. *An Enquiry into the Duties of the Female Sex* [1797]. Introduced by Gina Luria. New York: Garland, 1974.

Gladstone Papers. British Library MS. 44723 f. 282. A Digest of Roberts's *Memoirs*.

Gosse, Edmund. "Review of The Letters of Hannah More, Selected by R. Brimley Johnson." *Sunday Times*, 15 Nov. 1925, 15.

Green, Katharine Sobba. *The Courtship Novel, 1740–1820: A Feminized Genre*. Lexington: University Press of Kentucky, 1991.

Gregory, Dr. John. *A Father's Legacy to his Daughters*. London: W. Strahan and T. Cadell, 1781.

Hamilton, Catherine J. *Women Writers: Their Works and Ways* [1892]. Freeport, N.Y.: Books for Libraries Press, 1971.

Harford, Alice, ed. *Annals of the Harford Family*. London: Westminster Press, 1909.

Harford Papers. City of Bristol Record Office 28048. c. 1/2, 68/18, 74, 78, 82/1.

Harland, Marion (M.V. Terhune). *Hannah More*. New York: G.P. Putnam's Sons, 1900.

Hess, Marlene Alice. *The Didactic Art of Hannah More*. Ann Arbor: University Microfilms International, 1983.

The History of Barley Wood. Wrington: H.A.T. Group, 1980.

Hobsbawm, E.J., and Joan Wallach Scott. "Political Shoemakers." *Past and Present* 89 (1980): 86–114.

Hoole, John, translator. *Regulus. Dramas by Metastasio*. London, 1800.

Hopkins, Mary Alden. *Hannah More and Her Circle*. New York: Longmans, Green, 1947.

Jackson, J.R. de J. *Romantic Poetry by Women: A Bibliography, 1770–1835*. Oxford: Clarendon, 1993.

Jay, Elisabeth. *The Religion of the Heart: Anglican Evangelicalism and the Nineteenth-Century Novel*. Oxford: Clarendon, 1979.

Joceline, Elizabeth. *The Mothers Legacie, to Her Unborne Childe*. 7th Impression. London: Robert Allot, 1635.

Johnson, Claudia L. "Introduction." *Considerations on Religion and Public Education (First American Edition, 1794) Hannah More*. Augustan Reprint Society no. 268. Los Angeles: William Andrews Clark Memorial Library, 1990.

———. *Jane Austen: Women, Politics and the Novel*. Chicago: University of Chicago Press, 1988.

Jones, Ann H. *Ideas and Innovations: Best Sellers of Jane Austen's Age*. New York: AMS Press, 1986.

Jones, Mary Gwladys. *The Charity School Movement: A Study of Eighteenth-Century Puritanism in Action.* Cambridge: Cambridge University Press, 1938.

——. *Hannah More.* Cambridge: Cambridge University Press, 1952.

Kelly, Gary. *English Fiction of the Romantic Period, 1789–1830.* London: Longman, 1989.

Kelly, Gary, editor. *Millenium Hall.* Peterborough: Broadview, 1995.

Kelly, Gary. "Revolution, Reaction, and the Expropriation of Popular Culture: Hannah More's *Cheap Repository.*" *Man and Nature* 6 (1987): 147–59.

——. "Romantic Evangelicalism: Religion, Social Conflict, and Literary Form in Legh Richmond's *Annals of the Poor.*" *English Studies in Canada* 16 (1990): 165–86.

Kiernan, V. "Evangelicalism and the French Revolution." *Past and Present* 1 (1952): 44–56.

Knight, Mrs. Helen C. *A New Memoir of Hannah More; or, Life in Hall and Cottage.* New York: M.W. Dodd, 1851.

Knox, E.V. "'Percy' (The Tale of a Dramatic Success)." *London Mercury* 13 (1925–26): 509–15.

Kowaleski-Wallace, Elizabeth. *Their Fathers' Daughters: Hannah More, Maria Edgeworth, and Patriarchal Complicity.* New York: Oxford University Press, 1991.

Kraeling, Emil. *Rand McNally Bible Atlas.* New York: Rand McNally, 1966.

Lamoine, Georges. *La Vie Littéraire de Bath et de Bristol, 1750–1800.* 2 vols. Paris: Librairie Honoré Champion, 1978.

Landry, Donna. *The Muses of Resistance: Laboring-Class Women's Poetry in Britain, 1739–1796.* Cambridge: Cambridge University Press, 1990.

Laqueur, Thomas Walter. *Religion and Respectability: Sunday Schools and Working Class Culture, 1780–1850.* New Haven: Yale University Press, 1976.

Latimer, John. *The Annals of Bristol in the Eighteenth Century.* London: Butler and Tanner, 1893.

LeGates, Marlene. "The Cult of Womanhood in Eighteenth-Century Thought." *Eighteenth-Century Studies* 10 (1976–77): 21–39.

Leigh, Dorothy. *The Mothers Blessing; or, The Godly Counsule of a Gentle-woman, not long since deceased, left behind her for her Children.* London: John Budge, 1618.

Lewis, Paddy. "The little girl who wanted to see Bookshops and Bishops." *Illustrated Bristol News,* September 1963, 26–27.

Lewis, W.S., R.A. Smith, and C.H. Bennett, eds. *Horace Walpole's Correspondence with Hannah More. . . .* Vol. 31 of The *Correspondence* of Horace Walpole. New Haven: Yale University Press, 1961.

Locke, John. *Some Thoughts Concerning Education.* Edited by John W. and Jean S. Yolton. Oxford: Clarendon, 1989.

Macaulay, Catharine. *Letters on Education with Observations on Religious and Metaphysical Subjects* [1790]. Edited and introduced by Gina Luria. New York: Garland, 1974.

[Macaulay, Zachary]. "Mrs. H. More's Schools; or, The Blagdon Controversy." *Christian Observer* 1 (1802): 180–85.

————. "Review of *Coelebs in Search of a Wife.*" *Christian Observer* 8 (1809): 109–21.

McGrath, Patrick. *The Merchant Venturers of Bristol.* Bristol: Society of Merchant Venturers, 1975.

MacSarcasm, Rev. Sir Archibald [William Shaw]. *The Life of Hannah More, with A Critical Review of Her Writings.* London: T. Hurst, 1802.

Mahl, M.R., and H. Koon, eds. *The Female Spectator: English Women Writers before 1800.* Bloomington: University of Indiana Press, 1977.

Makin, Bathsua. *An Essay to Revive the Antient Education of Gentlewomen.* Introduced by Paula L. Barbour. Augustan Reprint Society no. 202. Los Angeles: William Andrews Clark Memorial Library, 1980.

Meakin, Annette M.B. *Hannah More: A Biographical Study.* London: John Murray, 1911.

Meissner, S.J., M.D., W.W. *Ignatius of Loyola: The Psychology of a Saint.* New Haven: Yale University Press, 1992.

Mellor, Anne K. "English Women Writers and the French Revolution." In *Rebel Daughters: Women and the French Revolution,* edited by S.E. Melzer and L.W. Rabine, 255–72. New York: Oxford University Press, 1992.

————. *Romanticism and Gender.* London: Routledge, 1993.

Merrett, Robert James. "Pictorialism in Eighteenth-Century Fiction: Visual Thinking and Narrative Diversity." In *Time, Literature and the Arts: Essays in Honor of S. L. Macey,* edited by T.L. Cleary, 157–91. Victoria: University of Victoria, English Literary Studies no. 61, 1994,

Mitford, Mary Russell. *Our Village: Sketches of Rural Character and Scenery.* 2d ed. London: G.B. Whittaker, 1827.

Hannah More's Cards of Wisdom, Intended as a conversation for two or more persons, to which is added a Game, as a further Amusement for a Party. Birmingham: J.T. Maund, n.d.

More, Martha. *Mendip Annals; or, A Narrative of the Charitable Labours of Hannah and Martha More in their Neighbourhood, Being the Journal of Martha More.* Edited by Arthur Roberts. London: James Nisbet, 1859.

Myers, Mitzi. "Hannah More's Tracts for the Times: Social Fiction and Female Ideology." In *Fetter'd or Free? British Women Novelists, 1670–1815,* edited by Mary Anne Schofield and Cecilia Macheski, 264–84. Athens: Ohio University Press, 1986.

————. "'A Peculiar Protection': Hannah More and the Cultural Politics of the Blagdon Controversy." In *History, Gender & Eighteenth-Century Literature,* edited by Beth Fowkes Tobin, 227–57. Athens: University of Georgia Press, 1994.

————. "Reform or Ruin: 'A Revolution in Female Manners'." *Studies in Eighteenth-Century Culture* 2 (1982): 199–216.

Myers, Sylvia Harcstark. "Learning, Virtue, and the Term 'Bluestocking'." *Studies in Eighteenth-Century Culture* 15 (1986): 279–88.

————. *The Bluestocking Circle; Women, Friendship, and the Life of the Mind in Eighteenth-Century England.* Oxford: Clarendon, 1990.

Newcastle, Margaret. *Nature's Pictures.* London: J. Martin and J. Allestrye, 1655.

Newman, Barbara. "On the Ethics of Feminist Historiography." *Exemplaria* 2 (1990): 702–7.

Nussbaum, Felicity A. *The Autobiographical Subject: Gender and Ideology in Eighteenth-Century England*. Baltimore: Johns Hopkins University Press, 1989.

Nussbaum, Felicity, and Laura Brown, eds. *The New Eighteenth Century: Theory, Politics, English Literature*. New York: Methuen, 1986.

Pearson, Norman. "The Lighter Side of Hannah More." *Nineteenth Century* 59 (1906): 842–58.

Pedersen, Susan. "Hannah More Meets Simple Simon: Tracts, Chapbooks, and Popular Culture in Late Eighteenth-Century England." *Journal of British Studies* 25 (1986): 84–113.

Pennington, Rev. Montagu. *Memoirs of the Life of Mrs. Elizabeth Carter, with a new edition of her Poems*. 2 vols. London: F.C. & J. Rivington, 1808.

Phillips, Marion, and W.S. Tomkinson. *English Women in Life and Letters*. Oxford: Clarendon, 1926.

Pickering, Sam. "Hannah More's *Coelebs in Search of a Wife* and the Respectability of the Novel in the Nineteenth Century." *Neuphilologische Mitteilungen* 78 (1977): 78–85.

Pindar, Peter [John Wolcot]. *The Works of Peter Pindar, Esq.* 5 vols. London: J. Walker, 1794–1801.

Poovey, Mary. *The Proper Lady and the Woman Writer: Ideology as Style in the Works of Mary Wollstonecraft, Mary Shelley, and Jane Austen*. Chicago: University of Chicago Press, 1984.

Prochaska, Frank K. *Women and Philanthropy in Nineteenth-Century England*. Oxford: Clarendon, 1980.

Proudfoot, Wayne. *Religious Experience*. Berkeley: University of California Press, 1985.

Quinlan, Maurice J. *Victorian Prelude: A History of English Manners, 1700–1830*. New York: Columbia University Press, 1941.

"Review of *An Address to Mrs. H. More* by T. Bere, *The Force of Contrast*, and *Truths respecting Mrs. More's Meeting-Houses* by Edward Spencer." *Monthly Review* 37 (1802): 203–4.

"Review of *Christian Morals*." *Monthly Review* 70 (1813): 374–86.

"Review of *Essays on Various Subjects*." *Monthly Review* 3 (1777): 201–7.

"Review of *A Letter to Mrs. H. More* by Rev. C. Daubeny." *Monthly Review* 31 (1800): 106–8.

"Review of *Percy*." *Monthly Review* 4 (1778): 23–28.

"Review of *A Poetical Review of Miss H. More's Strictures* by Sappho Search." *Monthly Review* 32 (1800): 315–16.

"Review of *Practical Piety*." *Monthly Review* 64 (1811): 390–400.

"Review of *Remarks on the Speech of M. Dupont*." *Monthly Review* 11 (1793): 118–19.

"Review of *Sir Eldred* and *The Bleeding Heart*." *Monthly Review* 2 (1776): 89–99.

"Review of *Strictures on the Modern System of Female Education*." *British Critic* 13 (1799): 643–51.

"Review of *Strictures on the Modern System of Female Education*." *Monthly Review* 30 (1799): 410–17.

Richardson, Samuel. *Pamela; or, Virtue Rewarded*. 2 vols. London: J.M. Dent & Sons, 1914.

Roberts, Arthur, ed. *Letters of Hannah More to Zachary Macaulay, Esq*. London: J. Nisbet, 1860.

Rogers, Katharine M. *Feminism in Eighteenth-Century England*. Urbana: University of Illinois Press, 1982.

Rutter, John. *Delineations of the North Western Division of the County of Somerset and Its Antediluvian Bone Caverns*. London: Longman, Rees, 1829.

Sanders, Valerie. *Reason over Passion: Harriet Martineau and the Victorian Novel*. Sussex: Harvester Press, 1986.

Sangster, Paul. *Pity My Simplicity: The Evangelical Revival and the Religious Education of Children, 1738–1800*. London: Epworth, 1963.

[Scott, Sarah.] *A Description of Millenium Hall, and the Country Adjacent: Together with the Characters of the Inhabitants, and such Historical Anecdotes and Reflections as may excite in the Reader proper sentiments of Humanity, and lead the Mind to the Love of Virtue*. London: J. Newbery, 1762.

Search, Sappho [John Black]. *A Poetical Review of Miss Hannah More's Strictures on Female Education*. In a series of Anapestic Epistles. London: T. Hurst, 1800.

Seward, Anna. "On visiting the Silvan Cottage Inhabited by Miss Hannah More and her sisters 1791." In *The Juvenile Forget Me Not*. Edited by Mrs. S. C. Hall. London: F. Westley and A. H. Davis, 1831.

Shiach, Morag. *Discourse on Popular Culture: Class, Gender and History in Cultural Analysis, 1730 to the Present*. Cambridge: Polity Press, 1989.

Signourney, Mrs. L.H. *Pleasant Memories of Pleasant Lands*. Boston: James Munroe, 1842.

Silvester, James. *Hannah More Christian Philanthropist*. London: Thynne, 1934.

Smith, Olivia. *The Politics of Language, 1791–1819*. Oxford: Oxford University Press, 1984.

Smith, Sidney. "Review of *Coelebs in Search of a Wife*." *Edinburgh Review* 14 (1809): 145–51.

The Something Wrong Developed; or, Free Remarks on Mrs. H. More's Conventicles. Bristol: Harris and Bryan, 1801.

Southey, Robert. *The Lives and Works of the Uneducated Poets*. Edited by J.S. Childers. London: Humphrey Milford, 1925.

Spacks, Patricia Meyer. " 'Always at Variance': Politics of Eighteenth-Century Adolescence." In *A Distant Prospect: Eighteenth-Century Views of Childhood*. Los Angeles: William Andrews Clark Memorial Library, 1982.

Spencer, Edward. *Truths, respecting Mrs. Hannah More's Meeting-Houses, and the Conduct of her Followers; Addressed to the Curate of Blagdon*. Bath: W. Meyler, 1802.

Spenser, Edmund. *The Faerie Queene: The Works of Edmund Spenser*. Edited by E. Greenlaw, C.G. Osgood, F.M. Padelford, *et al*. 9 vols. Baltimore: Johns Hopkins University Press, 1932–1949.

Spinney, G.H. "Cheap Repository Tracts: Hazard and Marshall Editions." *The Library* 20 (1939–40): 295–340.

Spring, David. "The Clapham Sect: Some Social and Political Aspects." *Victorian Studies* 5 (1961): 35–48.

Stapleton Parish Church Register. City of Bristol Record Office. P/HTS/R/1(a).

Stone, Lawrence. *The Family, Sex and Marriage in England, 1500–1800.* New York: Harper & Row, 1977.

The Story of the Theatre Royal Bristol. Bristol: Trustees of the Theatre Royal, 1971.

Stratford, J. *Robert Raikes and Others: The Founders of Sunday Schools.* London: Sunday School Union, 1880.

Swift, Jonathan. *Poetical Works.* Edited by Herbert Davis. Oxford: Clarendon, 1967.

Tabor, Margaret E. *Pioneer Women.* London: Sheldon Press, 1927.

Taylor, Thomas. *Memoir of Mrs. Hannah More: With Notices of Her Works, and Sketches of Her Contemporaries.* 2d edition. London: Joseph Rickerby, 1838.

Thompson, E.P. *The Making of the English Working Class.* London: V. Gollanz, 1963.

———. "The Moral Economy of the English Crowd in the Eighteenth Century." *Past and Present* 50 (1971): 76–136.

Thompson, Rev. Henry. *The Christian An Example. A Sermon Preached in the Parish Church of Wrington, Somerset, on the Sunday after the Funeral of Mrs. H. More.* London: J.G. and F. Rivington, 1833.

———. *The Life of Hannah More: With Notices of Her Sisters.* London: T. Cadell, 1838.

Thomson, James. *The Seasons.* Edited by O. Zippel. Berlin: Mayer & Muller, 1908.

Tobin, Beth Fowkes. *Superintending the Poor: Charitable Ladies and Paternal Landlords in British Fiction, 1770–1860.* New Haven: Yale University Press, 1993.

Todd, Janet. *The Sign of Angelica: Women, Writing, and Fiction, 1660–1800.* London: Virago, 1989.

Tompkins, J.M.S. *The Polite Marriage.* Cambridge: Cambridge University Press, 1938.

Torrens, Robert. *Coelibia Choosing a Husband: A Modern Novel.* 2 vols. London: J.F. Hughes, 1809.

Trevelyan, George Otto, ed. *The Life and Letters of Lord Macaulay.* 2 vols. New York: Harper, 1876.

Trimmer, Mrs. Sarah. *The Family Magazine; or, A Repository of Religious Instruction and Rational Amusement.* London: J. Marshall, January 1788–June 1789.

———. *The Oeconomy of Charity; or, An Address to Ladies Concerning Sunday Schools; the Establishing of Schools of Industry under Female Inspection; and the Distribution of Voluntary Benefaction.* London: T. Bansley, 1787.

Ty, Eleanor. *Unsex'd Revolutionaries: Five Women Novelists of the 1790s.* Toronto: University of Toronto Press, 1993.

Unwin, Rayner. *The Rural Muse: Studies in the Peasant Poetry of England.* London: George Allen and Unwin, 1954.

Valenze, Deborah. *Prophetic Sons and Daughters: Female Preaching and Popular Religion in Industrial England.* Princeton: Princeton University Press, 1985.

Vicinus, Martha. *The Industrial Muse: A Study of Nineteenth Century British Working-Class Literature*. New York: Barnes & Noble, 1974.

Waldron, Mary. "Ann Yearsley and the Clifton Records." *The Age of Johnson* 3 (1990): 301–29.

Walford, L.B. *Four Biographies from Blackwood*. Edinburgh: Wm. Blackwood, 1888.

Ware, Ciji. *Wicked Company: A Novel of the Eighteenth Century New York: Bantam Books, 1992*.

Weiss, Harry B. "Hannah More's Cheap Repository Tracts in America." *Bulletin of the New York Public Library* 50 (1946): 539–641.

Wilberforce, Robert Isaac and Samuel Wilberforce. *The Life of William Wilberforce*. 5 vols. London: Murray, 1838.

Wilberforce, William. *A Practical View of the Prevailing Religious System of Professed Christians, in the Higher and Middle Classes in this Country, contrasted with Real Christianity* [1797]. 13th ed. London: T. Cadell & W. Davies, 1818.

Wollstonecraft, Mary. *Vindication of the Rights of Woman: With Strictures on Political and Moral Subjects*, [1792]. Edited by Miriam Brody. London: Penguin Classics, 1983.

Yearsley, Ann. *Earl Goodwin, An Historical Play*. London: G.G.J. & J. Robinson, 1791.

———. *Poems on Several Occasions by Ann Yearsley A Milkwoman of Bristol*. London: T. Cadell, 1785.

———. *Poems on Various Subjects by a Milkwoman of Clifton near Bristol, Being Her Second Work*. London: G.G.J. & J. Robinson, 1787.

———. *Reflections on the Death of Louis XVI*. Bristol: Printed and sold by the Author at her Public Library, Crescent, Hotwells, 1793.

———. *Stanzas of Woe, addressed from the Heart on a Bed of Illness to Levi Eames, Esq., Late Mayor of the City of Bristol*. London: G.G.J. & J. Robinson, 1790.

Yeazell, Ruth Bernard. *Fiction of Modesty: Women and Courtship in the English Novel*. Chicago: University of Chicago Press, 1991.

Yonge, Charlotte. *Hannah More*. Boston: Roberts Brothers, 1890.

Index